W9-CXV-022

THE ART OF THE DRAMA

UNIFORM WITH THIS VOLUME

A FOREWORD TO FICTION

BY

James Weber Linn and Houghton Wells Taylor

APPROACHES TO POETRY

BY

Walter Blair and W. K. Chandler

The Art of the Drama

by

FRED B. MILLETT

PROFESSOR OF ENGLISH, WESLEYN UNIVERSITY

and

GERALD EADES BENTLEY

PROFESSOR OF ENGLISH, PRINCETON UNIVERSITY

Appleton-Century-Crofts, Inc.

NEW YORK

667-15

E64088

PRINTED IN THE UNITED STATES OF AMERICA

FOREWORD

This book is not a history of the drama. Nor is it a manual for the multitudes who aspire to write plays and sell them. It is a tool for the use of those who wish to deepen their understanding and enhance their enjoyment of plays witnessed in the theater or read in the study. As a textbook, it may prove useful in the study of the history of the drama or of the drama as a literary type, or in such a course as the Introduction to the Study of Drama as given at the University of Chicago.

The book is divided into three parts, each of which emphasizes a particular aspect of the drama. Part I is mainly devoted to the historical aspect of the drama, the spirit of the age, the nature of the theater and audience in each of the major periods in dramatic history. It also contains a general discussion of the major forms or types of drama—tragedy, comedy, melodrama, and farce—and a more detailed consideration of the types of drama and comedy characteristic of each period. Part II considers the major modes of drama—classicism, romanticism, realism, sentimentalism, symbolism, and expressionism. Part III concerns the major problems of dramatic technique and the characteristic solutions of those problems in the various types and modes and periods of drama.

There is no question that it would have been more logical to consider first the technical, second the æsthetic, and third the historical approach to the study of drama, and students of a logical turn of mind will have no difficulty in using the text in that order. But we have come to feel that it will, in general, be preferable for the student to master the facts in Part I before he ventures upon the more theoretical considerations of Parts II and III.

Both teacher and student will observe that this book makes no attempt to treat comprehensively any particular plays or the work of any particular playwrights, although many plays and many playwrights are drawn on for illustrative material. Rather is the book intended for use in connection with the reading and study of any series of plays in which the teacher or student may be interested. Inevitably, the plays, playwrights, and movements of each major period in the drama are discussed in each of the three parts of the book. But the very full index will make it easy for the reader to turn rapidly to our consideration, under various heads, of a particular play, playwright, or period. Moreover, the book is constructed in such a way that it will be possible to emphasize with ease any element that it seems desirable to emphasize in connection with the study of a particular period or form. For example, if it is desired to emphasize the treatment of plot in classical tragedy, the student may consult the treatment of tragedy under the heads of "Classical tragedy," "Classicism," and "Plot." Or, if the romantic elements in Shakespeare's comedies are to be emphasized, the student may well consult our treatment of Elizabethan comedy, romanticism, and setting.

The plan of the book, its general outline, and Part I are the work of Professor Bentley. Parts II and III are the work of Professor Millett. But the collaborators are willing to assume joint responsibility for whatever errors in facts, ideas, opinions, and judgments appear anywhere in this book.

F. B. M.
G. E. B.

CONTENTS

PART III

DRAMATIC TECHNIQUE

THE ART OF THE DRAMA

INTRODUCTION

THE STUDY OF THE DRAMA

Before we enter upon the study of the drama, it will be well to define the elements that differentiate the dramatic from the non-dramatic. The word *dramatic* is frequently used metaphorically to mean "startling," "thrilling," or "exciting," but such a loose use of the term will hardly be of service to us. A clue to the essential elements of drama is furnished by the first clause of the most famous of all definitions of tragedy, Aristotle's "Tragedy is an imitation of an action." Though the term *imitation* has provoked dozens of interpretations and controversies, the modern student may take it to mean "representation." In other words, drama is not life, but the representation of life. Not a real event, but the representation of a real (or an imagined) event, is the essence of drama. Furthermore, the element in representation that distinguishes the drama from the novel or painting or sculpture is impersonation—that is to say, the assumption by human beings of personalities, characters, natures, or entities other than their own. This impersonation differs from the attempt of a person to pass himself off as another person (as a detective in disguise or an imperial or princely impostor does) in that the impersonation involves participation not in *actual* but in *represented* action. The impersonation may involve the assumption of an animal personality, as in primitive dramas representing hunting, warfare, or religious invocation, or like the Cat and the Dog in Maeterlinck's *Blue Bird,* the alligator in Barrie's *Peter Pan,* or the White Horse and the Dormouse in *Alice in Wonderland.* Or the impersonation may be the assumption of the nature of an entity, like Mercy or Nought in the morality plays, or Deus in the biblical drama, or the pagan gods and goddesses in the classical or Oriental drama. The concept of impersonation may likewise be extended to cover the representation of imagined human beings by puppets or marionettes or by the shadow actors of Oriental drama.[1]

The dance, when it includes the element of impersonation, becomes a part of that representation that is drama, and monologue and pantomime, whether incidental to the spoken drama or given independently, are by-paths of the art of the drama. The concept of represen-

[1] See Loomis Havemeyer, *The Drama of Savage Peoples* (New Haven: Yale University Press, 1916), pp. 212–216.

tation also includes the moving or talking picture, since here, as in the drama acted by real persons in the presence of an audience, the element of impersonation is clearly concerned.

Another essential of drama, apparent in Aristotle's definition, is action. Drama, in both its philological and historical aspects, cannot exist without it. The action is usually overt—that is to say, physical. There is a change of status or relationship or circumstance, whether it be the violent change of murder or suicide or the subtler changes of economic disaster or amatory triumph. The action may, however, not be overt at all. The change, indicated by dialogue or pantomime, may be a change of state of mind or emotion or intellectual attitude. So long as the action represented concerns an impersonated character or entity, drama exists.

The indispensable elements in drama, then, are representation, impersonation, and action. Thus a represented incident or episode, a five-minute dialogue, a pantomime, a puppet-play, a moving-picture, a grand opera, or even an oratorio when it involves actual impersonation, all come under the broad ægis of drama. Acrobatic acts, tumbling, and sleight-of-hand performances become drama only when the participants impersonate figures, such as clowns and tramps, that are other than their own persons. A minstrel show, although it involves impersonation, becomes drama only when, as in an acted skit, it represents action as well.

The difference between drama and *a* drama is easy to discern. *A* drama, whether it last five minutes or five hours, is a particular example of the species drama. *A* drama may, and usually does, involve the technical elements of plot, character, setting, and dialogue, but even when these elements are reduced to a minimum, we still have drama, provided that the elements of representation, impersonation, and action are present. When we speak of *drama,* we have in mind the whole body of specific dramas produced by mankind throughout its recorded history. When we speak of *dramatic,* we intend to signify the virtual and not the carelessly metaphorical application of the term.

The drama is at once a literary type and a form of art which for its total effect involves the contribution of a large number of non-literary elements. These indispensable elements are actors, costumes, setting, and that nexus of these elements that is known as direction.

The drama may be studied as a type of literature or as a form of living art. As a literary type, it may be studied in its genres: tragedy, comedy, melodrama, and farce; in its æsthetic modes: classical, romantic, realistic, etc.; in its technical elements: plot, character, dialogue, and setting. Like other art-forms with a complex history, it may be studied in terms of such conventions as effect the choice of a subject, the presentation of characters as types, the tone or mood, and the style of dialogue. Like other forms of literature, the drama may be studied sociologically—that is to say, in terms of its relation to the life and thought of the particular age in which it was produced. Finally, it may be studied in its relation to its individual authors—that is, as an expression of the personality and the view of life of its creators.

The approaches we have indicated are shared by the drama with other types of literature. But the approach to the drama as a living art, as an art made possible only in the theater with the aid of actors and all the technical resources of the theater—such a method of study makes demands on the literary student such as are made by no other form of literature. It is to the processes involved in such a study that this book is primarily devoted.

The study of the drama outside the theater has become so conventional an approach that students need constantly to be reminded that the only proper place for the study of the drama is the theater. Especially at a time when, for reasons both æsthetic and economic, the experience of students of the drama in the theater is pitifully limited, it is necessary to insist that students accustom themselves to regarding the drama not as a literary type to be enjoyed, like the lyric, the novel, or the essay, in cloistered solitude but as a form of æsthetic experience to the maximum effectiveness of which a large number of non-literary elements must contribute.

In a very real sense, a play is not a play until it is acted in a theater before an audience, for, if the playwright knows what he is doing, he will never forget that he is creating out of words a form which the actor and the theater will endue with life. Moreover, the practical playwright assumes that his work will be submitted to the judgment, will touch the instincts, and will stimulate the emotions, not of a student coolly isolated in his study but of a mass of spectators of varied temperaments gathered in a theater. These spectators will influence each other's responses and, at best, will coalesce into a super-individual entity, whose experience is something more than the sum-total of the experiences of all the individuals in the theater.

The student of the drama, moreover, will fail to get a tithe of the values implicit in drama if he does not take constantly into consideration the fact that a play is written to be performed not in the abstract theater of an idealist's imaginings but in a theater characteristic of a particular period, with the advantages and limitations of any structure and organization of human contrivance. Consequently, it behooves the student to ascertain the nature of the theater as it existed in the period in which the play was written or performed and to keep in mind as vividly as possible the appearance, structure, and atmosphere of the playhouse for which the play in question was written.

The relationship between the drama and the theater is not, to be sure, perfectly easy to define. The late Brander Matthews was wont to write as though the play were a sort of inconsequential by-product of the theater, as though a careful study of theatrical architecture would explain the drama of Shakespeare and Molière, Aristophanes and Oscar Wilde. But the relationship between the theater and the drama is not the relatively simple one of cause and effect. The relationship, like marriage, is that of mutually influential agents. The theater is a changing form; the playwright is a changing and, in some instances, an innovating entity. The relationship, then, is that existing between two variables and therefore is constantly in need of being defined and re-defined, for every playwright and for every type of theatrical structure.

The theatrical structure itself has its own complexities; it is not merely architectural like a church, it is artificial and mechanical as well. At its simplest, it involves the element of setting. Some plays, to be sure, require no more in the way of scenery than a vaguely designated open place providing room for the action of the piece, while others require an elaborate series of sets and of stage properties. Any serious and imaginative study of the drama involves an investigation of what scenery is available in the theater concerned and what scenery is indicated in the play under study. As we shall see, various types of drama make varying demands upon scene-designers and scene-shifters, but every play raises some sort of problem as to setting, and that problem not merely the playwright and the producer, but also the student, must heed.

In theaters less exposed to the light of day than the open-air theaters of ancient Greece, the problem of lighting is involved. This is a matter which, it might seem, concerns only the architect, the theater owner, the producer, and the stage-mechanician. But the student of the drama in the theater will lose a great deal of the effectiveness of the drama unless he is at least generally aware of the history of lighting in the theater and of the resources of the modern switchboard and, what is more important, unless he is attentive to the crudity or subtlety, the ugliness or beauty, the crassness or suggestiveness with which a particular producer in a particular theater invests his production by means of lighting.

Nor will the serious student overlook the easily forgotten fact that plays are written to be acted by human beings.[2] In the barren-

[2] Or, in rare instances, by puppets or marionettes.

ness of the classroom, the student must not forget that the actor is an element indispensable to the drama. In the first place, the consciousness that dialogue was written to be delivered by the human voice may reveal hitherto unexpected aspects of clarity and beauty, grace and elegance, wit and humor, in dramatic dialogue. Further, and more significantly, the student unfamiliar with the theater must accustom himself to the idea that the actor makes a tremendously important contribution to the nexus of complex impressions a play produces in the theater. That contribution may be legitimate or illegitimate, but it cannot be ignored. Playwrights in ancient and modern times have sometimes imposed terrific burdens upon the actors of the parts they have imagined; playwrights in all ages have fitted parts more or less snugly to actors or actresses with whom they were acquainted or by whom they were commissioned, but playwrights have never been able to forget completely that human personalities are a part of their material, animated clay in the hands of the dramatic potter.

The actor temperament is a strange and in some ways a repellent thing. It has a plasticity far beyond the temperament of ordinary persons. It is capable of taking on a variety of forms so wide that they may seem mutually inconsistent and unrecognizable. Sometimes, this plasticity seems to be compensated for by an actual vacuity or imperfection of real "character." Sometimes, on the other hand, an absence of plasticity seems to be compensated for by a stable personality so charming and vital, so alluring or impressive, that impersonation seems needless. Indeed, it is not difficult to distinguish two types of actors: those who subordinate their own personalities to the part that they "take" and those who merely exploit their own personalities. There seems no doubt that real acting requires a personality of the first sort, but the history of the theater is replete with instances of actors (but more often of actresses) who have been such fascinating personalities that it has been possible for them to make heavy contributions from their own store of personal riches without the necessity of acting.

Whatever the nature of the actor may be, the student of the drama in the theater cannot afford to ignore his contribution. That contribution, whether from his own or his assumed personality, is a result of elaborate training and the most highly conscious artifice. A painful impression of the complexity of the art of acting can be gained from the unhappy experience of watching an amateur performance, in which at least ninety per cent of the effects are likely to be distressing. The amateur actor is incapable of walking or talking, of sitting or standing, effectively. He is mealy mouthed and monotonous. He is at once the consolation and the despair of the trained performer. A more delightful experience of the highly complex technique of acting can be gained by watching a skilled director in the rehearsal of a play. The pains expended on the utterance of every syllable, on the movement of every limb, are incalculable. If access to a rehearsal is forbidden, the student can gain a sharp impression of the technique of acting by watching two performances of the same play. Barring accidents, it will be found that they vary in only the most trivial respects. And the skill involved is not merely that of attaining complete control over tone and gesture, movements and posture, but of communicating an effect of spontaneity and artlessness to the two-hundredth or the two-thousandth performance. So great is the contribution of skilled acting to a play that it is sometimes extremely difficult to distinguish the values involved in the play from the values imparted by the acting and to decide what values the play possesses in and by itself.

Finally, the student of the drama in the theater should remember that the total effectiveness of a play, the unity wrought out of diverse elements is, in all probability, due to a producer or director who, from a lifeless manuscript, envious and egocentric actors, shabby or elegant scenery, bad-tempered mechanicians and technicians, may create upon the stage a few hours of life more glamorous and thrilling, more memorable and meaningful, than most of the hours spent by most human beings outside the theater. It is, after all, the unnoticed and anonymous producer who brings distinguished or trivial plays to transitory but vivid life.

PART I

DRAMATIC FORMS OR TYPES

CHAPTER I

DRAMATIC FORMS OR TYPES

There are four principal aspects of the drama which may be profitably studied in order to attain a better understanding of plays: dramatic forms, dramatic history, dramatic modes, and dramatic technique. A study of the drama may well begin with a consideration of forms.

The four most important dramatic forms—tragedy, comedy, melodrama, and farce—are worth the study of any one interested in plays and the theater. Such a study is worth-while, not because there is any particular value in definitions, nor because any one should be encouraged to murmur, "Ah, yes, a melodrama!" whenever a popular thriller is mentioned, but because it helps one to understand the purpose and the problems of any man who has written a play to be performed before an audience. The four principal dramatic forms have been worked out not by critics and teachers but by playwrights struggling to tell a story to an audience by means of actors and a stage and striving to make the audience understand the story as the playwright understands it and see the implications which he sees. Dramatic forms are the result of an analysis of the problem of directing the emotional responses of an audience in a theater. Many failures have taught playwrights a few principles of effective presentation, and each generation imitates the successes of its predecessors. Dramatic forms are one of the phases of this traditional knowledge. Critics simply observe and try to evaluate what successful playwrights have done. They write down the results of their observations for people who are interested in the ways of the drama, but who are not willing or able to discover them by trying to write a few plays themselves.

The chief difficulty involved in a study of these dramatic forms lies in the confusion which has arisen because various historical epochs have had somewhat different conceptions of them. The term *comedy* did not suggest quite the same thing to the audience of Aristophanes in the fifth century B. C. as to the audience of Robert Greene in the sixteenth century or to the audience of Molière in the seventeenth. Since these differences are due largely to the social and theatrical conditions under which the plays were written, we shall consider the two chief dramatic forms—tragedy and comedy—chronologically, attempting to outline the most important of these conditions for each of the great dramatic epochs.

There is a second difficulty which arises in a study of dramatic forms. This is the multiplicity of minor varieties, like chronicle plays, heroic plays, tragicomedies, burlesques, problem plays, and various combinations of standard forms.

Generally speaking, drama has tended to split up into an increasing number of forms as it developed. Apparently in the earliest days of dramatic development there was no adequate recognition of the differences between the various forms of dramatic appeal. We cannot be sure of this in the earliest appearance of drama in Europe, before the fifth century B. C. in ancient Greece, but it was certainly true in the Middle Ages when drama began to develop all over again after the disappearance of the classic drama. Plays were produced for centuries in medieval England before the average dramatist began to see that he could affect his audience more profoundly if he distinguished carefully between plays which were comic and plays which were tragic. It seems probable that the situation was analogous in the earliest developments in prehistoric Greece.

By the fifth century B. C., however, the Greek dramatists recognized clearly the distinction between comedy and tragedy. This understanding of the differences in purpose and method between the two forms was applied to the plays of the time, and in the fourth century B. C. Aristotle, the first great dramatic critic, discussed in his *Poetics* the essentials of comedy and tragedy as he saw them in the great plays of Æschylus, Sophocles, Euripides, and Aristophanes.

It was nearly two thousand years after Aristotle had written his *Poetics* before there was a general recognition that certain types of boisterous, humorous treatment, when separated from the more analytical methods of comedy, constituted a distinct form which came to be called farce. At about the same time (in England at the end of the seventeenth century and the beginning of the eighteenth) certain plays which limited their appeal to the more sensational and less significant aspects of tragedy were recognized as constituting a separate form called melodrama.

These two forms—melodrama and farce—are universally recognized to-day, but the dramatic student is frequently confused by the fact that most early dramatists made little attempt to distinguish farce from comedy or melodrama from tragedy. Thus, most of the comedies of Aristophanes and Plautus have large elements of farce in them, and Shakespeare's *Taming of the Shrew* and Jonson's *Epicœne,* which their authors called comedies in all honesty, are typical farces. In the same way, during the Renaissance the term *tragedy* was used to include melodrama. Some of the best Elizabethan tragedies, like Webster's *Duchess of Malfi* and Beaumont and Fletcher's *Maid's Tragedy,* made use of melodrama, while other plays called tragedies at the time, like Kyd's *Spanish Tragedy* and Shakespeare's *Titus Andronicus,* are melodrama pure and simple.

The minor forms of drama, like chronicle plays, heroic plays, tragicomedies, burlesques, and problem plays, belong to the study of particular periods of dramatic history and not to a general introductory survey of the principal dramatic forms. These minor forms rise out of peculiar interests which have dominated certain audiences and led to the development of a type of play which appeals to this interest. Generally the interest has died out after a generation or so and the type of play has disappeared with it. Thus the chronicle history play grew out of the absorbing interest of the Elizabethan audience in history, and for about a quarter of a century plays of this type rivaled comedies and tragedies in popularity. But by the time of the death of Shakespeare, the great interest in history had waned and chronicle history plays had lost their popularity. Since Shakespeare's time they have been so rare as to demand consideration in only the most exhaustive studies. In the same way, the problem play, which attained a great vogue in the last quarter of the nineteenth century and the first quarter of the twentieth through the efforts of Ibsen and Galsworthy and other social-dramatic reformers, has been rapidly disappearing from our theaters in the last ten or fifteen years.

Since these minor forms have been ephemeral interests in the long history of the drama, we shall neglect them in our consideration of the principal dramatic forms and confine our attention to the more enduring types of tragedy, comedy, melodrama, and farce.

CHAPTER II

TRAGEDY

Of all the chief dramatic forms (tragedy, comedy, melodrama, and farce), certainly the most honorable, if not the most ancient, is tragedy. It is most honorable because more than any other dramatic form it has contributed to civilized man's most constant purpose: his never-ending struggle to understand himself and the world he lives in—to understand life. It is fitting, therefore, that tragedy should come first in our consideration of the dramatic forms.

As the most aspiring of these forms, tragedy has occupied the attention of writers on the drama more than all the others. Yet for the modern student beginning a study of the drama, the definitions and discussions of these writers are often more confusing than helpful. There are two chief reasons for this confusion.

First, as we have already noted, confusion arises because different historic epochs have had different conceptions of the form, and the critics of these epochs have emphasized different aspects of tragedy. Thus Aristotle, writing in the fourth century B.C. and thinking of the plays which had been written in his and the preceding century, said, "Tragedy, then, is an imitation of an action that is serious, complete, and of a certain magnitude; in language embellished with each kind of artistic ornament, the several kinds being found in separate parts of the play; in the form of action, not of narrative; through pity and fear affecting the proper purgation of these emotions." [1]

In the Renaissance, just before the great development of English tragedy in the plays of Shakespeare and Marlowe and Webster, the English critic, William Webbe, wrote *A Discourse of English Poetrie,* which was published in 1586. In this book, Webbe speaks of tragedies as "expressing only sorrowful and lamentable histories, bringing in the persons of gods, goddesses, kings, and queens, and great state, whose parts were chiefly to express most miserable calamities and dreadful chances, which increased worse and worse, till they came to the most woeful plight that might be devised." [2]

[1] S. H. Butcher, *The Poetics of Aristotle* (London: Macmillan & Co., Ltd., 1922), p. 23.

[2] G. Gregory Smith, *Elizabethan Critical Essays* (Oxford: Clarendon Press, 1904), I, 249. We have modernized the spelling.

Finally, a modern American teacher of the drama in an attempt to frame a definition of tragedy which would apply to modern plays of the type and yet not exclude the dramatic masterpieces of the past, has said, "A tragedy is a play in which the treatment is serious, profound, and lofty, and the ending is both disastrous and inevitable."[3]

These three definitions serve to illustrate the variations in the critical statements which have been made about tragedy. Aristotle wrote of the form, the magnitude of the action, and the emotional function of tragedy. Webbe was concerned primarily with the "sorrowful" action and the high estate of the characters. Carpenter emphasized the treatment of the subject and the character of the ending. All three men seem to have certain conceptions in common; yet there is a great difference in their emphasis and in their selection of essentials.

The second reason for the confusion which often results from a study of tragedy which begins with definitions is the student's unfamiliarity with the plays. He has no means of testing the adequacy of the definitions. This being the case, there is a strong temptation simply to memorize any definition proposed and then to attempt to judge plays without having had any broad dramatic experience. Such a procedure, of course, leads to confusion. It is much better to attempt first to understand certain famous tragedies as well as possible. Then, after becoming thoroughly acquainted with a number of effective tragedies of different periods, the student may be in a position to broaden his understanding by examining these plays in the light of a definition.

We shall begin our study of tragedy, therefore, not with a concise definition but with some consideration of various elements which appear again and again in great tragedies. We are not yet in a position to decide whether *all* good tragedies *must* have these characteristics, or whether they are peculiar to tragedy.

Perhaps the characteristic which the average person is most likely to associate with tragedy is an unhappy ending, usually the death of the most important character. It cannot be denied that most tragedies do end unhappily, but it does not require a knowledge of very many plays to see that an unhappy ending can scarcely be called the most essential trait of the form. Would *As You Like It* be a tragedy if Rosalind were accidentally stabbed in the last scene? Would *The School for Scandal* be a tragedy if Sir Peter and Lady Teazle had another quarrel in the last act, and if Sir Peter, in a fit of rage, shot his wife and then committed suicide in remorse?

[3] Bruce Carpenter, *The Way of the Drama* (New York: Prentice-Hall, Inc., 1929), p. 36.

It does not take much thought about the effect of an unhappy ending to see that it is not death or a disappointed love affair which makes a play a tragedy. In fact, there are a few good tragedies—Euripides' *Iphigenia in Tauris* for example—which end happily.

A characteristic much more important to great tragedies than an unhappy ending is their treatment of a serious subject, a significant struggle between a character or a group of characters and some great force. In *Œdipus Rex* Sophocles writes of the struggle of a man against fate or the gods; Shakespeare shows Hamlet struggling to throw off the shackles of his own character; Ibsen's *Ghosts* depicts a woman fighting against heredity and the hypocritical code of society. Each dramatist has selected a conflict which had great significance for the audience of his time, and in the finest tragedies this struggle has been depicted with such a depth of understanding and such an honesty of purpose that the plays have never lost their power to move and to ennoble thinking men even though the conflict itself may seem less important or less real than it once did. This selection of a subject or theme of great consequence has been characteristic of the greatest tragedy since the time of the ancient Greeks.

Closely connected with the treatment of a serious subject is another characteristic of tragedy equally important but more difficult to define. All great tragedies which have come to be acknowledged as plays of permanent value have been so written that they convince an audience of their universal significance. The spectator feels that he is seeing not simply a few events in the life of an individual but an action whose importance extends beyond the life of one man or even of one age. Many devices have been used by the dramatists of different ages to obtain this effect, but, however produced, it is a familiar element in the appeal of great tragedies. People no longer believe in the Olympian gods who decreed the horrible fate of Œdipus; yet Sophocles' tragedy, which portrays the working out of that fate, has for thinking men the same universal appeal it had more than two thousand years ago. Likewise the black magic, the diabolical presence, and the literal hell of Marlowe's *Dr. Faustus* have become unreal for most moderns, but the tormented figure of the doctor as he cries,

> Ah, Faustus,
> Now hast thou but one bare hour to live,
> And then thou must be damn'd perpetually!
> Stand still, you ever-moving spheres of Heaven,
> That time may cease, and midnight never come!

has the same universal tragic significance it had for Marlowe's Elizabethan contemporaries.

This universality in the appeal of great tragedies is so important that it will be worth while to examine some of the means which tragic dramatists have used to attain it. One of the earliest devices was the selection of a hero or protagonist [4] whose rank was such that he seemed more important than ordinary men. In the days when the fate of a king was likely to influence greatly the welfare of the people of his kingdom, tragic writers usually selected a king or a prince for their chief character. Æschylus wrote about Orestes, son of the King of Argos; Sophocles' greatest play is concerned with the tragic career of Œdipus, King of Thebes; Shakespeare selected Hamlet, Prince of Denmark, and Lear, King of Britain. When we see the tragic fate of these men, we seem to see the ruin of the whole nation which they represent, and the magnitude of the catastrophe makes us feel that we are witnessing an action of universal significance.

Often tragic dramatists gain this effect through the use of some force that is more than human in its power, and we feel that we ourselves, or any other human being, would have been as completely overwhelmed as the hero of the tragedy. We have already noticed Sophocles' use of fate and Marlowe's employment of the supernatural in *Dr. Faustus*. Shakespeare makes a similar use of the ghost in *Hamlet* and the witches in *Macbeth*. Modern dramatists, of course, are restricted in their use of gods and ghosts because of the changes in popular belief, but they make use of other forces greater than man which have a like effect on the audience. In Synge's *Riders to the Sea,* old Maurya is just as powerless in her struggle against the sea as Œdipus was in his struggles against the decree of the gods. Mrs. Alving, in *Ghosts,* fights for her son, but she is just as hopelessly doomed to defeat as Hamlet or Dr. Faustus, because she is fighting heredity. Thus the type of superhuman force used in tragedy may vary as popular beliefs change, but the effectiveness of employing such a force as a means of giving universal significance to the action remains the same.[5]

Another quality which will be found to distinguish the work of great tragic dramatists is honesty. Perhaps this term is not familiar as applied to plays, but it is not difficult to understand. All plays, if they are successful, *seem* to be true to life, at least during the performance. But we realize before we have witnessed any large number of plays that many of them have simply been made to appear true for the moment; that the dramatist is not trying to

[4] See Chapter II, Section A, for a discussion of Greek tragedy.

[5] These are by no means all the devices which dramatists have used to give universal significance to the action of their tragedies, but they are enough to illustrate the value of the characteristic and some of the means of its attainment.

show us life as he really sees it but is willing to write anything that will bring customers to the box office. As a matter of fact, most plays are written this way. The dramatist has learned what the average audience—as unintelligent as most *average* groups—would like to see, and he shows it to them in his play, regardless of how false or misleading or trivial it may be. Every one has seen plays of this sort; nine out of ten "movies" scarcely pretend to be anything else. Such plays are fundamentally dishonest.

A tragedy, however, cannot be written in this way. The dramatist must be honest; he must show his audience life as he really sees it. As we have already noted, the tragic dramatist deals with serious subjects and tries to give his action universal significance. He is concerned with something more than mere entertainment. Under these circumstances, sincerity is the least that the audience can demand, and all noteworthy tragedies are fundamentally honest.

Perhaps this initial discussion is enough to guide the student who is approaching the study of the form tragedy for the first time. In his study of the plays of each of the great tragic periods, a consideration of the characteristics of the plays of that period will be more pertinent than it is here. It will, furthermore, help him to distinguish between the permanent and the temporal traits of tragedy. Then, after he has become familiar with a few of the world's tragic masterpieces and with the peculiar conditions affecting the Greek, the Elizabethan, the neo-classic, and the modern conception of tragedy, he may with profit study the generalizations and the definitions of Aristotle and Rymer and Schiller and Brunetière.

A. GREEK TRAGEDY

Tragedy was first developed by the ancient Greeks. Not only is this dramatic form their invention, but they brought it to such a high state of perfection that Greek tragedy after nearly 2,500 years is still thought of as the standard of greatness.

But the modern playgoer who reads a play of Æschylus or Sophocles or Euripides with no preparation is likely to be disappointed. He will surely recognize fine poetry, but the play is apt to seem unreal—full of irrelevant lyrics, of impossible action, and altogether much more a series of poems than a play. This strangeness is not surprising when we stop to think of the innumerable changes which 2,500 years have necessarily made in the theater, the technique of the actors, the circumstances of production, and, most of all, in the ideas, tastes, and prejudices of the audience. So that if he is to appreciate the full greatness of Greek tragedy, the reader must begin with some consideration of the people for whom it was written and the circumstances of its production.

The Times

All the great tragedies of the Greeks were produced at Athens between 500 B.C. and 400 B.C. This century included the period of Athenian glory—the Golden Age, the Age of Pericles—and part of the period of disillusionment which followed it. To understand the plays we must know something of the beliefs and customs of the people of Athens during this time.

Perhaps the ideas or conceptions of the Athenian which seem most foreign to us and which, because of their great importance in the theater, stand most in the way of our full understanding of the tragedies are his attitude toward religion and the gods and his attitude toward the state. Greek tragedy was religious in origin and purpose, and it was produced by the state for the people as a whole.

Greek religion is confusing to the modern student because it includes so much that he does not think of as religious and excludes so much that he does so think of. Whatever his personal attitude toward religion, the modern student is likely to associate it with morality and churches and probably with creeds. All these were unimportant or unknown to the religious Greek. Religion for him suggested Poetry and Music and Nature, his ancestors, and the history of his country. His gods were the impersonations of the powers of Nature and of his own passions and attributes, of the Earth and the Sky and the Sea, fire, wind, and thunder, of Love and Wisdom. The gods were, furthermore, his own ancestors—every family traced its origin to some hero who was the son of a god and a mortal. In form and desires the gods were beings like men. Like men, they loved and fought and quarreled; they had their favorites and their enemies; they often thwarted each other in their desires and frequently bore grudges against certain mortals or against other gods; and a great deal of their time was spent on earth, interfering—helping or hindering—in the affairs of men.

All this system of belief brought religion and the gods into more intimate touch with the lives of the people than is the case to-day. A man did not succeed or fail because of luck or his own efforts. If his ship were dashed on the rocks in a storm, Poseidon was angry because of some slight. If Athens won an important battle, the sole credit was due not to the victorious general or the Athenian soldiers but to Athena, who had fought on the side of her city. If the rain came just at the time it was most needed, Zeus had heard the prayers of the people and had been pleased with their offerings. The Greek was thus brought into constant touch with his gods; every event of his day had a religious significance, and good fortune or catastrophe was not meaningless. By his religion, in Dickinson's phrase, the ancient Greek was "made at home in the world."

In his worship of these familiar gods, the Greek of the fifth century B.C. was again different from the modern religious man. This difference was due in part to the close relationship between religion and the state. The gods were not only the ancestors of men; they were the founders and protectors of the various Greek city-states and even of particular institutions of the government. Thus the state itself was in part a religious institution and performed many of the functions which we associate with an organized church. The ancient Greek had no such church. His priests were simply public officials appointed to perform certain rites. The observances which we might characterize as "the duty of all good Christians" he would think of as "the duty of all good citizens"; his religious life was a phase of his political life. Religious and political affairs were so bound up together that the average Greek probably did not always distinguish clearly between them. Political alliances were frequently made to support the cult of some god, and the influence of the omens of the gods on political or military undertakings was profound.

This close relationship between political and religious activities explains the peculiar character of the Greek festivals of which the tragedies were a part. Fundamentally these festivals were religious, but they were also what we should call legal holidays, and the celebrations were organized and financed by the state. Under the auspices of the state they were one of the most important of the religious observances of the Greeks. Though there were many of them, they were all accompanied by contests and processions, songs and dances, which were designed to express the fundamental religious conceptions of the people.

Since the performing of tragedies was one part of the celebrating of two such religious festivals, the City Dionysia and the Lenæa, it is worth while to notice more closely certain particular Greek religious beliefs which, not quite familiar to us, may otherwise prove confusing when we find them playing an important part in the tragedies.

One of the ideas, basic in Greek tragedy but rather unfamiliar to us, is the conception of the sin of pride and its inevitable punishment. The Greeks associated this punishment with the goddess Nemesis, the scourge of the man who forgot the part of the gods in his successes and became presumptuous because of his long-continued prosperity. To the Greek audience nothing in a tragedy more ominously foreshadowed the downfall of the hero than an expression of his pride. Thus when Æschylus wrote his play *The Persians* in celebration of the Greek victory over the hosts of Xerxes, he was careful not to show the Greeks in triumph but to fill his play with the mourning of the Persians. On the other hand, when Sophocles in *Œdipus Rex* made his hero refer to himself in his first speech as "world-honored Œdipus," the audience must have shuddered at his presumption. And when in *Agamemnon* Clytemnestra persuaded her husband that, as conqueror of Troy, he should not set his foot on the common earth but should walk from his chariot into the palace over a tapestry, the audience must have held its breath as Agamemnon hesitated to indulge his pride in this ostentation. When he succumbed, the audience felt that he had invited his doom.

Another religious idea common to tragedy was the dangerous course of the unbalanced man or the man who, because of personal tastes or preferences, neglected certain phases of the activities and interests of the well-balanced man. In the Greek conception such a man flattered the gods of his choice and neglected others, and jealousy was common among the gods. Hippolytus, for instance, was a young man whose interests centered in what we should call the sporting world. He was a great hunter and charioteer. Naturally enough, since the athletic outdoor life was his hobby, he was little interested in women and love—his devotion to Artemis brought about his neglect of Aphrodite. When Euripides wrote the tragedy of *Hippolytus* he emphasized this defect as a foreshadowing of disaster, a foreshadowing which no Greek in his audience would miss. Aphrodite herself in the prologue calls attention to his neglect of her; the statues of Artemis and of Aphrodite stand in full view of the audience throughout the performance; and very early in the play an old huntsman warns Hippolytus that only evil can follow his constant devotion to Artemis and his neglect of Aphrodite.

Again and again in Greek tragedy the dramatist is concerned with the religious ideas of sin and punishment. Æschylus, in particular, seems never to lose sight of them. But the Greek idea of sin was not the same as ours. It did not involve any interest in what we call the conscience of the sinner. Sometimes the sin was committed lightly and forgotten; sometimes it was unconscious; sometimes the sin for which a man was punished had been committed by his fathers. In any case there was none of the morbid brooding, the "consciousness of sin," which occupies such a prominent place in Christian literature.

Usually the sins for which the characters in the plays suffer have been committed before the tragedy opens. Agamemnon suffers for the sins of the House of Atreus committed before he was born and for his own sins committed before the fall of Troy; the crimes for which Œdipus suffers have nearly all been committed before the play opens; Antigone and Creon, in Sophocles' *Antigone,* suffer for crimes which the audience has not seen. Often these tragedies involve the punishment which a man undergoes for the sins of his fathers, as in *Agamemnon* and *The Libation-Bearers* and Euripides' *Electra.* The Greek dramatist could generally assume a knowledge of these stories on the part of his audience, but the modern reader, if he is fully to understand a play, must first review the myth upon which it was based.

The Origin of Greek Tragedy and the Occasions of Its Production

Greek tragedy, then, was religious in character, not only because the performance of the tragedies was always part of a religious festival, but because the form itself had been developed out of an ancient religious observance. It is not necessary here to consider very fully the origin of tragedy, but some reference to it will make clearer the form and method of production of the plays of Æschylus, Sophocles, and Euripides.

Tragedy originated in and was always associated with the worship of Dionysus (Bacchus), the god of wine. Performances of plays in ancient Greece were always part of the festivals in his honor, and his altar was always in the theater in full view of the spectators. The tragedies which have come down to us are full of relics of the dances in honor of Dionysus which antedate by many years the birth of tragedy. The most striking of these relics is the chorus itself. The institution of the chorus seems very strange to the modern theater-goer, but long before there were any characters, this chorus was associated with the worship of Dionysus; its members danced in honor of the god. When tragedy first developed, only one actor appeared with the chorus, and he carried on dialogues with its leader. The precise nature of this earliest form of tragedy is obscure now, but it seems that stories from the Greek myths were represented by means of mimetic action on the part of the one actor, by dialogues between this actor and the leader of the chorus, and by songs and symbolic dances by the chorus. The songs and dances must have been by far the most important part of these earliest tragedies. It is with these early one-actor plays that the name of the actor-dramatist, Thespis, is associated.

When historic tragedy appears in the plays of the first great dramatist, Æschylus, certain conventional features are well established. The first is the chorus, a group of dancers, at first fifty in number but later reduced to twelve and then raised to fifteen. The second is the subject matter, which is taken from the religious myths, though there are a few plays based on Greek history, since the early Greeks did not distinguish sharply between history and myth. A third convention is the limited number of actors. In the earliest plays of Æschylus only two are used, but in most Greek tragedies there are three. The Greeks usually called the first of these tragic actors the *protagonist* and the second the *deuteragonist.* It is from this Greek designation that the leading character in the tragedy of later periods is often called the protagonist.

The Greek limitation of the number of actors in a tragedy to three does not mean that only three characters could appear in the play, or that only three men [6] might be on the stage at once. It means that all the speaking parts were taken by three actors, though mutes, or what we should call "extras," could appear on the stage with them. Thus all plays were so planned that not more than three characters ever spoke in the same scene. This number does not include the leader of the chorus, who often spoke to the characters. He did not, however, have a name part; he might be "An Old Man," or "A Huntsman," or "A Theban Elder."

Another unfamiliar convention in the Greek tragedies is the avoidance of violence on the stage. This convention was due partly to the type of production and partly to the religious character of the plays. The old taboos of the ancient ritual prevented the murder of one actor by another on the stage. Of course Greek tragedies do involve violence. They are full of it. But all murders and most other violent acts occur off stage and are reported by messengers or overheard by the audience, or the bodies are revealed by one of the machines of the Greek stage called the *eccyclema.*

Closely associated with the religious origin of tragedy is the influence of the occasions of its production in the fifth century. In ancient Greece, tragedies were never given in private or for commercial purposes. They were presented in Athens twice a year, once at the Lenæa, a festival which took place late in January, and again at the festival of the City Dionysia, in March. In each case the tragedies were presented in competition. Three tragic poets were selected to compete by the archons, or city officials. Each poet wrote three tragedies and a satyr play for the contest. Then after long and strenuous rehearsal these twelve plays were publicly produced as part of the festival. They were presented at the expense of the city; that is, the city either paid directly or persuaded some public-spirited wealthy citizen to pay for the trainer, the actors,

[6] Greek actors were always men; women never appeared on the stage.

the chorus, and the flute player, to purchase or rent the costumes and masks, and to care for the theater. There was a small charge for admission, but this charge kept no one away for the city paid the admission of any citizen who could not pay for himself.

At the performances of the plays, ten officially selected judges were present. When they had seen all the plays, they awarded the prize to the author of the best group. From fragmentary inscriptions and occasional references, we know the outcome of certain of these contests, and several of the winning plays are still extant. Thus at the contest of the City Dionysia in 458 B.C. Æschylus won with his tragedies *Agamemnon, The Libation-Bearers,* and *The Eumenides.*

The Theater and the Performance

One of the most powerful of the influences on the drama of any time is the theater in which the plays are presented. The more plays one reads, the more striking this fact becomes. The theater at Athens not only influenced greatly the plays which were written to be acted in it, but was so different from ours that it requires rather full discussion.

To the modern theater-goer, the Athenian theater of the fifth century B.C. seems much more like an amphitheater or a stadium than it does like a playhouse. It was not really a building at all, but a semi-circular series of seats on a hillside about an open dancing place, a stage elevated little or not at all above the level of the dancing place, and a scene building which furnished a background and dressing-rooms. This theater, much larger than any modern one, held as many as 17,000 spectators.[7]

The most prominent part of this theater was the dancing place which the Greeks called the *orchestra.*[8] In the fifth-century theater at Athens this was a circular place sixty feet in diameter. Here the chorus danced and sang, or stood during the dialogue. Though they occasionally went onto the stage, they usually stayed in the orchestra during the entire performance. In the center of this orchestra was a small stone altar to Dionysus called a *thymele,* a constant reminder of the religious character of the plays.

The stage of this theater, the place for the actors as opposed to the chorus, was directly behind the orchestra. The most recent investigations seem to indicate that it was on the same level as the orchestra, or not elevated more than one or two steps at the most.

[7] The average New York theater holds about 1,000 people.

[8] This is the original meaning of the word. Our use of it to indicate a group of musicians did not develop for more than 2,000 years and was taken from the part of our theater in which they sit.

It was as wide as the orchestra, though it must have been rather shallow. Though this stage was the normal acting place, the actors sometimes came out into the orchestra, just as the chorus occasionally left the orchestra for the stage.

Behind this stage was the building called the *scæna* or scene-building, which was used for the background of the action, and for the dressing-rooms of the players. This building had several doors which were used as entrances onto the stage. Across the front of the scene-building was a row of columns called the *proscenium.* A roof from the scene-building to this row of columns and the roof of the scene-building itself formed convenient high places—house-tops or walls or hills—for use in the plays. The lonely sentinel watching for the signal fires from Troy at the beginning of *Agamemnon* evidently stood on the roof. The front of the scene-building was, of course, the same for all plays and formed what we should call a permanent set. This is the reason why the action of Greek tragedies nearly always takes place in front of a palace or a temple, from which the actors are supposed to be coming when they appear on the stage from the scene-building. Thus, when Œdipus entered from the palace at the beginning of *Œdipus Rex,* the actor really came out of the scene-building.

But actors did not always come onto the stage from a building; there were other entrances to the Greek stage. The most important ones were right and left between the seats of the auditorium and the scene-building. They were really exits from the theater which were used by the audience before and after the performance. Though they were used by all characters who came onto the stage from some out-of-door place (i.e., not the scene-building), they were most convenient for the entrance of processions and crowds of people. Such entrances could be made much more telling in this way than they can on most modern stages. These side entrances would make most effective the procession which comes upon the stage in *Agammenon* with the soldiers back from Troy and the chariots of Agamemnon and Cassandra. The chorus usually entered and left the orchestra by these entrances.

Some time in the fifth century, wings which were called the *parascenia* were added at either end of the scene-building. In the later plays, especially in the plays of Euripides, the appearance of gods on the stage became popular. When the gods appeared in the earlier plays, they had walked on or been drawn across the stage in cars or chariots, but in the later plays the gods descended from above or spoke from mid-air. This was managed by means of a crane called the *machine* operating from the roof of one of the *parascenia.* By the use of this crane Medea was carried off at the end of Euripides' *Medea.* The dramatist used it again to manage the appearance and disappearance of Artemis in a cloud at the end of *Hippolytus* and of Dionysus at the close of *The Bacchæ.*

In the later Greek tragedies, especially in the plays of Euripides, it became increasingly common to introduce a god in this machine, so common in fact that *the god from the machine* (often given in its Latin form, *deus ex machina*) became a common phrase. The phrase is often used in a derogatory fashion to indicate that the dramatist has resorted to the miraculous appearance of a god to disentangle his too-complicated plot.

Another device which was used in the Greek plays was the *eccyclema.* Modern students of the Athenian drama are not quite sure about the character of this piece of apparatus, though there are numerous examples of its use. The *eccyclema* was utilized to make sudden revelations of tableaux, the result of some action, frequently a murder, which had occurred indoors out of sight of the audience. Thus, in Euripides' *Madness of Heracles,* Heracles, who has slain his wife and children, has been bound to a pillar inside the palace. As the chorus chants about the deed, Heracles suddenly appears, bound to his pillar. Again, in Sophocles' *Ajax,* the protagonist suddenly appears among the bodies of the cattle he has slaughtered. There are several references to the device by which these revelations were made, and from these references certain authorities have concluded that there were two types of *eccyclema.* One was a simple platform on wheels which was rolled out through a door of the scene-building with the proper actors posed upon it when the time for the revelation came. The other type of *eccyclema* was a circular platform on a pivot placed in one of the open doorways. Across the diameter of this circular platform was a screen, dividing it into two parts. A tableau was set on one part and then the other part, the empty half, was turned toward the audience until the proper moment for the revelation. At this moment (in *The Madness of Heracles* the moment when the chorus chants, "Alas! Behold the doors of the stately palace fall asunder."), the *eccyclema* was turned on its pivot in the doorway. The empty half of the circular platform disappeared from the view of the audience, and the half with the tableau upon it swung into view. After the proper interval, the *eccyclema* was turned again, swinging the tableau out of sight and revealing the back of the screen again.

These are the main characteristics of the Greek theater and the chief devices used in its production. The plan of the theater itself may be made somewhat more clear by the diagram on page 27.

The production of a Greek tragedy at this open-air theater in Athens during the City Dionysia or the Lenæa was, of course, very different from any modern performance. The characteristics of the Greek theater and the religious origin and occasion of the plays made this inevitable.

There are two general distinctions which will be found most helpful to keep in mind when trying to visualize the performance of a Greek tragedy. The first is the fact that while Elizabethan and modern tragedy is primarily only a form of entertainment, Greek tragedy was a religious ritual. The second distinction is that in

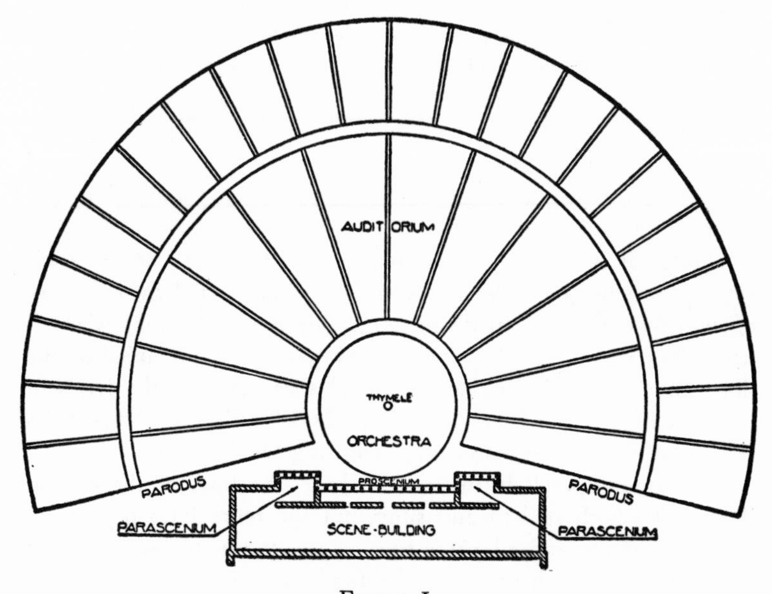

FIGURE I

GROUND PLAN OF A GREEK THEATER

Reprinted from R. C. Flickinger, *The Greek Theater and Its Drama* by permission of the University of Chicago Press.

many ways the performance of a tragedy in Athens must have been more like a modern opera than a modern play.

The religious element, as we have seen, was prominent in the minds of the audience. The occasion was a religious festival; the theater was a temple of Dionysus; the priests occupied a prominent place in the theater; the plot of the play was always a familiar religious one; the gods themselves frequently appeared on the stage; and in many of the tragedies, particularly those of Æschylus, the theme of the play was a profoundly religious one. On the other hand, we must not make the mistake of thinking of the religious attitude in modern terms. The Greek audience was far from being subdued and meekly reverent. Bad actors were sometimes hissed off the stage and occasionally even had stones thrown at them. A peculiarly Athenian expression of disapproval was the beating of the heels of sandals against the front of the stone benches. Thirty thousand sandals pounding in this fashion must have made quite a din for the actor who spoke his lines badly.

The musical character of Greek tragedy is not so unfamiliar to us as the religious element, since we have something similar in opera. A fine voice, not only a good speaking voice but also a fine singing voice, was by far the most important qualification for the Greek actor. Since there were at the most only three speaking actors in a tragedy, each actor had to be able to vary his intonations and the quality of his voice when he appeared in different rôles in the same play, and this was particularly difficult since, as we have seen, the actor had to play not only men's parts but women's parts as well. This required a voice of great flexibility and compass as well as the great power necessary to reach seventeen thousand people in an outdoor theater.

Though it is not always possible to tell just what parts of their rôles were sung by these actors and what parts spoken, it is easy enough to make general distinctions. The lyrical portions were almost always sung as solos, duets, or trios, often accompanied by the flute. In general, the highly emotional speeches, like the lyrics of Œdipus after he has been blinded or Hippolytus' prayer to Artemis before he goes out to his death, were sung by the actor.

The same general distinctions apply to the lines of the chorus. They were both spoken and sung, but the more lyric parts were sung. There are, indeed, some lines of the chorus so beautiful that they almost sing themselves, like those just before the death of Phædra in *Hippolytus,* "Could I take me to some cavern for mine hiding."

This chorus and its function in the tragedies are likely to present the greatest puzzle to the modern reader. We have nothing at all like it. The chorus of the modern musical play, though it bears the same name and though it dances and tries to sing, is utterly different in function. We must remember that the Greek chorus was a relic of the days before tragedy had evolved. In many ways it was an anachronism in a play, and in the later days of Greek tragedy it was given a more and more subordinate place. But the ritualistic character of the plays made it impossible that the chorus be abolished, and with that amazing Greek artistic ingenuity which seemed always able to transform a handicap into an advantage, the tragic dramatists made of the chorus a most effective dramatic instrument.

The use of the chorus varies in different plays and in different parts of the same play. Sometimes the members of the chorus are simply minor characters who fill out the scene and give expression to miscellaneous ideas of the crowd like Shakespeare's first, second, and third citizen. Æschylus uses them in this way in *Agamemnon* when they hear the cries of Agamemnon from inside the palace, and Euripides makes them serve the same purpose in *Hippolytus* when Phædra admits her love for her stepson.

Sometimes, as a group, the chorus becomes the protagonist of the play, as in *The Trojan Women,* where the members of the chorus are the Trojan women. Again they are used to emphasize the position of important characters. Thus, in Sophocles' *Antigone,* the chorus of Theban senators who disapprove of her illegal acts build up the bitter loneliness of Antigone in the play. This function is closely allied to another which the chorus often performs, that of an ideal audience. That is, the dramatist makes the chorus react to events upon the stage in the same way in which he hopes his audience will react, but more articulately. They express horror when he would have his audience shudder, sorrow when he would have them despair. This function is sometimes performed directly simply by comments on the action of the play, but in its most effective and most peculiarly Greek form it is indirect, as in the foreboding song of the chorus after the King and Queen have entered the palace in *Agamemnon,* or in the beautiful song of escape in *Hippolytus* after Phædra has rushed off the stage to kill herself. Of course the possibility of subtle effects like these was greatly increased in Greek tragedy by the fact that the audience already knew the general outline of the plot of the play. The dramatist could concern himself with nuances of dramatic effect instead of simple efforts to keep the movement of the action clear and the situation of the characters unconfused.[9]

But the songs of the chorus do not puzzle the modern reader so much as their dances which, to us, seem highly inappropriate in a tragedy. To us the word *dance* suggests something trivial however much we may enjoy it. But to the Greeks, the dance was a form of art, like music or poetry. It was not merely a gay movement of the feet but an expression of ideas by means of the human body, just as music was an expression of ideas in sound and sculpture an expression of ideas in stone. Aristotle defined dancing as an imitation of "actions, characters, and passions, by means of postures and rhythmical movements." The choral dance was thus essentially

[9] An excellent example of the use of the audience's knowledge of the story for subtle effects is found in the superb tragic irony which Sophocles has built into *Œdipus Rex.*

mimetic in character; it supplied the action of a scene reported on the stage, or it suggested the passion underlying the emotional outburst of an actor.

When we think of the dance in this way, we are not surprised to learn that it demanded especially a skilful use of the arms. A famous dancer who appeared in the plays of Æschylus is said to have been able to "depict events with his hands." One writer of antiquity in telling a man how to show off his accomplishments advises him to dance, "if his arms are flexible." One of our scraps of information about the chorus tells us that the various dances or postures were classified, but we know only a few of them, such as thrusting with the sword and shaking the fist in menace. These choral movements accompanying a tragedy were slow, majestic, and portentous; the dumb show was grave and dignified. A dance of this type, a sensitive response of the whole body to certain ideas in the play and not simply a mechanical rhythmic movement of the feet, would be far from disconcerting; rather would it serve to increase the vividness of the tragic story unfolding on the stage.

The twelve or fifteen members of the chorus were made to look as much alike as possible. They all wore the same inconspicuous costume and identical masks; there was no distraction because of the individual characteristics of any one dancer. They had been rigorously trained in their part for weeks before the performance and were expected to be perfect in execution. Their movements were partially military, and the dancers were never scattered about the orchestra like a crowd, but were always in precise formation.

The action which went on behind the orchestra on the stage is not so unfamiliar to us as the action of the chorus, but it was still quite different from the acting in a modern theater. Most of the differences result from the characteristics of the Greek theater and Greek productions which we have already seen. First there was the very large theater. The modern type of production in such a theater would have made the actors look puny and the action ridiculous. Furthermore, nine-tenths of the audience would have heard nothing. Since the characters in Greek tragedies were mostly heroes and prophets and gods, they could not appear puny or ridiculous, and several devices helped them to avoid such a contretemps. Their features were made distinct by masks which were always worn and which served much the same purpose as make-up in our theater.[10] These masks are said also to have increased the resonance of

[10] These masks were not all alike, but were made to bear the expression most characteristic of the individual. They could be changed when necessary. In *Œdipus Rex,* for instance, when Œdipus returned to the stage blinded, he certainly wore a new mask. The masks meant, of course, that the actor's expression could not change

the actors' voices. The robes worn on the stage were colorful and distinctive to give the characters individuality, just as the costumes of the chorus were uniform and inconspicuous to keep individuality subordinated. These robes were flowing and dignified. The danger that the actor might appear dwarfed in the huge theater was avoided by increasing his size, though keeping his proportions perfect. His chest and limbs were padded, and his height was increased by means of a special shoe with a huge wooden sole, called a *cothurnus*. A cone-shaped prolongation of the upper part of the mask (which was made to look like hair or a wreath or a helmet, depending upon the character) also served to give the actor height and dignity.

These details of production, like the lines of the tragedies themselves, show that the keynote of a Greek tragedy was dignity. The ideas and the characters and the plot of the play demanded it, and the staging contributed to it.

These various characteristics of the Greek plays, theaters, and productions combine to develop certain characteristics in the tragedies. One was the method of introducing characters. Since there were no playbills or programs to give the *dramatis personæ,* characters were generally introduced on their first appearance, often by the chorus.

Another of the repeated problems of the dramatist was the necessity of explaining the constant presence of the chorus, which also offered almost insuperable difficulties to any change of place or time. This is the chief reason why Greek tragedies generally had unity of place and tried to have unity of time. Unity of time was sometimes obtained, however, by simply ignoring the necessary lapse of time, as Æschylus in *Agamemnon* ignored the time required by the Greeks to get back from Troy.

Another peculiar feature of Greek tragedy is the consistent avoidance of interior scenes. On the modern stage interiors are common because in our theaters an indoor scene can be presented more easily than an outdoor one and because we spend most of our lives indoors. Just the opposite was true in Greece. The average Greek spent the majority of his waking hours out-of-doors and, perhaps a more conclusive reason, it was impossible to present an interior scene in an open-air theater.

while he was on the stage. This immobility of expression is likely to appear to us as a serious handicap, but we must remember that in a huge daylight theater changes of expression could have been seen by only a few hundred people even if the actors had worn no masks. Even in a modern theater, where changes of expression can be seen, there is a great deal to be said for the use of masks. Some successful modern dramatists, Eugene O'Neill for instance, are very enthusiastic about them and only reluctantly forego their use.

The Tragic Dramatists

After such a long-winded discussion of Greek tragedy as this, it ought not to be necessary to say very much about the men who wrote it. A little information, however, will make the plays themselves somewhat clearer.

Greek tragedy, as the term is commonly used, always refers to the extant plays of three dramatists, Æschylus, Sophocles, and Euripides. All three of them wrote in the fifth century B. C.

Æschylus, the oldest, was born 525 B. C. and lived until 456. His father was a member of the "old nobility" of Athens. Æschylus as a young man fought in the wars against Persia, so distinguishing himself in the famous battle of Marathon that his prowess as a soldier was never forgotten in Athens even after he had become her greatest dramatist.

When Æschylus first began to write, tragedy was still near to its prehistoric origins. He added a second actor to the one who had taken all the parts before, invented many of the tragic costumes and accoutrements, and developed the stage. He acted in his plays himself and trained his own chorus. Since he was writing in the early days when religious beliefs had not been questioned and the glory of Athens was every man's theme, his plays are profoundly religious in conception and patriotic in tone. They are less modern in technique than the others, and the chorus still has a very large part of the lines in his plays. He is said to have written ninety plays, but only seven are extant.

Sophocles was born in 497 B. C. and died in 405. He had a great contemporary reputation, but his love of Athens led him to reject many invitations to visit the courts of rich princes. Tradition says that he held civic offices and even went on foreign embassies. When he was fifty-five, he was appointed general with Pericles in the Samian war.

Tragedy was a much more highly developed form when Sophocles began to write. He was less interested in religious truths than Æschylus and more interested in dramatic technique and in character. He added the third actor in the production of the plays and invented many of the devices used in the theater. In his plays the chorus is less important than in the plays of Æschylus, but the characters are more closely studied, assuming more the characteristics of human beings and less those of huge figures representing human woes. He wrote over a hundred plays, of which eight are extant.

Euripides, the youngest of the tragic poets, was born in 485 B. C. and died in 406. Though only twelve years younger than Sophocles he represented a new age. For him the gods were no longer the center of the universe, as they had been for Æschylus, and Athens was not the perfect state which could do no wrong. He attacked the Athenians for their tyranny and sordidness, and he hated the gods for their cruelty and injustice. He was a doubter and a questioner. Although while he lived the old beliefs were beginning to die out, still he was ahead of his time, and like all such men was accused of being an atheist, a teacher of immorality, and a corrupter of youth. This unpopularity was increased because he was not a "mixer" but preferred to live by himself. In his old age Athens became so unfriendly to him that he went into voluntary exile.

It is partly for these reasons that the plays of Euripides seem to us more modern than the others. In them he reduces still further the part of the chorus and treats his characters more as individuals than did his predecessors. He is particularly interested in women and frequently presents problems which are peculiarly women's problems. Unlike the earlier dramatists, he did not think a love affair unfit to be treated in a tragedy. It was partly because of these innovations and of his unconventional treatment of women that the Athenians of his time called him immoral and a woman-hater.

In his plays Euripides is forced to do more explaining of the myths upon which his tragedies are based than Æschylus and Sophocles did, partly because the myths were not so well known in his time and partly because he was inclined to use the less familiar versions of the mythical stories and not the popular versions utilized by Æschylus and Sophocles. Thus the prologue with which so many of his plays begin was really necessary.

Though he was not popular in his own day, Euripides became one of the most admired poets of Greece within a century of his death. And to the modern reader he seems to write with a knowledge of humanity and a sympathy with it not found in Æschylus or Sophocles. Only eighteen of the ninety plays he wrote are extant.

B. MEDIEVAL TRAGEDY

The great tragedies of fifth-century Athens were imitated by lesser Greek poets and by the Romans, especially Seneca, but they had no worthy successors in the ancient world. In early Christian times, the old drama was stamped out through the efforts of the barbarians and the Christian Church. For centuries there was nothing in Europe which we should call drama at all.

When the drama did appear again, it had to develop from the most rudimentary beginnings, almost as if plays had never been known in the world before. As it has always done, it began in religious observances, and it grew for more than five hundred years in England before it was weaned from the Church. This medieval drama never did develop a body of what we should call fine plays, but for centuries it kept alive the taste for drama in England. It is from these medieval plays and not from the tragedies and comedies of ancient Greece that our modern drama has grown.

Properly speaking, there were no real tragedies and very few real comedies written in medieval times. The plays were usually dramatic hash—serious scenes and comic scenes mixed higgledy-piggledy with very little conception of dramatic unity. A few of the plays, however, show a surprising knowledge of comic technique and stand out as well-developed comedies. Though there are no fully developed tragedies in the medieval drama of England, there are serious plays which display an effective handling of situation and character, of pathos and suspense. It is in these plays that we are interested here, because even though they are not tragedies themselves, they did perform something of the function of tragedy in medieval England.

The Times

Though the medieval drama of England was developed slowly during the course of more than five hundred years, its most characteristic plays are products of the fourteenth and fifteenth centuries. The period is much closer to our own than the period of Greek tragedy, but this fact does not necessarily mean that it is much more familiar; in fact most modern American readers have probably heard more and thought more about ancient Greece than about fourteenth-century England. Many of the medieval institutions are closer to our own than Greek institutions, but some knowledge of the culture of Greece is a part of the intellectual equipment of every educated man.

Probably the most important institution in medieval times, certainly by all odds the most important institution so far as the drama is concerned, was the Church. It touched the affairs of every man, woman, and child as no institution of our time can ever hope to do. Not only did it have a great deal of power as a church; it was the schools and universities, the hospitals, the charitable foundations, the provider of art, literature, music, and entertainment as well. In most countries of Europe it was more wealthy and powerful than the government itself; it was a super-state which often forced kings to give way before it and which provided a closer bond of union between the people than any sense of national unity or patriotism.

So far as the drama was concerned, the institution of most importance in medieval England after the Church was the trade gild.

Perhaps modern trade unions are as much like medieval trade gilds as any institution we have, but there are at least as many points of difference as of similarity between the two.

The medieval gild was not simply an organization of employees, but included employers as well. Thus the goldsmiths' gild of London included both the senior workers in the goldsmiths' shops and all the wealthiest jewelers and bankers (since the banking of the time was done by the goldsmiths) in the city. This gild, under authority from the city, regulated very strictly all the business affairs of its members. Membership in the gild and payment of its fees were absolutely essential before a man could do business as a goldsmith in London. The gild dictated not only wages and hours of labor but also the standard of quality for merchandise, the conditions of its manufacture, and the prices to be charged for it. The gild had power to levy heavy fines on its members, and could even confiscate a man's stock or destroy his business for infringements of its regulations.

These prerogatives make it obvious that the medieval gilds were much more powerful and wealthy than the modern trade unions. Though the activities of any particular gild were confined to its own city, in that city the gild was a real power. The government of the city was in the hands of the gilds and city officials were usually gild members who had risen to office within their particular gilds. In the overseeing of industry and commerce, the regulation of living conditions in the city, and the administration of justice, the gilds were really instruments of government.

Gilds were not only commercial and political organizations; they had social and religious functions as well. They attempted to assist their members in times of illness or misfortune, to provide for them in their old age and to protect their widows and children. As for the religious aspect, each gild had its patron saint, and on specified occasions appeared in a body at church. The organization contributed regularly to the Church, and in many of the religious festivals each gild took part as a body.

Such bodies, of course, called forth the intense loyalty and pride of their members. They combined in one organization most of the functions of modern trade unions, business and professional clubs, fraternal and benevolent orders, religious societies, and civic clubs. It is not surprising to find them in more or less friendly rivalry at civic and religious festivals or to discover that in the eyes of their members they occupied a position of importance almost as great as that of the Church itself.

The medieval townsmen who, with the folk from the surrounding villages and countryside, made up the audience at medieval plays, were by no means the equals of the Greeks who listened to the verses of Æschylus and Euripides. Most of them were illiterate, and as a group they were ignorant and credulous. The religion which dominated their plays was much more a thing of churches and creeds and priests than was the religion which had dominated the Athenian plays. Their religion had rather less to do with their everyday lives and much more to do with promises of rewards and punishments after death than had that of the Greeks. At their plays they found entertainment and spectacle and specific moral instruction—the devout and obedient man will receive God's blessing; the proud and disobedient are in danger of hell fire.

The Origin and Occasion of Medieval Plays

The drama of medieval times, like the drama of ancient Greece, had its beginnings in religious observances. The medieval church was always anxious to make its mysteries and the biblical narrative real and vivid to its uneducated members. The churches were filled with stained glass and carved wood and stone, with wall paintings and pictures, all of which portrayed the biblical stories and the essential mysteries for the people. The Mass itself was an attempt of this sort. It was very natural that the same attempt should be made by means of impersonation and dialogue.

The earliest attempts to use impersonation and dialogue in teaching the people were made, as might be expected, in connection with the two greatest occasions in the church calendar, Easter and Christmas. By the ninth century additional words were being written (in Latin, of course, like all the service of the Church) for the ecclesiastical music of the Easter service, words which put into the mouths of choristers the very speeches which the biblical account assigns to the angel and to the three Maries on the first Easter morning. When these choristers sang antiphonally—that is, one man or group of men singing the question and another the answer—the beginning of dialogue had appeared in the Church. In the course of time, these chanted dialogues (tropes, as they were called) were detached from the regular service and allowed to develop more independently. The choristers who represented the angels and the Maries were dressed to indicate their parts and were instructed to make interpretive gestures. With this development, embryo plays had appeared.

Such an effective addition to the services of the Church did not long remain unknown; it was rapidly developed and widely imitated. Just as the account of the first Easter morning could be enacted, so could the first Christmas story, and the story of Good Friday and the Annunciation, and so on through the whole New

Testament narrative. These representations were elaborated until they included not only the events of the holy day itself but also the antecedent and succeeding events. The presentation of the Nativity, for instance, developed until the audience was shown not simply the events at Bethlehem but the Old Testament prophecies of the birth of Jesus as well, and thus gradually all the Old Testament narrative.

The developments here so glibly recounted did not take place in a few months, but were the slow growth of centuries. They were taking place in most European countries as well as in England. Churchmen, as they traveled about, reported what they had seen, and the new additions of France or Italy were imitated in Germany and England. Most of the great churches of Europe and even many of the smaller ones presented these ecclesiastical plays in Latin at various times during the year.

As the plays became more and more elaborate in structure and in presentation, however, the Church found increasing difficulty in keeping them purely religious in character. At first they had been presented in the church, in direct connection with the service, in the language of the Church, and had been written and acted entirely by priests and choristers. But how was it possible to keep the plays entirely in the hands of churchmen when a hundred or more actors were required? Gradually certain parts, minor ones at first, were given to laymen. Since very few of the laymen knew Latin, little by little, bits of the vernacular were written into the plays.

The size of the crowds attracted and the size of the playing place demanded were another difficulty. The earliest tropes required very little playing space as only a few robes and a tomb were necessary, but as the plays developed, more and more properties had to be used—mangers and crosses and stars and arks and tables and fiery furnaces and thrones and mountains. As the spectacle grew, the crowds grew. Soon even the greatest cathedrals were scarcely large enough to provide all the numerous playing places and to accommodate the crowds from all the surrounding countryside. The plays were taken outside the churches to the cathedral close or the market place. And once outside the consecrated building, secularization became more rapid. More and more laymen were given parts, until they dominated the plays; more and more of the Latin was translated into the vernacular until the common people could understand nearly all the words. Bits of everyday life were worked into the plays to entertain the crowds, and gradually the direct responsibility for the plays came to rest with the city rather than with the Church.

After the plays reached the point where they were written in the vernacular, acted by laymen, and controlled by non-ecclesiastical bodies, they began to lose the universal character which had marked them as long as they were entirely in the hands of the Church, and to become more and more national in character. It is in this national stage of the development of the medieval drama that the most interesting of the English plays appear.

The Performance of the Medieval Plays in England

In England, the secular organizations which took over the religious plays after they had outgrown the Church were the trade gilds. By the time of this transition, the plays were vast in extent, really great series of from twenty-five to fifty plays which presented all the biblical story from the fall of Lucifer and the creation of the world to the resurrection and the last judgment. They required hundreds of actors and many hours, often several days, for complete presentation. Such a series of plays was called a cycle, and such cycles of religious plays or mystery plays (as they were called because they presented the mysteries of the Christian religion) were being performed in a score of market towns and cities all over England in the fourteenth and fifteenth centuries. But of all the English cycles, only five have been preserved in anything like their entirety. The best of them are the cycles presented at Chester and at York and one presented at an unknown place, probably Wakefield in Yorkshire.[11]

In the hands of the gilds these plays were given not one or two at a time on appropriate days as they had been in the churches, but all at once on a special gala occasion for which preparations had been made weeks in advance and which was a holiday in the city, celebrated by all the citizens and by hundreds of visitors who came from miles about to see the plays. The occasion usually selected in England was Whitsuntide (seven weeks after Easter) or Corpus Christi Day (eight and one-half weeks after Easter). Both were religious fête days, and both fell at a time of year when the weather was likely to be suitable for out-of-door performances in the streets of the city.

The normal plan was for the city to assign each play of the cycle to some particular gild, as often as possible to a gild which had special facilities for presenting the play. Thus at York the gild of shipwrights was selected to stage the play of *The Building of the Ark,* and at Chester the cooks and innkeepers acted the fiery play of *The Harrowing of Hell.* The gild which the city made respon-

[11] All these plays are of unknown authorship. Probably many of them were written by monks; certainly there was no such thing as a professional playwright at the time.

sible for a play had to take complete charge of its production—furnish the stage, the properties, the costumes, and the decorations, hire the actors, and superintend the rehearsals. Sometime before the performance the members of the city government inspected rehearsals, and woe betide any gild whose play was not properly in hand. The city then made general arrangements for the great day. The stations (street corners and open spaces) for the performance of the plays were selected; the houses and buildings about these places were decorated for the occasion; scaffolds or bleachers were built at the best station for the civic dignitaries and any visiting nobility or royalty; and the advertising of the plays (usually public announcements made in the surrounding towns and villages by gorgeously dressed horsemen or by the town crier) was provided for.

When the great day arrived, the city was sure to be crowded with visitors and holiday-making citizens. Very early in the morning the crowds collected at the various appointed stations and waited excitedly for the first play. At the designated time (in York this was 4:30 A. M.) a team of horses was driven up to the station pulling a pageant wagon, or what we should probably call an elaborate float. These pageants were huge double-decked wagons, gaily decorated with paint and brass, streamers and pennons, cloth-of-gold and brightly colored hangings, and displaying to as great advantage as possible the insignia of the gild which was to present the play. The lower deck, from the wagon-bed to a platform six or seven feet above it, was curtained from the view of the crowd and used as a dressing-room, or as hell, if the play was one in which hell could be used. The platform which served as the roof of this lower story was the stage upon which the action of the play took place. It was fitted with the necessary properties and covered with a canopy, usually tasseled and fringed.[12]

Upon this pageant wagon the first play of the cycle, *The Fall of Lucifer,* was presented to the crowd. When it was finished, the horses were driven to the second appointed station and the play was performed again. In the meantime the pageant wagon for the second play, *The Creation and Fall of Man,* had been driven

[12] This is the type of pageant wagon which most of the extant records indicate and which was probably most common, but it is sometimes said that the pageant wagons were three-decked. Though this is perhaps true of the pageants built for a few of the plays which required part of the action in heaven and part on earth (like *The Expelling of Adam and Eve out of Paradise,* where the first two-thirds of the action takes place in Paradise, after which the angel drives out Adam and Eve, and a stage direction says, "Then Man and Woman departyth to the nether parte of the pageant," and then the last third of the action takes place on earth), most of the plays required only one stage level.

up to the first station, and the crowd watched the second episode in the history of the universe. When it was finished, the first pageant wagon drove to the third station, the second pageant wagon drove to the second station, and the third wagon came to the first station. And so the plays continued until the crowd at each station had witnessed every play from *The Fall of Lucifer* to *Doomsday* and the last judgment of the resurrected souls. In Chester the performance of this series took three days, and even an avid medieval crowd must have had its fill of dramatized salvation by the time the last pageant wagon rolled away.

The Plays

There are certain recurrent peculiarities in these medieval plays which are sometimes confusing to the modern reader. In almost every play anachronisms are common. This was due in part no doubt to ignorance, as in many popular modern plays on historical subjects, but often it was undoubtedly a conscious use of contemporary terms and local references in an attempt to make the biblical stories vivid for an audience which knew little or nothing of life in ancient Palestine. Thus the Judean winter is cold and snowy at Christmas time, Herod is Sir Herod, Noah's wife and her tipsy gossips drink the popular malmsey, shepherds complain of English taxes, and the money mentioned is generally pounds, shillings, and pence. In other ways the biblical narrative was amended or expanded to suit the audience. Characters who were simply mentioned or who did not appear at all in the Bible were brought upon the stage to complete the picture. If the shepherds watched their flocks by night, the medieval dramatists thought they probably had something to watch for; so sheep stealers are brought into the plays of the Nativity. If Noah had three sons, he certainly had a wife, and if wives in Noah's time were anything like wives in medieval Chester, Mrs. Noah probably objected strenuously when commanded to desert her home and her friends; so Noah is given a spouse who speaks her mind with vigor and abandon.

Often the conceptions of time and place in medieval plays make it difficult for modern readers to imagine their production. How did Abraham and Isaac make a journey of several days on a platform that could not have been much more than thirty or forty feet long? How did the Ark sail about for forty days and forty nights in a play that lasted about thirty minutes?

In general these feats were accomplished by simply ignoring the difficulties, just as we ignore the impossibility of the lapse of two or three months between the acts of a modern play. When Noah closed the window of the Ark, sang a Psalm, and then opened the window and announced that forty days had passed, the audience accepted his statement without astonishment. The situation is treated precisely the same way in our plays. We lower the curtain instead of opening a window and announce the forty-day interval in a program instead of from the stage.

The change of place in the medieval plays is slightly more confusing. Since their stage was isolated and could not be concealed from the audience by a curtain, our modern tricks to disguise the impossibility of a change of place were not available. If the play required two or more places, at least one was indicated by properties which were self-explanatory.

The place designated by properties remained the same throughout the action; it was usually at one end of the pageant. Such definitely localized places were called *sedes*. Other places in the action of the same play were indicated simply by the words of the characters. One part of the pageant was an unlocalized place, or *platea,* which, when not in use, was no place, and which became a definite locality only as the speeches of the characters identified it. Thus in the Chester play of *The Deluge,* one end of the pageant is the Ark, a definitely localized place (*sedes*) quite clearly indicated by the ship-like form of the Ark with the pictures of animals painted upon it as indicated in the stage directions. The other end of the pageant was the unlocalized place (*platea*) which was no place when the Noah family was packed into the Ark, but which was thought of as Noah's home when his wife was drinking there with her cronies. After the flood, when the Noah family had landed, it became Mount Ararat. In *The Sacrifice of Isaac,* the localized place is the mount with the altar. The rest of the stage represented definite places only as the words of the characters indicated that the audience must think of some particular locality.

These principles of medieval staging, though somewhat confusing at first, are really not difficult to follow; it is from them that our modern principles of staging have developed. And the medieval plays, however crude and naïve they may seem at first, will be found to present subtleties of dramatic effect which have only been elaborated in modern plays; they are the beginning of our modern drama.

C. ELIZABETHAN TRAGEDY

The drama generally called Elizabethan is that written for the London theaters between the years 1584 and 1642.[13] The best of

[13] The name, of course, comes from Queen Elizabeth, though the period of the Elizabethan drama does not exactly coincide with the years of her reign. Elizabeth was Queen of England from 1558 to 1603, but the plays to which her name is given

these plays, of course, are Shakespeare's, but there were others who helped to make the plays of the Elizabethan period the greatest ever written in English. Marlowe and Jonson, Heywood and Webster, all had some of Shakespeare's genius—a fine ear for the melody of words, a depth of human understanding, an amazing vitality, and a brilliant creative imagination which could send upon the stage hundreds of characters as alive as those who walked the London streets. And there were others besides Shakespeare, Marlowe, Jonson, Heywood, and Webster. In this time it seemed that almost any hack dramatist could get at least one or two fine scenes into a play.

Whenever such an abundance of fine plays is written for the stage, there is invariably an unusual audience which is partially responsible for them. The Elizabethan dramatist, like any modern dramatist who succeeds in getting his plays produced, wrote for the taste, the understanding, and the prejudices of his audience. It was, in part, the characteristics of the audience and the time which developed the Elizabethan drama. For this reason it is worthwhile to have some understanding of the times in which Shakespeare and Marlowe lived and of the audience for which they worked. Furthermore, such an understanding is not only enlightening but really necessary if one is to read Elizabethan plays intelligently. Since the tastes and prejudices of the twentieth-century audience are not the same as those of the Elizabethan, we must see the plays of Shakespeare and his contemporaries not with a modern crowd in a modern theater but as a member of an Elizabethan audience watching the performance at a great Elizabethan playhouse like the Fortune or the Globe.

The Times

Many of the characteristics of these Elizabethan playgoers were due to the stirring times in which they lived. Every Elizabethan felt himself part of a new world, the new world that was developing out of the Middle Ages, the world of the Renaissance. Many of the things which he believed had been unknown to his grandfather. The earth was not the center of the universe; it moved around the sun. The earth was not flat; it was round. The very ship in which Sir Francis Drake had sailed around the world could

were written during the last third of her reign and the reigns of her two successors. The first plays of Lyly, Kyd, and Marlowe (1584, 1587, 1589) mark the beginning of the period, and the Puritan law closing all the London theaters in 1642 marks its close. Since the Puritans managed to keep all theaters shut for eighteen years, 1642 marks the end of an epoch in English drama. The theaters and plays were quite different when dramatic production began again at the restoration of Charles II in 1660.

be seen any day lying at a wharf near London. Far to the west were vast countries swarming with strange people whose very pots and pans were made of pure gold. *The* church was no longer the Roman Catholic Church but the English Church. The head of the Church was the Queen, not the Pope at Rome. The Pope was not an object of veneration but a vicious English-hating anti-Christ who was baited and laughed at in plays like Marlowe's *Dr. Faustus.* England was the greatest nation on earth, the conqueror of the mighty Spanish Armada, the Mistress of the Seas. England's history was not a dim record of the past, but a series of glorious stories which might be read in popular chronicles and poems or seen on any stage in London. The future was not a vague continuation of the past, but a series of exciting possibilities in which a poor boy might become a great actor, make a fortune, retire, and endow a college, like Edward Alleyn, or in which a hard-working shoemaker might make a lucky investment and become a capitalist and Lord Mayor of London, like Simon Eyre in Thomas Dekker's play, *The Shoemaker's Holiday.*

In all these ways the conceptions of the typical Elizabethan differed from those of his forebears who had watched the mystery plays at York and Chester. He was living in a time of rapid changes, a time of peace and prosperity, of great intellectual stimulation and comparative freedom of ideas. These facts help to explain the great brilliance of the period. The Italian Renaissance following the rediscovery of Greek and Latin literature had begun to influence England more than fifty years before Elizabeth's time, but it was not until her reign that its immense effect on English literature had become apparent.

With all these new developments and stimuli, however, London was not the highly civilized place that it is sometimes thought to have been. In fact, sharp contrasts of the good and the bad were one of its most striking characteristics. Its citizens wrote and listened to the finest poetry ever created in England, but they lived in a filthy city of open sewers and frequent raging epidemics. They cultivated fine music as one of the essential accomplishments of any man who pretended to be educated; yet they were equally interested in the torture of animals at bull-baitings and bear-baitings and in the beheading of men on the scaffold. Beauty and violence were almost equally a part of their lives. The poets themselves, creators of beauty, were violent men. Jonson killed a man in a duel, Raleigh died on the scaffold, Sidney was killed in battle, and Marlowe was stabbed to death in a tavern brawl. These startling incongruities—poetry and filth, music and blood lust, beauty and violence—are characteristics of the Elizabethan times which formed the background of the plays of Marlowe and Shakespeare and their great contemporaries.

The Elizabethan Theater

Equally important in an understanding of Elizabethan plays are the peculiar physical characteristics of the theaters, or playhouses, as they were more frequently called.

Elizabethan dramatists, like all other dramatists, were very greatly influenced by the theaters in which their plays were to be produced. Every scene was planned to utilize the advantages or to avoid the defects of the stage of some Elizabethan theater, and the plays as they have come down to us to-day bear throughout the marks of such planning. If this fact is forgotten, certain passages seem absurd because the reader tries to fit them into the conditions of a modern stage, or some highly dramatic speech loses its theatrical effectiveness because he does not remember how it was acted at the Fortune or the Globe. A knowledge of the general characteristics of the Elizabethan theaters should always furnish the background for the reading or producing of a play of Shakespeare's time.

First of all, the Elizabethan theater was, in part, an open-air place. It was built in the form of a hollow square or octagon, with no roof over the central part. This central part was simply the bare ground, called the pit or yard, where the people stood who had paid only the general admission of a penny or two. Usually there were three galleries about this pit, the lowest raised two or three feet above the ground. These galleries formed the sides of the square or octagon, and in them the people who had the price of a reserved seat could sit. They were roofed, of course, to protect the fine clothes of the ladies and gentlemen who had paid for seats. The people in the pit (the groundlings or stinkards, they were often called, for obvious reasons) got wet if it rained.[14]

The most significant differences between this theater and a mod-

[14] This description applies to the public theater of Elizabethan times. As a matter of fact, there were two types of theaters in use then which were distinguished as "public playhouses" and "private playhouses." Though most of the great Elizabethan plays were written for the public theaters, and though it is these houses which are generally referred to by the term "Elizabethan theaters," the private playhouses deserve some consideration as the antecedents of the Restoration theaters.

Private theaters were really open to any one who could pay the price of admission, but they were more exclusive because more expensive. They were smaller than the public playhouses, and unlike them were completely enclosed—large rectangular rooms with a stage at one end. In the pit they had benches instead of standing room, and they provided boxes for the more distinguished spectators. Though the performance at these playhouses was normally in the afternoon, it could be given at night, and artificial lighting was quite common. From 1576 to 1642 there was nearly always at least one private theater running in London.

ern theater were in the stage. The Elizabethan stage was divided into three parts. The largest and most important part, the one upon which most of the action took place, was a low platform jutting right out into the middle of the crowd in the pit. Shaped like a truncated triangle (or, in some theaters, like a rectangle), it was raised two or three feet above the ground and, in most theaters, seems to have had a low railing about the outer edge. (See the diagram on p. 47.) This part of the stage was called the outer stage or the platform. It was always in full view of the audience since there was no kind of curtain to shut it off at any time.

Behind this platform were the two other parts of the stage, continuations of the galleries. The people sat in all sections of these galleries except the section behind the outer stage. Thus if the theater were octagonal, the people who had paid for reserved seats sat in the galleries on seven sides, but the galleries on the eighth side, the side behind the platform, were adapted for use as parts of the stage. The lowest of these, the one whose floor was level with that of the outer stage, was called the inner stage. It did not occupy the full width of the platform but was really a small room behind the central part of the outer stage and open to the audience on one side. This inner stage, unlike the outer stage, had a curtain by which it could be shut off from the view of the audience. It was frequently used for small scenes, like studies or bedrooms, and set with properties—beds, chairs, tables, books, etc. These properties were set in place while the curtains shut off the view of the audience, and generally while some scene was being acted on the outer stage. When the Elizabethan dramatist wanted the curtains of this inner stage pulled back to disclose the scene within, he wrote in his stage directions, "Discovered."

Thus in *Dr. Faustus* Marlowe has conceived his play with the devices of the Elizabethan theater in his mind. He has planned for the chorus to appear on the outer stage, perhaps just in front of the inner stage curtains where its last line could be delivered most effectively. But Faustus himself will be more effective if he appears first in his study, probably surrounded by his books and his chemical apparatus, and pretty surely dressed in his black doctor's gown. Thus the audience will get its first impression of him as a scholar.

With something like this in his mind, Marlowe wrote the last line of the chorus, "And this the man that in his study sits," and then the stage direction, "FAUSTUS *discovered in his study.*" It was a familiar direction to the Elizabethan stage manager, but if it is read with no thought of the characteristics of the Elizabethan theater, it is sure to be confusing.

The third part was the upper stage. It was immediately above the inner stage, a continuation of the *second* gallery which ran behind the platform. The upper stage was about the same size as the inner, and like the inner stage it had a curtain by which it could be shut off from the view of the audience. Across the front there was a low railing, like the one about the platform. This upper stage was used when the action of the play demanded that some one appear in a high place—an upper room, or the wall of a city, or a hill, or the rigging of a ship. It is generally indicated in the stage directions by "above." Thus in the fourth act of *Antony and Cleopatra* when Shakespeare wishes to indicate that Cleopatra and her attendants who appear on the top of a monument are to use the upper stage, he writes the stage direction, "*Enter, above,* CLEOPATRA, CHARMIAN, *and* IRAS."

All three parts of this stage were well supplied with trapdoors, since sudden disappearances and apparitions which rose through the ground were very common in Elizabethan plays. Descending gods and angels and flying creatures of various sorts were also common. These were managed from a room which overhung the outer stage at the level of the third balcony. This room was built up higher than any other part of the theater and was called the hut. It was necessary to the presentation of plays, but it was not a part of the stage proper.

The three essential parts of an Elizabethan stage, then, were the outer stage, the inner stage, and the upper stage. In a ground plan the theater would look something like the diagram on p. 47.

Obviously a stage so different from ours gave the dramatist and the producer advantages and disadvantages unlike those of modern times. A little study will show what some of them were. Perhaps the most obvious advantage is flexibility. No modern theater can stage a play with a large number of scenes as easily as the average Elizabethan theater could. Any playhouse in Shakespeare's London could produce the forty-two scenes of *Antony and Cleopatra,* but it is out of the question for most theaters to-day. Of course the Elizabethans had a great advantage in that they used no scenery. This increased greatly the speed of their productions and the flexibility of their stage. To a modern theater-goer, accustomed to the conventions of scenery, an unset stage seems crude, but a little thought will show that the creation of scenery by the imagination of the audience is just another convention, like many similar ones which we accept as a matter of course. Most of the world's greatest plays have been written for stages which had no elaborate scenery.

Another advantage of the Elizabethan stage is not quite so

obvious. The platform stage, as contrasted with the modern picture-frame stage set back behind a proscenium arch, gave the actor a much closer contact with his audience. Thus, not only could the actor get his effects more surely and more rapidly, but the dramatist could also rely on a greater sense of intimacy between his char-

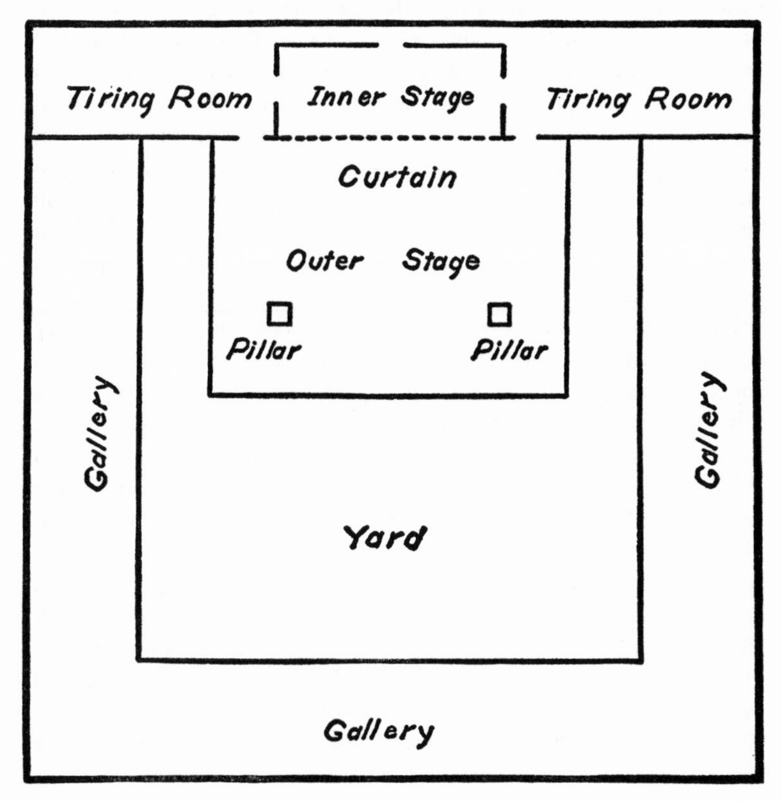

FIGURE II

GROUND PLAN OF AN ELIZABETHAN THEATER, THE FORTUNE

Reprinted by permission from Isidore J. Semper, *A Shakspere Study Guide* (New York: The Century Co., 1931).

acters and the audience than the modern playwright can. He had a little of the advantage of the novelist who can address to his reader an exposition of the motives of his characters.

Perhaps this advantage of actor-audience intimacy which the Elizabethan stage afforded is not made quite clear by the diagram. Note that the Elizabethan actor on the outer stage (where most of the action took place) was out in the midst of his audience. If he stood at the edge of the stage he could reach out and touch some of them. The modern actor is separated from the closest member of his audience by footlights and orchestra pit. He could not possibly touch any spectator. Instead of talking to the people all about him, the modern actor must throw his voice out through the proscenium archway and into the audience. If you want to see what sort of a difference this makes, try telling a story to a group of a dozen or more people in the manner of a modern actor and then in the manner of an Elizabethan actor. When you tell it like a modern actor, you must go out of the room in which your audience is sitting and stand five or ten feet on the other side of an open door. Now tell the story through the door. You must speak very distinctly and not too rapidly, so that your words will carry. You must be careful to face your audience as much as possible and to direct your voice *always* toward the open door, your proscenium arch. This is the way the modern actor must present himself.

Now, stand in the midst of your audience and tell your story again. Turn whichever way you like, speak more rapidly and more naturally; you can even interpolate occasional side remarks. This is the way the Elizabethan actor performed. And every Elizabethan dramatist knew that he could rely upon the intimacy with the audience which naturally followed. In a hilarious scene where a youth—whom the audience knew to be a girl in disguise—was about to be forced to fight a duel, the dramatist could direct the terrified girl to turn to some person standing in the pit and say, aside, "Pray God defend me! A little thing would make me tell them how much I lack of a man." Of course the man spoken to would laugh, and those standing about him would laugh, and probably most of the rest of the audience as well. This is just what Shakespeare did in the fifth scene of the third act of *Twelfth Night.*

In our modern theater, to deliver an aside the actor must strain his voice in a "stage whisper" which will carry out across the footlights, over the orchestra pit, and into the midst of the crowd in the darkness beyond. Of course it is absurd, and so we say that all asides are absurd, forgetting that Shakespeare wrote his for a theater in which they could be easily delivered and in which they served to make the audience feel that they were being let in on the joke.

There were other conventions of Elizabethan play production, not quite so closely connected with the physical characteristics of the stage, but equally a part of the regular procedure in the playhouses and equally confusing to the reader who thinks of all plays as scripts for the modern theater.

One of these conventions was the use of boy actors in the parts of women and girls. The Elizabethan stage had no actresses. This seems a more serious difficulty than in Greek and medieval plays, because, unlike the earlier dramatists, the Elizabethans often created very feminine characters, but it was not the difficulty we are likely to think. Boys in women's parts suggest to us college boys playing female parts in musical shows. We can be perfectly sure that the parts of Juliet and Rosalind and Cleopatra and Viola would never have been written had Elizabethan boy actors been anything like this.

First of all, these boys had years of thorough training. The Elizabethan acting company was a repertory company, a permanent organization in which the same actors appeared together year after year. This meant that they could develop a perfection of ensemble, a highly effective team work, which is seldom seen on the American stage. Such permanent organizations as these repertory companies could be very exacting in training their actors. Boys of only seven or eight were often apprenticed to a member of one of these companies, and this apprenticeship meant that the boy was entirely under the control of the actor to whom he was bound. The actor practically adopted him; the boy left his own parents and lived and worked with the actors.

Suppose a bright, good-looking boy, with a good singing voice (the actors were always hunting handsome boys with good voices) had been apprenticed at the age of eight to a very successful actor. For five years he lived with that actor, heard stage talk at all hours of the day and night, attended hundreds of rehearsals, saw plays nearly every afternoon, and had small parts himself, holding trains, running errands, shouting in a crowd. At odd moments he studied carefully the technique of the actors in his company whom he saw day after day; he learned the parts of some successful older boy; he tried to mimic women on every possible occasion. Is it any wonder that when he was thirteen this boy was able to play a woman's part almost as well as an actress? There are several Elizabethan stories of the skill of these boys. One of them, a very famous boy in Shakespeare's company, was once taken, dressed as a woman, to a London gossip session. He was quite the hit of the party, and at the end of the afternoon only the woman who had introduced him knew that he was really a boy and not a lawyer's wife, as he pretended.

This Elizabethan custom of putting boys in women's parts made effective certain dramatic situations which cannot be plausibly presented on our stage. The most common, of course, was the disguise of a girl as a boy. How simple it was for Shakespeare to have Viola or Rosalind who was really a boy acting a girl's part—disguise herself as a boy! Such a confusing disguise was convincing and entertaining for an Elizabethan audience. Even a modern audience can be entertained by it, though it is very rarely that a modern actress can make herself a really convincing boy. The modern audience—or more often the modern reader—forgetting that Shakespeare was very effectively taking advantage of a convention of his own stage, is apt to think that these disguise plots are silly when staged.

There is one other characteristic of Elizabethan productions which is likely to confuse the modern reader. This is the conception of location or place which is somewhat like the medieval conception. The Elizabethan theater-goer concentrated on the characters and the action far more than we do. Setting meant very little. The important thing was—"What are these people saying and doing?"—not "Where are they doing it?" Not only was there no scenery to indicate the place, but often the place was of no importance. If the scene was a hot argument growing into a desperate fight between the two suitors for the hand of the heroine, the audience did not care whether the fight occurred in the heroine's house, in the street, or in a field. The important thing was the fight. Elizabethan playwrights generally gave very little indication of the place of the action; often they paid no attention to it at all. The action took place on the outer stage, and nobody bothered his head about what particular place the outer stage was supposed to represent at that moment. Modern editors often write in their guesses as to the location of the scene, but the Elizabethan editions of the plays seldom indicate it.

This subordination of place is also evident in the scene divisions of an Elizabethan play. We think of a scene as the action of a play between two lowerings of the curtain. On Shakespeare's stage, one scene succeeded another without a break. There was no intermission in the action except between acts, and not always even then. Thus an Elizabthan play was not so choppy as the printed page seems to indicate. Most of the audience probably did not know and certainly did not care where one scene ended and another began.

The Elizabethan Audience

The audience in this Elizabethan theater had certain likes and dislikes which had a great deal of influence on the plays the dramatists wrote; it differed sharply from the theater audiences of most other times. Certainly one of its most striking characteristics was its great appetite for plays. In a city of 100,000 to 150,000 population, fourteen theaters were built in this period, five or six times as many as exist in most modern cities of this size. Often as many as six different theaters were competing, and under the repertory system, presenting eight or ten times as many plays a month as the average modern theater. Such a full program could be supported only by an audience which included a very large proportion of the entire population of the city.

No other audience, with the possible exception of the Athenian, has ever been so representative of all classes of society. All London was to be found in Shakespeare's theater—there were noblemen and beggars, court ladies and prostitutes, soldiers and poets, city apprentices who stole their master's time to go to see the play, and courtiers who came to see if the piece might be suitable for performance before Queen Elizabeth at Windsor Castle, rich city merchants who could buy up several theaters, and pickpockets who came to find the price of the next meal. All of them came to the playhouses and all of them expected to be pleased by the dramatist.

Such a conglomerate audience meant that the successful dramatist must provide a variety of appeals in his plays: beautiful poetry, slapstick comedy, romantic scenes, heroic characters, punning dialogue, patriotic spouting, spectacular events, penetrating characterization. Because he had to please all sorts of people, as a rule, Elizabethan plays offer an unusually varied appeal.

But there were some demands in which nearly all this heterogeneous audience united. They were always interested in a story so that the play which succeeded with them had to have much more narrative interest than most modern plays. This interest, coupled with the characteristics of the stage which made certain types of theatrical endings impossible, is the reason for the *completion* of the story, which people so often think undramatic, at the end of Elizabethan tragedies. *Antony and Cleopatra* does not end with the death of Cleopatra, as a modern tragedy would, but with the speech of Cæsar giving orders for her burial in the same tomb with Antony. And *Romeo and Juliet* continues after the death of the lovers until the audience has learned of the reconciliation of the two families.

The Elizabethan audience also demanded action. The modern type of play in which people simply sit about and talk would have been driven off the stage of the Globe or the Fortune, driven off not by falling receipts or unkind reviews but by hisses and jeers and flying nut shells and apple cores. The stinkards in the pit were not known for their good manners. They were standing, and they were not inclined to tolerate anything that bored them; the oranges and apples regularly sold in the theaters were ready to hand, and there is more than one record of an occasion when the distaste of the crowd in the pit was riotously expressed to the extreme discomfort of the actors. So the Elizabethan plays regularly provide the action which the audience demanded. The tragedies and histories especially are filled with the violence of the age, with battles and street fights, with murder and suicide, and even with torture and mutilation.

Another demand of the audience, or at least of that part of the audience which stood in the pit, was for comic scenes. This often presented a serious difficulty in tragedy. It demanded a peculiar type of genius which could give the groundlings their comic scenes without violating the tragic tone of the play. Shakespeare could do it with the old nurse in *Romeo and Juliet* or the grave-digger in *Hamlet* or with Charmian and the clown in *Antony and Cleopatra,* but others were not so successful. The comic scenes in Marlowe's *Dr. Faustus* are serious blemishes in the play, though they no doubt pleased the groundlings.

The Elizabethan audience was very fond of color and display. This delight in brilliance was manifested outside the theater as well as inside. Their clothes were gorgeous and costly, generally more costly than they could afford. Men frequently bankrupted themselves to dress well, or as one playwright says, "put their acres on their backs." Both men's and women's clothes were elaborately embroidered and brocaded, and those of the courtiers were often sewn with jewels. Color was as common in men's dress as in women's, and it was not unusual to see a gallant dressed in crimson and gold and silver and green. This taste for color was reflected on the stage. The costumes for an Elizabethan play were more of the sort that we associate with opera and revue than with comedy and tragedy. Some of the theatrical records of the time show that the producer paid the tailor more for the hero's costume than he paid the dramatist for the play.

The plays themselves regularly tried to satisfy the taste of the audience for display. Masques and balls and gorgeous state ceremonials were repeatedly introduced. We can be sure that the entrance of the cardinals and the bishops, the archbishops and the pope in *Dr. Faustus* was a grand procession of brilliant robes and gold and silver ornaments, and that when Cleopatra came upon the stage with her attendants in the first scene of *Antony and Cleopatra,* the audience was dazzled with all the resplendent costumes which the theater could afford.

All these characteristics of the typical Elizabethan audience are responsible for differences between the theatrical fare of their time and of ours. The great Elizabethan drama cannot be fully appreciated or even understood without some consideration of these differences in the reading of the plays.

D. NEO-CLASSICAL TRAGEDY

The greatest period in French dramatic history falls in the second and third quarters of the seventeenth century, when the tragedies of Corneille and Racine and the comedies of Molière were first presented. This period immediately follows the Elizabethan era in England, but the French drama by no means derives from the English. In fact the differences between the greatest dramatic achievements of France and of England are so fundamental that one familiar with the English tradition has no little difficulty in appreciating the most celebrated manifestations of French dramatic genius. These differences between Elizabethan tragedy and French neo-classic tragedy are due in part to the dissimilarities in the times which produced these two notable dramatic outbursts.

The Times

French neo-classicism flowered in the reign of Louis XIV, the Roi-Soleil. The absolutism of the government of Louis is a political counterpart of the rigidity of neo-classicism. Louis had ascended the throne as a child, and France had been made the most powerful nation in Europe before he attained his majority. His long and brilliant reign was largely spent in an attempt to consolidate the power of France and to organize and refine the manifestations of French genius. The king himself was the center not only of French political existence but of artistic and literary life as well.

For many people the symbol of the grandeur, extravagance, and formality of the reign of Louis XIV is Versailles. Here the king created a magnificent center for the life of the French court, the apex of the social, political, and artistic life of the kingdom. It was planned and decorated by the greatest French artists, it was the gathering place of the most brilliant French society, and its entertainment was frequently provided by the greatest French dramatist, Molière.

This aristocratic character of the life of the time is one of its most essential features. The critics thought of literature and drama not as expressions of the life of the whole nation, but as "the delectation of refined and educated people," and such people were, of course, generally connected with the court of Louis.

It would be a mistake, however, to think of the drama of seventeenth-century France as exclusively aristocratic, significant though this element was. The life of Paris was as important to it as the life of the court. The literature of this period has a distinctly urban character. Good sense and sophistication are as conspicuous in it as the more courtly form and polish and, however deeply the dramatists were affected by the standards of the court, their plays were produced more often before a Parisian audience than before a courtly one.

The Theater

The typical Parisian theater in the reign of Louis XIV derived from an indoor tennis court, just as the typical Elizabethan public theater derived from an inn yard. Indeed, certain Parisian and many provincial theaters were simply remodeled tennis courts. Such a court, perhaps 100 by 40 feet, was adapted for dramatic performances by the erection of a shallow stage at one end. Along either side of these tennis courts ran galleries for the spectators which were used for the same purpose when the hall was converted into a temporary theater. Other spectators stood on the floor of the court itself. As in Shakespeare's playhouse, it was usual for young gallants to be seated on the stage much to the hindrance of the actors. Little if any scenery was used in these temporary theaters; often there were only simple hangings about the stage in the manner of many modern amateur performances on improvised stages. Such tennis court theaters were lighted by candles about the stage and sometimes in a chandelier suspended above it.

Such remodeled theaters were not, of course, the equal of the more famous playhouses, like the Petit Bourbon Theatre and the Palais Royal. These two theaters, both royal property, were, of course, much more splendid than the old tennis courts, but they differed in stage facilities and in the permanence of their arrangements rather than in fundamental plan. The Palais Royal, the theater with which Molière was associated for the longest period and for which most of his great plays were written, was the finest in Paris. It had been built at great expense by Cardinal Richelieu in 1640 for private performances and later bequeathed to Louis XIV.

The Palais Royal was some 100 by 50 feet in size. Along each side were two galleries, one above the other, divided into boxes and generally occupied by ladies and their escorts. The main floor was divided into two parts. The front half, next the stage, had no seats and was called the *parterre*. The 300-odd spectators who could be accommodated in this part of the theater, which corresponded to the pit in an Elizabethan playhouse, stood throughout the performance and consequently were inclined to be noisy and restless. Admission to the *parterre* was less than to any other part of the house.

Behind the *parterre,* the rear half of the main floor rose in steps, so that the stage would be visible over the heads of those standing in front. These steps were fitted with benches which ran from wall to wall in straight lines, not in arcs as in most modern theaters. Since the spectators on these benches behind the *parterre* sat at some distance from the stage, and since Racine's theater, unlike Shakespeare's, was always dependent upon artificial lighting, it was none too easy for them to see the details of the action which took place on the stage. Certainly facial expression could have been none too clear, for this theater was lighted by candles in chandeliers over the stage, and there seems to have been little attempt to direct the light onto the faces of the actors and to keep it out of the eyes of the spectators.

The stage of this theater was modern in its essentials; that is, it was built behind a proscenium arch and shut off from the view of the audience whenever the actors wished by a curtain, and it was fitted with scenery which indicated the location of the scenes to the audience and incidentally, limited the dramatist in the number of scenes he could use. Scenery was of the wings and drop type.[15] In the plays of the time, it generally depicted either an open square with houses on two sides which could be used as the homes of various characters as in *L'École des Femmes* and *L'École des Maris* of Molière; or a single interior as in Racine's *Andromaque* and *Britannicus,* and Molière's *Le Misanthrope, L'Avare,* and *Tartuffe;* or the façade of a palace as in Racine's *Phèdre*. Changes of scene were few; in practically all neo-classic tragedies and in most of the comedies only one set was used.

The fact that there were gallants seated on the stage helps to explain certain other practices at the Palais Royal and other Parisian theaters of the time. Scenes never ended in a tableau, as so many modern scenes do; invariably all characters walked off at the end of the act. Heavy properties were generally limited to a few chairs, with perhaps a table; often even these were eliminated, and the characters stood during their conversations. The dramatist generally worked his action down stage so that the actors were nearer the audience, under the chandeliers, and comparatively remote from the set. Thus the scenery in a neo-classic play was not of great importance; it simply indicated the place and had little relation to the actors.

From this account, the Parisian theater of the reign of Louis XIV may seem quite different from modern ones, but the difference is a matter of details, like the standing audience in the *parterre* and the gallants on the stage. In its essentials this theater was modern: it was an indoor theater with a stage behind a proscenium arch, equipped with scenery and artificial light. More than once the important fact has been pointed out that essentially Shakespeare's

[15] See p. 64 for a description of this type of scenery.

theater was a medieval one, and that the theater of Corneille and Racine and Molière was modern.

The Audience

To the theater-goer of to-day, the audience of Corneille and Racine seems an unaccountable contradiction, for it was both more intellectual and more rowdy than the average modern audience. The intellectual element in the audience found satisfaction in the austerity and lucidity, the subtle analyses of problems of conduct or of emotional states of the neo-classical drama, and in the social conception of comedy held by Molière.[16]

The rowdiness of the audience is illustrated by numerous accounts of violent disturbances in the theaters. It was not uncommon for noblemen or officers to force themselves in past the doorkeeper, sometimes with great violence. There are records of doorkeepers being beaten, stabbed, and shot at in the performance of their duties. On the occasion of one of the performances of Molière's *L'Amour médecin,* there was a great disturbance in which a number of pages beat the spectators and finally took possession of the *parterre.* Such violence as this was by no means a daily occurrence, but it is a clear indication that the audience at the Palais Royal could scarcely be called well-behaved.

Probably the actors really suffered more from the fine gentlemen on the stage than from the ruffians in the *parterre.* As in Shakespeare's theater, gentry of this sort were often much more interested in a display of their fine clothes and their arrogant manners than in the subtleties of the play.[17] Even when they were quiet and orderly, however, they were a handicap to the performance; they forced the actors to rely almost wholly on their lines to create the illusion of the play, and they seriously restricted the action.

These two groups in the neo-classic theater, the dandies on the stage and the swaggerers in the *parterre,* were simply the most conspicuous part of the audience; they formed only a small minority of the spectators, probably not more than one-fifth at most. Certainly it was the other four-fifths whose interests and tastes most

[16] For a fuller discussion of this conception of comedy, see below Chapter III, Section E.

[17] Molière gives an amusing account of the conduct of one of these empty-headed gentlemen in his *Les Fâcheux*. This gallant strode onto the stage after the play had begun, sat insolently between the audience and the actors, shouted orders and conversed in a loud voice during the dialogue, and finally walked across the stage and left the theater in the midst of the performance. It is amusing to note how much this account of Molière's has in common with Thomas Dekker's account of a similar occurrence on a London stage some fifty-odd years before. Dekker's account may be found in his *Guls Hornbook*.

concerned Racine and Molière, for any practical dramatist, most of all a manager-dramatist like Molière, is perfectly well aware that it is the opinion of the bulk of his audience which determines the fate of the play, not the whims of noisy minorities.

The largest group in this theater was made up of the burghers of Paris, solid middle-class citizens with sufficient interest in dramatic entertainment to support in 1661 six different companies, each performing three or four afternoons a week.[18] It was this section of his audience upon which the dramatist had chiefly to rely for the support of his plays. Their taste was not limited to any one dramatic form; this is the audience which first witnessed the tragedies of Corneille and Racine, the great comedies of Molière, and the farces of the Italian comedians and of Molière's own company. If the plays which are written for it may be taken as the measure of an audience, then the finest groups of spectators in the history of the drama have been the Athenians of the fifth century B.C., the Londoners of the reigns of Elizabeth and James I, and the Parisians of the reign of Louis XIV.

The Tragedies

Neo-classical tragedy is a form of tragedy that resulted from the attempt to produce plays on the model of the tragedies of ancient Greece and Rome and in accordance with what the Renaissance had come to regard as the Aristotelian "rules." The rules of the neo-classicists were, however, pseudo-Aristotelian rather than Aristotelian. The most controversial of these rules concerned the three unities of time, place, and action. Unity of action is treated in Aristotle's *Poetics* as an important æsthetic principle of tragedy. Unity of time, that is, the limitation of the time of action of a tragedy to a single day, is mentioned by Aristotle as a matter of common practice rather than as a matter of principle. Unity of place is not mentioned at all. The three unities of neo-classicism, then, were based not on the text of the *Poetics* itself but on Italian and French critical interpretation and development of Aristotle. In sixteenth-century France, the rules came to have greater and greater prestige, without influencing the popular secular drama in any important respect. In seventeenth-century France, however, not only did the rules tend to take on the aspect of immutable universal laws but at the height of the neo-classical movement, the drama was almost completely subdued to the form and mode implied in the rules.

In view of the social, religious, and æsthetic differences in the ages which produced Greek and neo-classical tragedies, it is in-

[18] See Karl Mantzius, *History of Theatrical Art* (London: Duckworth & Company, 1905), IV, 170–171.

evitable that neo-classical tragedy should differ in a number of respects from the tragedies of Æschylus, Sophocles, and Euripides. But the similarities were even more important. In both types of tragedy, the subject was likely to be historical or legendary, and the important characters concerned were almost exclusively persons of royal or noble birth. The sequence of painful or disastrous events in which the noble persons were involved ended usually in disaster, although occasionally, as in Euripides' *Iphigenia in Tauris* and Corneille's *The Cid,* happy endings were permitted. Both types of tragedy display a very considerable simplification and abstraction in the treatment of character, with Corneille's practice closer to the typical characterization of Sophocles, and Racine's closer to the more individual characterization of Euripides. In both types of tragedy the element of idealization is all-important; mundane and realistic details are steadily suppressed, and the characters live, move, and have their being in a world free from economic and physiological complexities.

But the differences between classical and neo-classical tragedy are really more interesting than their inevitable resemblances. On the whole, as we have indicated, neo-classical tragedy is a stricter and more rigid form than classical tragedy because of its subservience to the doctrines of the three unities.[19] Neo-classical tragedy, besides, is more unified in tone than classical tragedy, since the former rigorously excludes personages from humble life, touches of humor, or lyrical alleviations of the unrelentingly heroic tone. This unity of tone is intensified by the severely unified style of neo-classical tragedy. The metrical complexity of ancient tragedy permitted a range of poetic effects that neo-classical tragedy denied itself in its constant use of the rimed Alexandrine.[20]

The diction and imagery of neo-classical tragedy are infinitely more limited and selective than the diction and imagery of classical tragedy. This limited vocabulary and this fastidious elimination of inappropriate metaphors and similes were the results of that passion for decorum that was so integral an element of neo-classical thought and art. It should also be said that the process of abstraction and idealization common to both forms of tragedy probably advanced further in the later form than in any other type of tragedy produced in the western world. The manners and the preoccupations

[19] Professor George Sherburn has said that the French can endure their classical tragedies only because they are acted romantically. One encounter with the curious but highly traditional thespian phenomena of the Théâtre Français is sufficient to convince one of the truth of his observation.

[20] Like the English practitioners of the rimed couplet, the French tragic writers contrived to play a considerable variety of tunes on the Alexandrine, but even at its best, it remains a more restrictive instrument than the English iambic pentameter.

of the characters are even more super-mundane than those of the heroes and heroines of classical tragedy.

The omnipresent confidants of neo-classical tragedy developed as a result of the strict adherence to the unities, the consequent minimization of the action represented on the stage, and the almost complete elimination of the chorus of classical tragedy. The confidant is usually a colorless and unopinionated parasite attached to each of the major persons of the drama, in order to supply the necessary auditor for the revelation of the past and the soul-agonies of the present.

The Dramatists

Neo-classical tragedy developed to its final and perfect form only after a prolonged struggle with the relatively formless and undifferentiated types of popular drama, which in early seventeenth-century France took the forms of tragedy, tragicomedy, melodrama, and pastoral drama. The career of Pierre Corneille (1606–84) illustrates the gradually increasing domination of a somewhat recalcitrant personality by neo-classical doctrine.[21] Corneille's first sensationally successful play, *The Cid,* so affronted the neo-classical party under the dominance of Cardinal Richelieu that the play was submitted for judgment to the newly formed French Academy. Despite some qualifications, the play was condemned for a number of serious violations of the classical proprieties. From this experience, Corneille learned his lesson, and in most of his plays written thereafter took greater pains to make his practice coincide with the accepted æsthetic dramatic code. But his conscience was uneasy, and he repeatedly attempted, in critical appendices to his published plays, to defend himself from the charge of violating neo-classical principles. Corneille's was really a romantic spirit struggling to pour itself into the rigid neo-classical mould. His enthusiasm for the sensational and the supernatural marks him as romantic rather than as austerely classical. But his tragedies are among the glories of neo-classicism. They draw their heroic power from his treatment of character in terms of basic and dominating passion, his conception of drama as a conflict between opposed elements in a single character or between personalities holding opposing views, and his apotheosis of the human will.

It was Jean Racine (1639–1699) whose more feminine spirit found the neo-classical formula a perfect stimulus for his particular powers. Racine's forte was the analysis of emotion—especially of amatory emotion, and consequently the minimization of action and

[21] Corneille's major plays are *The Cid* (1635), *Horace* (1639), *Cinna* (1640), *Polyeucte* (1643), and *Rodogune* (1644).

the limitations of time and space bore less heavily on him than upon Corneille. Racine's plays usually resolve themselves into a passionate analysis of the emotions of characters involved in a complex situation the dénouement of which is undecided but imminent.[22] Racine's characters, especially his women characters, are more roundly and complexly drawn than Corneille's. They are not semi-heroic figures like the heroines of Æschylus or Sophocles, but seventeenth-century *grandes dames* with all the elegancies of speech and feeling of the most elegant of courts. His use of the rimed Alexandrine is subtle, but restrained. It has the complex and Virgilian beauty of the grand style at its best.

E. RESTORATION TRAGEDY

After eighteen years of "blue laws" in England, theatrical production began again when the exiled King Charles II returned to his throne in 1660. Since the closing of the theaters by the Puritans in 1642, there had been only surreptitious, semi-private performances of plays; some of the Elizabethan playhouses had been destroyed, others partially dismantled; all the old dramatic companies had been broken up and many of the actors had died; all but one or two of the Elizabethan dramatists were gone. The taste and make-up of the audience had also been changed by these years of Civil War and Puritan rule. As a consequence the drama of the Restoration (the period from 1660 to 1700) is quite distinct from that which precedes it. New dramatists write for a new method of production in a new theater, and, most important of all, they write for a new type of audience.

The Audience

The audience for which the plays of the Restoration were written was strikingly different from Shakespeare's. His theater was filled with people of every class in London, from noblemen to pickpockets; the Restoration theaters were run for one class only, and they were seldom filled anyhow. During a large part of the Elizabethan period, six different theaters were competing with each other to satisfy the Londoner's demand for plays. In the Restoration, though London had more than doubled its population since Shakespeare's day, it could scarcely support two theaters; when one was full, the other was almost sure to be empty. For a dozen years, indeed, only one theater was running in the whole city. This surprising difference is due largely to the character of the audience

[22] Racine's major plays are *Andromaque* (1667), *Britannicus* (1669), *Iphigénie* (1674), and *Phèdre* (1677)

and the character of the plays which were written to be presented in the Restoration theater.

When Charles II returned to ascend his father's throne in 1660, most Londoners were thoroughly tired of Puritan rule and eager for the restoration of the monarchy. Not all the old inhibitions, however, had been forgotten, and many a London merchant who cheered the return of the King still thought that playhouses were dens of vice. Perhaps this great middle-class audience might have been won over, had the Restoration theater managers tried to be conciliatory, but they were precisely the opposite. From the very first, the old Puritans and the middle classes were satirized and jeered at; the plays derided or ignored the favorite middle-class virtues and dwelt long and lovingly on the vices the Puritans most abhorred. Restoration plays were written for and about courtiers, and soon the fashionable wits and their parasites, male and female, were the only people to be found in the audience.

This courtly audience was interested in seeing itself on the stage, sympathetically treated, of course, and in seeing presentations of virtue and honor so exalted, so wholly removed from anything possible of human attainment, that no conceivable reflection on its own shortcomings could be implied. Thus the most characteristic products of the Restoration theater are all-too-human comedies and utterly super-human tragedies. Diverse as they are, both grow out of the characteristics and tastes of the wits of the Restoration audience.

The Restoration fop was a gorgeous creature, very much concerned with all matters of style and wit and taste and not at all concerned with morals. He admired extravagance, dissoluteness, brilliance and insolence; he was a wit and a philanderer. Gay and cynical, he could scarcely conceive of innocence; certainly he could not take it seriously. He thought of the theater, and of most other resorts of the fashionable world, as places to meet other gallants and to ogle and if possible to arrange rendezvous with the women in the audience and the actresses on the stage. Very often the gallants were much more interested in affairs in the audience—conversations, flirtations, quarrels, and even an occasional duel—than in affairs on the stage.

This does not mean that these Restoration wits were incapable of appreciating dramatic art. Far from it. Many of the plays of the time and some of the best were written by gallants; they set themselves up as critics and patrons of the arts; nearly all the most prominent courtiers were at least dabblers in literature. But they could not allow themselves to take drama or anything else too seriously. The Restoration wit was a professed dilettante: his play was the amusing product of a few idle hours, his poems had beguiled a convalescence, his science was a pleasant relief from too strenuous dissipation. Even his most serious occupation, love, was not to be taken too seriously; he did not allow his infatuations to get out of hand; he felt it vulgar to confine his attentions too long or too exclusively to one woman.

This characteristic attitude made the drama a toy of the court circles. The theater was a fashionable place and its plays were eminently suitable for polite conversation, but the Restoration fop felt that the drama was nothing to command very great respect or very deep interest. In the comedies he liked to see himself, his extravagances and his love affairs and mild satires of his pet foibles. In the tragedies he enjoyed exaggerated conflicts of love and honor, conduct so scrupulously high-minded as to be mostly outside the bounds of human probability and therefore no reflection on his own conduct which was generally unscrupulous and low-minded. These tragedies always incorporated an elegance which was distinctly a part of the spirit of the age. The love of form and polish could be expressed in plays as well as in courtly manners. In a tragedy the logic of the classic unities and the even flow of polished and regular verse had the appeal of the perfectly tailored coat and the practised bow in the drawing room.

Naturally the courtiers knew and admired the classical standards of Augustan Rome. Furthermore, many of them had spent years of exile with King Charles in France and had returned to England thoroughly imbued with the neo-classicism of the contemporary French stage. The tragedies of the Restoration are the nearest to the French classical ideal of any that have been written in English.

The Theater and the Performance

The theater of the Restoration was not developed from the typical public playhouse of Shakespeare's time, but from the private playhouse [23] which was much more suitable to the requirements of a select courtly audience. The typical Restoration theater was a remodeled indoor tennis court, very much like the theater of Corneille and Racine in Paris. A stage was built in at one end, the court itself became the pit, now supplied with benches and much more respectable than formerly, and the old spectators' galleries became the galleries and boxes of the theater. Such a playhouse held a smaller audience than the old out-of-door one, and its productions, of course, required artificial light.

The most important innovation in the Restoration theater was the stage. Though based on the old Elizabethan type, it was suffi-

[23] See p. 44, n. 14

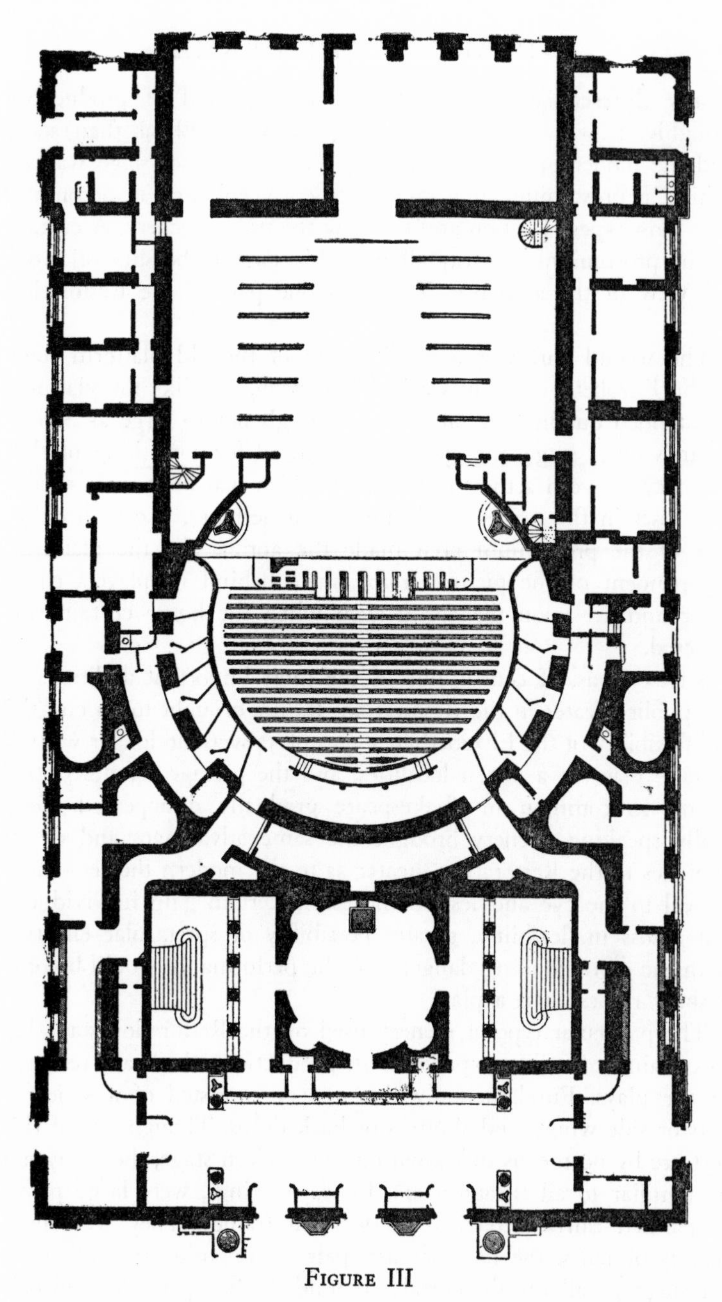

FIGURE III

PLAN OF THE GROUND-FLOOR OF DRURY LANE THEATER AS REBUILT IN 1812

This reconstructed nineteenth-century theater shows clearly the arrangement of flats and backdrops inherited from the Restoration theaters. Adapted from Benjamin Wyatt, *Observations on the Design for the Theatre Royal, Drury Lane* (London: J. Taylor, 1813).

ciently different to bring about a new method of production. Roughly, it was the middle step between the Elizabethan stage and the modern picture frame stage. The old inner stage was set behind a proscenium arch, and sufficiently enlarged to accommodate most types of action and to allow the use of scenery. A curtain in the proscenium archway allowed this stage to be shut off from the view of the audience. This was one part of the Restoration stage.

The second part was a modification of the old platform stage of the Elizabethans; it was called the apron, and like the platform it extended out into the audience. Though not so large as Shakespeare's outer stage, the apron still allowed for something of that intimacy between actor and spectator which had been such a valuable asset in the earlier productions. Furthermore, doors on either side of the proscenium arch made the apron, like the platform, independent of the picture frame stage behind it; players could enter and act upon the apron even when the house curtain was lowered.

Scenery was, of course, one of the most important additions to the public theater in the Restoration. Its use brought to an end the old flexibility of the Elizabethan stage; plays were no longer written to take place in a dozen localities, and the passages of descriptive poetry so common in Shakespeare gradually disappeared. Generally speaking, scenery brought the same advantages and disadvantages to the Restoration theater as to the modern theater—more appeal to the eye and less to the ear, a certain gain in vividness, but a loss in flexibility, greater possibility of spectacular effects—with the corresponding danger that the performance would become a show rather than a play.

The particular type of scenery used on the Restoration stage led to certain unfamiliar expedients in production which are reflected in the plays. Fundamentally the scenery consisted of a series of flats or side wings, and shutters or back drops. Though sets of this sort are by no means unknown on the modern stage, they may not be familiar to all theater-goers. Flats, or wings, were large pieces of painted canvas stretched on wooden frames. They were used in sets of pairs, the flats of each pair set opposite each other on the stage, parallel to the curtain. Behind the first pair a second pair was set, behind the second a third, and so on. The two flats or wings of the first pair were placed nearly as far apart as the sides of the proscenium arch, so that only the inside edges, perhaps two feet of a four or five foot flat, were visible to the audience. The second pair came a little nearer together than the first, the third pair nearer than the second, and so on. The last pair of flats (there were usually four or five pairs) lacked several feet of meeting in the middle of the stage. This gap was filled by a shutter or back drop (another piece of painted canvas) placed three or four feet behind the last pair of flats, so that the audience sitting out in front saw a stage apparently shut in on the sides by the painted wings and at the back by the shutter.

These flats and shutters were painted in perspective, so that the spectators seemed to see the houses facing each other along two sides of a street, or pillars along the sides of a hall or gallery, or trees bordering an open space in the forest. Each pair of houses or pillars or trees was, of course, painted at the ends of a pair of flats in diminishing size and height to give the effect of distance. On the back drop or shutter, the perspective was continued to some object in the background, or sometimes the shutter was painted to represent the third wall, or a clump of trees in the distance, or a building cutting off the end of the street.

A set of this sort could be changed in the course of the play by lowering the curtain and setting up new wings and a new shutter, but such changes were both difficult and expensive in a theater where the average play ran only three days, and ten or twelve new productions might be called for in the course of a single month. Instead of lowering the curtain and changing the entire set for a new scene, it was more common to shut off the view of the audience by pushing one pair of wings together in the middle of the stage. Since these wings all ran in grooves, it was a very simple matter to push one pair along its grooves until the two flats met. A scene could be acted on this half stage and the apron as well as on the whole stage. When the scene changed again, the pair of wings could be pulled apart to open up the stage behind. Often such changes occur in the midst of the action, where the stage directions say, "the scene opens," or "the scene closes."

Thus in the fourth act of Congreve's comedy, *Love for Love,* Sir Sampson Legend goes to call upon his son Valentine who is pretending illness. He is received by Jeremy, Valentine's servant, who tells of his master's condition. The scene was evidently performed in front of two flats pushed together across the stage, for when Sir Sampson breaks off the discussion and demands to see his son, Jeremy replies, "I'll knock at the door." After this speech, the stage directions say, *"Goes to the Scene, which opens"* and then, *"Valentine upon a Couch disorderly dress'd."* Evidently, at Jeremy's knock the two flats were pulled apart to disclose the bedroom scene which had been set behind. Similarly in the fifth act of Otway's tragedy, *Venice Preserved,* Belvidera was evidently on the apron when she was seized and carried off, for as soon as the stage is empty, the directions say, *"Scene opening discovers a Scaffold and a Wheel prepared for the executing of Pierre,"* and the execution scene begins immediately. At the close of this scene there is another stage direction, *"Scene shuts upon them,"* and immediately Belvidera is led upon the stage again.

This new type of theater which provided for the use of scenery was perhaps the greatest difference between the Elizabethan and the typical Restoration production. But another very important change was the introduction of actresses, a change which affected the plays in several ways. For one thing, after the new convention had become well established, there were more women's parts in the plays than before when playwrights had been limited by the number of well-trained boys available. Not only do Restoration plays have more parts for women, but these parts are more important and more varied than in the earlier plays. Actresses naturally became one of the greatest attractions of the theaters; men came to see Moll Davis in a new part or to admire Nell Gwyn disguised as a boy.

The Plays

With a few exceptions, the tragedies of the Restoration are not great plays; certainly they do not measure up to the tragedies of Shakespeare and Marlowe. The super-human characters and the noble sentiments which are so commonly found make them appear a bit absurd to the modern reader, accustomed to a more realistic type of play. A further difficulty in the tragedy of the Restoration is the intellectual, the unemotional quality which characterizes many of the plays. It is not that there is a consistent avoidance of emotional scenes, though as a matter of fact there are fewer than in Elizabethan plays; but when emotion does enter, it is not genuine and convincing. Instead of the deeply moving speeches of Shakespeare and Marlowe, the Restoration tragic dramatists write shrill, ranting, raving tirades—violent speeches which make a great deal of noise but which sound hollow and unconvincing. This was a very serious handicap, as passionless tragedy must be written with consummate skill if it is to avoid dullness or even absurdity.

For such reasons as these, the most typical heroic tragedies of the Restoration are not the best. Plays like Dryden's *Indian Emperor* and *The Conquest of Granada,* Settle's *Empress of Morocco,* and the Earl of Orrery's *Tragedy of Mustapha* are interesting as specimens of the taste of an age but not as moving plays.

The best tragedies of the Restoration, while possessing much of the characteristic restraint and classic form admired in the time, do not conform to all the requirements of heroic tragedy. They abandon the standard heroic couplets for more flexible and moving blank verse; they treat the leading characters a little less like demigods. Though written to please the classic taste of the typical courtly audience and though similar to true heroic tragedy in many respects, the best tragedies of the Restoration still have the power to move a modern reader. Such plays as Dryden's *All for Love* and Otway's *Venice Preserved* and *The Orphan* are tragedies worthy of consideration on their own merits.

Probably the most interesting and enlightening of these plays is Dryden's *All for Love*. It is both a very good tragedy and an excellent illustration of the taste of the Restoration. Dryden wrote it in confessed imitation of Shakespeare's *Antony and Cleopatra,* in an attempt to maintain the grandeur of Shakespeare's tragic effect without those irregularities and excesses of romanticism which so annoyed the classic taste of the Restoration. The play is not simply a revision, however; it is an entirely new play written on the same plot. Dryden's straining for the unities and his emphasis of the love versus honor theme, his consistent simplification and toning down of the old story which Shakespeare had used is an eloquent exposition of the divergent ideals of the Elizabethan and Restoration theaters.

F. MODERN TRAGEDY

The term modern tragedy is here used to refer to the plays written since the advent of Henrik Ibsen, the plays from 1880 to the present day. Since these are the plays of our own time, they do not require the same consideration of background necessary for an appreciation of a Greek or an Elizabethan tragedy. We are all more or less familiar with the characteristic ideas and interests of the typical modern audience and with the type of performance in twentieth-century theaters. Yet this very familiarity is likely to lead us astray; we assume that certain dramatic conventions are fundamental to all good plays when they are merely passing twentieth-century customs; we neglect the most significant interests in our enthusiasm for trifles. Because of this difficulty of seeing the modern drama in any proper perspective, it may be helpful to review briefly some of the characteristics of the audience, the theaters, and the tragedies of our own time—to try to see ourselves as we see the ancient Greeks, or as the students of 3934 may see us.

The Audience

In comparing modern tragedies with those written for an ancient Greek or an Elizabethan audience, it is well to remember that in many ways the typical modern audience is the least representative group of the three. The plays of Æschylus and Sophocles were witnessed by most of the free men of Athens, from the meanest citizen to the priests of Dionysus and Pericles himself. When a play of Shakespeare's was performed at the Globe, the greatest noblemen in the land were likely to be found in the gallery, while tradesmen and beggars, pickpockets and prostitutes, jostled each other in the pit. Modern theater audiences are not so representative as this. The largest classes in our city populations—laborers, unskilled workmen and their families—have deserted the theaters entirely for the movies. The distinction between the modern and the Greek and Elizabethan audiences applies not only to the classes represented but to the actual number of people who see plays. Only a small proportion of the total population supports the present-day theater. In Periclean Athens and Elizabethan London, most of the people were more or less familiar with their theater. In modern London, New York, and Chicago, probably the great majority of the population has never seen a play; certainly it has never seen a tragedy.

In this respect the modern audience resembles the audience of Restoration London or the Parisian audience in the reign of Louis XIV. This resemblance is sometimes obscured for us by the fact that London and New York have so many more theaters now than they had in the Restoration. We think that if modern London has thirty-five or forty times as many theaters now as then, and that if New York, which had none in 1675, has more than a hundred now, the modern audience *must* be more representative than the Restoration one. We forget that London has multiplied its population by about thirty and New York by even more.

This leads to another characteristic of the modern audience. In the other periods we have noticed, the theater audience was almost entirely a local audience. Sophocles wrote for Athenians, Shakespeare and Congreve for Londoners; they knew that the vast majority of people who watched their plays were thoroughly familiar with the life of the city. This is no longer true. The average audience in London and New York and Chicago is about half made up of visitors to the city. Furthermore, the modern play which has any sort of success is sure to be produced in other cities and even in other countries. In one season the active modern theatergoer may see American, English, Irish, German, French, Italian, Russian, and Norwegian plays. Obviously the successful modern dramatist cannot rely on local interests and local enthusiasms as Sophocles and Shakespeare and Congreve did.

These two characteristics of the modern audience which we have noted are in a sense contradictory. The modern audience is more restricted than the Greek or Elizabethan as far as classes and the total population are concerned. It is less restricted geographically than any earlier audience. Thus one characteristic prompts the dramatist to narrow his appeal; the other prompts him to broaden it.

Our audience of the early twentieth century is again distinguished by its interest in, or at least its lip service to, democracy. A great deal of this interest is artificial or sentimental; nevertheless, a larger proportion of plays center about lower class characters in our time than in any previous period. The heroes of modern plays are more likely to be sailors or bookkeepers than princes. In fact, there is a tendency to sentimentalize the lower classes, to assume not that the laborer is as good as the millionaire, but that he is much better. This is not the place to analyze this rather curious state of affairs; it is enough for us to note its existence, and to realize that modern dramatists are simply being conventional when they select for their heroes common soldiers or paupers, just as Shakespeare was conventional in selecting generals and princes for his heroes.

Perhaps it is most important of all to notice that the modern audience differs from all earlier audiences in that it is dominated by women. There have been women in the audience of all the theaters we have studied, but heretofore they have always been in the minority. In the twentieth century not only are there large numbers of women in the audience, but it is the opinion of the women which is most important in determining the success or failure of the play. When men and women attend the theater together, it is generally the women who decide which play it is to be. Numerically, women are in the majority in most audiences; at matinees there are often ten or twelve women for every man.

This predominance of women is greater in the United States than in any other country, but the same tendency is apparent everywhere. It is not easy to determine just what effect this characteristic of modern audiences has had on the drama. We may be sure, however, that it helps to account for the larger proportion of women's parts in plays, for the increasing attention to women's problems, and for the tendency to endow heroes and heroines with traits which will appeal especially to women. It would be false to say that all modern plays are written for women, but the plays of the twentieth century are certainly much less masculine in their appeal than the plays of the sixteenth century or the plays of the fifth century B. C.

Finally, we should take into consideration the fact that the modern audience has less interest in tragedy and less interest in or understanding of verse than earlier audiences. Whatever the reason for this, it is a conspicuous fact. In the twentieth-century American theater, a smaller proportion of the plays produced are tragedies than in any of the other theaters we have studied. Even the tragedies which are produced are likely to be timorously disguised in the advertisements as "poignant dramas." There is a close relationship between this fact and the modern distaste for poetry. Again and again in contemporary tragedies we see the dramatists struggling for an effect which an Elizabethan playwright would have achieved by the use of poetry. In *Riders to the Sea* Synge tries to attain the old tragic grandeur by giving an artificial beauty to his prose; he uses various poetic devices, but he does not quite dare to cast his dialogue in poetic form. In Eugene O'Neill's one-act play, *Bound East for Cardiff,* we can see the dramatist striving for an effect of imagined beauty and peace when the dying sailor says musingly,

> It must be great to stay on dry land all your life and have a farm with a house of your own with cows and pigs and chickens, 'way in the middle of the land where yuh'd never smell the sea or see a ship. It must be great to have a wife, and kids to play with at night after supper when your work was done. It must be great to have a home of your own, Drisc.

This is a theme for poetry, but because of the conventions of the modern theater, O'Neill has restrained himself to poetic prose.

This distaste for poetry and tragedy is a phase of the modern subservience to realism.[24] Poetry is taboo because it is not an accurate imitation of what people actually say in ordinary conversation. Tragedy generally involves an action somewhat more exalted than the realist can find in everyday life. Probably there are other reasons more intimately connected with modern thinking, but our primary interest here is to note these prejudices in connection with modern tragedies. They constitute one of the chief handicaps under which serious modern dramatists labor.

The Theater and the Performance

Modern plays are influenced just as much by the type of theater and the type of performance for which they are written as were Greek plays. Modern theaters, however, are comparatively familiar; our purpose is not to visualize a twentieth-century performance, but to consider those characteristics of our theaters which must be remembered in comparing contemporary plays with the plays of earlier periods. With this purpose in mind, we must limit our discussion to the typical modern theater. The most advanced of twentieth-century stages and performances, while very interesting,

[24] See Chapter VIII.

are not particularly significant for the study of typical modern plays. The great majority of plays, good and bad, are written for a conventional performance in a conventional theater.

By far the most important new device in the modern theater is the electric light; more than anything else it has influenced the development of the modern performance. One experienced producer has written: "The only invention of the first importance to the theater, made between the time of Euripides and our own day, is the electric light. And it was invented with no thought of the theater at all. The other mechanical devices were known to the Greeks, or have been of passing consequence. The switchboard is the only powerful new instrument."[25]

If we think of the electric light only as an aid to superficial realism in the theater—the dawn, brilliant sunlight, deepening twilight—it does not seem so important as this quotation indicates. Of course, it is an aid to the dramatist to have his audience *see* that darkness is coming on or that moonlight is making it easier for his characters to see, but such things are not the most essential elements of drama. Shakespeare got around the difficulty adroitly enough by making his characters talk about the sunrise or the darkness. In fact, the more sensitive members of an audience probably get a much more vivid picture from Romeo's lines,

> . . . look, love, what envious streaks
> Do lace the severing clouds in yonder east:
> Night's candles are burnt out, and jocund day
> Stands tiptoe on the misty mountain tops,

than from the most gorgeous sunrise that any stage electrician ever devised.

The chief contribution of the electric light is to a much more essential function of the drama than this. An important purpose of the dramatic writer in any period is to play upon the emotions of his audience, and this is the function of the dramatist upon which the electric light has exercised the most profound influence. Everyone has observed certain effects of light upon our emotions—fear is more easily aroused in a dim light or in darkness than in the full glare of the sun; joy is more contagious on a bright spring afternoon than on a gray winter morning; melancholy thoughts are more easily suggested to us at twilight than at noon. These effects are known to all, but there are others just as sure to influence an audience though not quite so universally recognized. We respond to colors just as readily as we do to degrees of light. The

[25] Thomas Wood Stevens, *The Theatre from Athens to Broadway* (New York: D. Appleton & Co., 1932), p. 211.

stage manager who knows how the mood of the audience will change as he gradually alters the yellow light to blue or the green light to rose can be of great assistance to the dramatist in building up the mood of his play.

It must not be thought, however, that this new device in the theater is a simple automatic machine to be used by any fool; its effective use is a result of skill and of long patient work. If the lighting of a play is to be effective, it must, like every other device of the dramatist or actor, be subtly used; ninety-eight per cent of the audience must be unconscious of the lighting changes deliberately calculated to influence them. Of course most productions do not achieve this subtlety. The light changes are jerky or too fast; the increasing light from the rising sun looks like the result of a flash-light bomb, or the change from yellow light to blue is so abrupt as to suggest that an indigo cloud has passed over the sun. But when skilfully used, the switchboard is the greatest aid to the dramatist that has been developed since the day of Euripides. When Shakespeare wanted his audience to feel the despair of Hamlet, he had only the magic of his lines and the art of the actor to effect his purpose; the modern dramatist can add to these the cunning use of lights.

Much less important than electric light, but more apparent to the average theater-goer, is the use of realistic scenery in the modern theater. These sets relieve the dramatist of the necessity of making his characters describe the setting, but they are at least as much of a handicap to him as an advantage. Since the modern audience is accustomed to the convention of realistic backgrounds, the dramatist is hampered by the limitations of a scene designer and a stage manager as earlier dramatists were not.[26] In the average theater the playwright must confine himself to three or four different scenes for his action. Sometimes he can arrange for more, but not usually; in fact, his chances of selling his play are greatly increased if he can limit himself to one set. Certain mechanical devices—revolving stages, wagon stages, elevator stages—have ameliorated this difficulty somewhat, but not much. In the first place, these devices have increased the possible number of sets only a little; a dramatist writing for a theater equipped with all of them is still more limited than Shakespeare was. In the second place, comparatively few theaters, except in Germany, are able to use these moving stages.

[26] The habit of the modern audience of relying on the scene designer for the background instead of relying on the lines of the characters or on its own imagination is one of the greatest difficulties with which modern producers of Shakespeare's plays have to contend.

The convention of realistic scenery handicaps the modern dramatist not only in the number of scenes he may use in his play, but also in the type of scene. In general he must limit himself to places easily reconstructed by the scene designer. The cliffs of Dover, or the forest of Arden, or even the chariot way before the palace of Agamemnon are not scenes which the average producer is glad to attempt. In general, out-of-door scenes are much less common in modern plays than in earlier ones. Most of our plays are so constructed that the action takes place in two or three comparatively small rooms, with an occasional garden or terrace which calls for more of the works of man than of nature.

It is worth noting that these limitations of the conventional realistic set have proved so annoying that there is a strong tendency at present to get away from them. Good scene designers are relying more and more on suggestion—a single tree to represent a forest, one huge column to suggest the interior of a church—and refusing to attempt to give photographic reproductions. Some go even further and set the stage so as to convey an idea rather than depict a place. Certainly the most advanced modern productions rely less and less on realistic backgrounds and more and more on the imagination of the audience and the art of the actor as Sophocles and Shakespeare did. The great majority of modern plays, however, have not yet been affected by these advances; they are written for conventional productions with sets constructed to look as much like the real thing as possible.

Some of the characteristics of modern plays are due to the fact that the average theater of our time is smaller and more comfortable than many of the earlier playing places. This condition has abetted the modern interest in realism in developing a type of acting that is more subdued, more conversational, than the acting on the Greek or Elizabethan stage. Ordinary tones of voice can be heard in a modern theater as they could not have been in the Theater of Dionysus at Athens. The physical comfort of the upholstered seats of a twentieth-century theater has something to do with the elimination from many of our plays of the ranting speeches and constant action necessary to hold the attention of the standing audience crowded into the pit of an Elizabethan playhouse. Generally speaking, the dialogue of a modern play is written to be spoken in conversational tones, and fights and murders are comparatively few. It would certainly be inaccurate to attribute this change entirely to the characteristics of the modern theater, but this has been one of the causes.

In most of the plays of our time the action is broken up into several clearly defined movements, or acts. Usually there is a heightening of interest at the end of each act and an interval in time before the beginning of the next. It does not take a very close comparison of plays written for modern theaters with plays written for earlier theaters to discover that the act is more of a unit in our plays than in many earlier ones. In general, modern plays tend to follow the classic divisions of the action which were characteristic in the ancient Greek theater and in the neo-classic theater. Twentieth-century dramatists are not quite so strict in their observance of these formal divisions as Sophocles and Corneille, but they are much more conscious of the requirements of form than the Elizabethan dramatists were.

One of the chief reasons for this new attention to form is the use of the curtain in the modern theater. Even in the earlier playhouses which had them, curtains were not used with the same finality, partly because of a different conception of the construction of a play and partly because of the difficulty of controlling the house lights. In modern theaters, the fall of the curtain is used to mark the end of something—the stage and all its illusions disappear, the lights are turned up—the audience ceases to be a group with a single interest and a single emotion and breaks up into individual units; people think and talk about something else, they even leave the theater. So far as the mood and the illusion are concerned, the play must begin all over again at the start of the next act. This customary use of the curtain to make a sharp break in the performance has led modern dramatists to build their plays so that this break will seem as natural as possible. It has also led most of them to plan each act so that some dramatic situation—a ludicrous discovery, a tragic revelation, a startling admission—gains emphasis when the action is suddenly blotted out by the curtain, like the vivid memory of the last minute before the earthquake. So far as the construction or planning of modern plays is concerned, this peculiar development of the act unit is one of the most striking characteristics of our plays.

More than most people realize, costume is an important factor in play production. Up to the end of the nineteenth century, the variety and color of costumes were a great source of interest, not only on the stage, but in real life as well. Though the dress of women still maintains some of its variety, it has nothing like as much as in Shakespeare's day, or Congreve's; men's clothes have become standardized in drab monotony. Since most of our plays are laid in the present, it is easy to see that the average performance cannot have the variety so easily attained on earlier stages. But costume has other uses. For purposes of characterization it has always been of great importance, but the modern dramatist is very much more limited in this regard than his predecessors have been. If a lawyer, a grocer, and a barber walked onto the Elizabethan stage, the audience needed no dialogue about professional matters to identify the men, but the modern audience, because of the standardization of men's clothes, has no means of distinguishing except by dialogue. This regular use of dialogue instead of costume, coupled with the modern use of explanatory *dramatis personæ* and full stage directions, helps to make modern plays easier to read than any others; more of the necessary information is written into the lines and less is left to the experience of the actor and the stage manager.

The lack of variety in modern costume has helped to bring about another change in our plays. Certain types of plot very easily staged in earlier times can no longer be made convincing because of the uniformity of modern dress and appearance. The most conspicuous of these is the disguise plot. If a young, smooth-shaven Elizabethan courtier removed his plumed and jeweled hat, his gray and crimson doublet with huge puffed sleeves slashed to show their purple lining, his short, stiff, embroidered hose, his long silk stockings, his crimson shoes, and his azure cloak lined with orchid and laced with gold, and then disguised himself in black shoes and stockings, close-fitting black doublet and hose, a tight-fitting black cap, a long black robe, and a full set of gray whiskers, he would have attracted no more attention on the streets of Shakespeare's London than any other doctor, but even his best friends might have had trouble in recognizing him as the gaily dressed, smooth-faced young courtier. All sorts of complications might easily have followed. Indeed, disguises were not uncommon in real life in the sixteenth and seventeenth centuries. But if a modern dramatist wants to disguise a rising young politician as a doctor, there is very little that he can do. Every item of the politician's dress might be worn equally well by the doctor; a beard or a concealing cloak would make the young politician too conspicuous. The problem is almost hopeless. The disguise plot, therefore, has become as rare in the modern theater as in modern life. Most people think that Elizabethan disguises are just an evidence of the improbability of old plots, forgetting that it is standards of dress which have changed and not the intelligence of the audience or the dramatist.

Finally, the complete commercialization of the modern theater has had its effects on our plays. In some periods, for instance the Greek and medieval, the theater has not been a money-making institution at all. In the Elizabethan period it certainly was, but it was largely in the hands of men devoted to its interests. Now many of the men who derive an income from the theater have no interest in it whatever, except as a source of profit. Theaters are owned by men who rent them just as they rent office buildings and apartment houses, with no interest in the tenants save that they pay their rent. Individual plays are even financed by men who have no interest in or knowledge of the play at all, but who are simply gambling on the success of the play just as they would on the rise of common stocks, often with even less knowledge of the business. One phase of this commercialization is the star system. Plays, like any other commercial product, are pushed by the advertising value of a popular name. Not infrequently the play is distorted to fit the talents or defects of a star, and often minor parts are given to incompetent actors to save money to pay the salary of the "lead."

All this is unfortunate, but not often disastrous. Many great plays have been produced primarily to make money; certainly Shakespeare and Molière paid very close attention to the box office. The dominant commercial interests of our own time probably will not wreck the theater, but it is well to consider their influence when reading modern plays.

The Plays

We have seen how the characteristics of the modern audience and the modern theater and performance influence the plays of our time. Certain other influences are not peculiar to the theater. One of them is to be seen in the preoccupation of modern playwrights (like other modern thinkers) with social themes and domestic problems. Since the time of Ibsen, subjects of this type have been by far the most popular for serious plays. As the Greek tragedies were likely to depend on a religious interest in the audience, and Elizabethan tragedies on the analysis of an individual, so modern tragedies generally center about a social problem.

Of course such problems cannot be considered in the abstract, however general they are in their significance. The dramatist usually selects an individual to stand for a type or a class. In *Justice* Galsworthy makes Falder stand for the thousands of ordinary men who are led into crime through their own weakness rather than viciousness, and the play becomes an indictment of the blind stupidity of the criminal courts; in *Loyalties* he makes De Levis stand for the Jew in modern society, and the play becomes an attack on race prejudice. There are scores of other plays with similar interests. The tragedy of Mrs. Alving in *Ghosts* is constructed to enable Ibsen to show up the fatal hypocrisy of modern society. O'Neill's *Anna Christie* is not primarily an individual but any poor girl driven close to disaster by overwhelming economic and moral forces. It is themes of this sort which dominate most serious modern plays.

Closely associated with the social interest of modern dramatists is the tendency to set plays in the here and now rather than in any past time or unfamiliar place. The social problems considered are contemporary problems, and the scene must therefore be a familiar one. So far as setting or background is concerned, the playwright is generally concerned not in making it beautiful or strange, but in making it as familiar and real as possible. All this is simply another way of saying that the dominant interest of most modern dramatists is realism.[27]

Another interest more popular in the plays of our times than of earlier periods is the domestic; more plays than ever before are written about home life, or family life. This is a phase of the modern preoccupation with sex. Marriage and divorce, love (love as a social problem, rather than romantic love) and parenthood, interest our serious dramatists as they have interested those of no other time. Comedies have always been written on these subjects, but before the time of Ibsen they were seldom very popular as material for serious plays. In the modern period Ibsen has written of marriage problems in *The Doll's House* and *The Wild Duck;* Strindberg has made bitter studies of love and marriage and parenthood in *Miss Julia* and *The Dance of Death* and *The Father;* Eugene O'Neill has considered love and parenthood in *Anna Christie* and *Strange Interlude* and *Mourning Becomes Electra.* In all these plays, the authors are interested in a social problem or a psychological diagnosis and not in a romantic story.

These tendencies in the serious drama of modern times are not, of course, universal. There are successful playwrights who ignore social problems, playwrights like Rostand and Yeats and Barrie and Maxwell Anderson who frequently write romantic plays of unfamiliar places and long-past times. Some of these men are fine dramatists, but their work is out of the main current of modern dramatic interests. The most characteristic serious plays of our times are realistic studies of domestic problems and social forces.

[27] See the discussion of realism, Chapter VIII.

CHAPTER III

COMEDY

Comedy is the most miscellaneous of all the dramatic forms. In fact, it might almost be said that comedy is simply what is left after all the tragedies, melodramas, farces, problem plays, tragicomedies, burlesques, and chronicle plays have been taken away. This vagueness about the limits of the form comedy may be somewhat surprising to the casual theater-goer who has assumed that all plays which end happily are comedies and all which end unhappily are tragedies. We have already noted the inadequacy of this distinction in our discussion of tragedy. Not only do some tragedies end happily, but most melodramas and all tragicomedies do. Furthermore, there are comedies which do not end happily in the ordinary meaning of the phrase; Molière's *Misanthrope* does not, nor does Jonson's *Volpone* or Rostand's *Cyrano de Bergerac;* yet all these plays were called comedies by their authors. The nature of the dénouement is no more reliable as a distinguishing mark for all comedies than it is for all tragedies. We must look for more fundamental characteristics of the form.

One of the difficulties standing in the way of an attempt to understand the essentials of comedy, from Aristophanes to S. N. Behrman, is the fact that different nations and different epochs have not agreed as to the most important characteristics of the form. For some audiences the chief distinction of comedy has been the social class of its characters. Thus the Romans and many of their successors up through the Renaissance thought of the characters of comedy as members of the middle and lower classes, in opposition to the kings and princes who were the chief characters of tragedy. But this distinction was not accepted by Greene and Shakespeare and the writers of Elizabethan romantic comedy, who presented dukes and kings and princes in their comedies as well as in their tragedies. The dramatists of the Restoration even tended to eliminate from their comedies bourgeois and lower class characters. To the English audiences of the eighteenth and nineteenth centuries comedy generally meant the happy ending, or the dénouement which involved rewards for the virtuous and sympathetic characters, and punishment or reformation for the wicked or unsympathetic ones.

Because of this variation in the standards of comic dramatists, one of the best approaches to an understanding of the general characteristics of the form is a hasty survey of what various notable theater audiences have been accustomed to expect in comedy. Such a sketch will indicate the reasons for the variety of the conceptions of comedy and may lead to a perception of certain qualities inherent in all.[1]

Comedy, like tragedy, first appeared in ancient Greece as an outgrowth of the religious celebrations in honor of Dionysus. It reached its highest form in the hands of Aristophanes, the only Greek comic dramatist whose work has come down to us in anything like a representative quantity. These plays of Aristophanes are an odd mixture of hilarity and satire and lyric beauty, of keen analyses of the ideas and practices of contemporary Athenians mixed with the wildest extravaganzas of the poets in hell and the city of birds. Evidently to Aristophanes, comedy meant three things: rollicking scenes of farce which would urge his audience to shouts of unrestrained laughter; satire, often very personal, of his contemporaries and their work, satire which would make his audience think about political or intellectual or social matters and which might perhaps lead to reform; and songs of haunting beauty which would give to his audience an æsthetic satisfaction of the sort modern audiences associate with operas or concerts rather than with plays.

The Roman comedies of Plautus and Terence were quite different from those of Aristophanes. The Roman comic dramatists had little interest in lyric beauty or in contemporary ideas and problems; the element of farce in their plays was not the fantastic fooling of the old Greek plays but a much more realistic and limited form of buffoonery. Their characters were not individuals but well-recognized middle-class city types who appeared in play after play. The comic dramatists presented to their audience these familiar figures in a great variety of situations. They expected to hold interest by the complicated intrigues of the plot and to arouse laughter at the ingeniously contrived situations displaying the cowardice of the boasting soldier, the elaborate lying of the clever servant, or the embarrassing predicament of the young prodigal. To Plautus and Terence comedy meant an intricate plot ingeniously devised to present a number of ludicrous situations in which certain stock figures were made ridiculous, frequently by violent means.

[1] This brief survey attempts to point out only the type of comedy most commonly associated with each of the periods mentioned. In most periods, several types of comedy were acted, but there is usually one which is the outstanding achievement of the time.

In Elizabethan and Jacobean England there were two popular types of comedy, the romantic type of Shakespeare and the realistic type of Ben Jonson. The romantic appeal of Shakespeare's *Midsummer Night's Dream, As You Like It,* and *Twelfth Night* is familiar. These comedies, which admit characters of all classes, present light-hearted stories of love and adventure in which the happy union of the lovers in the last act is always an important part of the appeal. Part of the action nearly always takes place in a wood or a garden, and the setting tends to be idyllic in opposition to the setting of city streets and houses in the realistic type of comedy. Shakespeare and his fellow writers of romantic comedy were not primarily interested in contemporary satire or in the humor rising out of ingeniously contrived situations; they planned their comedies to appeal to the audience's interest in a story, to their sympathetic satisfaction in the triumph of lovers, and to their appetite for music and poetry.

The realistic comedy of Ben Jonson and his followers was almost the complete antithesis of the light-hearted, fun-loving romantic comedy of Shakespeare. It was satiric and sometimes bitter, depending on ridicule rather than on humor for its laughs. Jonson thought that comedy had a social function to perform. It should benefit society by selecting the foibles and petty vices of the time and holding them up to ridicule on the stage. Furthermore, Jonson thought that comedies should not deal with princes and great noblemen but that the characters should be drawn exclusively from the middle and lower classes. In accordance with these principles, Jonson set his comedies in contemporary London, he modeled his characters on typical middle and lower class people whom he saw about him, and he attempted so to display these characters that the audience would laugh at their vanity and their greed and in so doing would laugh themselves out of their own addiction to these same vices.

The comedy which Molière wrote for the Parisians of the reign of Louis XIV resembles Jonson's more than it does that of any of the other comic dramatists whose work we have noticed. His best plays are set in contemporary Paris, his characters are drawn from the life about him, and he is conscious of the social function of comedy; but Molière was more good-humored than Jonson (for he recognized the futility of most attempts to reform people), and he was a much more profound student of character than his English predecessor. His best plays depend for their chief interest upon the inevitable clash between characters of opposed ideas and temperaments. Though he did ridicule the foibles and petty vices of his time, he was more interested in the fundamental relationships of men and women with each other and with the society of which they are a part. Molière expected from his audience not the roars of laughter provoked by the situations of Plautus and Terence, nor the delighted applause elicited by Shakespeare's charming songs and his happy dénouements of united lovers, nor yet the derisive glee prompted by Jonson's pompous fools and greedy schemers, but he sought to evoke that "thoughtful laughter" which greets the revelations of comedy of character or high comedy.

The comic dramatists of the period of the Restoration in England had certain interests in common with both Jonson and Molière; yet they had neither Jonson's reforming zeal nor Molière's profound interest in character. Their comedies were usually set in their own city and in their own time, and they were fond of revealing the follies of their contemporaries, but these revelations of folly had no moral purpose; they were intended purely for entertainment. The best dramatists of the Restoration tried to make their comedies reflect the manners of the more exclusive social groups of the time and to write brilliant dialogue whose wit would delight the sophisticated audience. In this comedy of manners and of wit the audience laughed at the affectations and vanities of their friends and acquaintances set forth on the stage and applauded the witty sallies of characters whose chief interests were fashionable manners and clever conversation.

In the eighteenth century and the first half of the nineteenth a few dramatists, like Sheridan and Goldsmith, tried to imitate the Restoration comedy of manners, but most of the comedies were of another sort, quite different in tone and purpose from the gay, brilliant, and none too decorous plays of Congreve, Wycherley, and Etherege. These comedies were somewhat like the Elizabethan romantic comedies in their interest in story, in the trials of lovers, and in the happy ending, rather than in satire or manners or wit or fundamental character conflicts, but in spite of these similarities eighteenth-century comedy differed sharply from Shakespeare's romantic variety. These comedies exploited the contemporary interest in preaching from the stage, the interest in the supposedly inevitable triumph of the soft-hearted and virtuous over the hard-headed and wicked, and the tearful interest in the pitiful and lugubrious for its own sake. This sentimental comedy of the eighteenth and early nineteenth centuries made three regular appeals to the audience: it gave them moralizing speeches, miniature sermons spoken by virtuous characters, for their self-righteous applause; it gave them pitiful scenes of virtue in distress for their ever-ready, sympathetic tears; and it gave them the gratifying triumph of virtue and modesty and honor at the end of the play for their comfortable satisfaction in the moral solidarity of their world.

On the modern stage all these types of comedy, except the Greek and perhaps the romantic comedy of the Elizabethans, are to be found. We have not worked out any new varieties, unless Bernard Shaw's challenging mixture of farce, comedy of wit, and propaganda is to be called a new type.

In this survey of the comedy of several historic epochs, we have noted the frequent combinations of comedy and farce, especially in the Greek and Roman plays. As a matter of fact, dramatists and critics did not distinguish between the two until the time of the Restoration, and even then the distinctions were not at first the ones which we should make to-day. To the modern critic, farce and comedy are different forms, and though they are still frequently combined, we recognize the existence of a type of humorous play, low in its appeal, which is not comedy and which we call farce. Since farce is now recognized as having certain peculiar characteristics of its own, we shall not consider it here as one of the varieties of comedy, but discuss it later in a separate chapter as one of the four fundamental dramatic forms—tragedy, comedy, melodrama, and farce.[2]

Our hurried survey of what various notable theater audiences have been accustomed to expect in comedy has pointed then, to seven different ideas of this form. First, there was the Greek mixture, which, because of the peculiarities of Greek conditions of performance disappeared from the popular stage more than two thousand years ago and which, therefore, we need not consider. There still remain the Roman type which depends primarily upon intrigue or situation, the Elizabethan romantic comedy, the Jacobean realistic or satiric comedy, Molière's high comedy or comedy of character, the Restoration comedy of wit or comedy of manners, and the eighteenth- and nineteenth-century sentimental comedy.

It is the presence on the modern stage of all six of these types of comedy, from the Roman comedy of intrigue or situation to the eighteenth-century sentimental comedy, which makes our modern conception of the form such a miscellaneous one. Not only are there examples of all these types to be seen in our theaters, but modern comedies are often a mixture of two or more of the old types.[3] It is no wonder that one has great difficulty in finding out just what a comedy is.

If we look closely, however, at these six types of comedy, we shall see that they all depend upon varying combinations of two quite different sorts of appeal to the audience. The first is an ap-

[2] See Chapter IV.

[3] See Section H of this Chapter for a discussion of the variety of modern comedy.

peal to the sense of humor, to the sense of the ridiculous. In the comedies based upon this appeal, the dramatist makes no very serious attempt to arouse the emotions or to engage strongly the sympathies of the audience; he tries to interest them mainly in the action and the dialogue of each particular scene in and for itself, and he is not interested in rousing any deep concern about the success of some characters and the failure of others. Dramatists making this type of appeal to their audience almost invariably rely more or less upon satire. Their comedies are intellectual rather than emotional. They may be far from profound, but the playwright does rely upon the audience's intelligent perception of those contrasts, incongruities, and inconsistencies which lead to laughter, and he makes little attempt to arouse the sympathies or the admiration or the pity or the hatred of the audience for any of the characters.

The second general type of appeal found in comedy is the opposite of the first; it is emotional rather than intellectual. In the plays dominated by this type of appeal, the dramatist tries to get his audience deeply interested in the outcome of the action, usually a love affair; he tries to build up a strong sympathy for certain characters and a dislike or even a hatred for certain others, and he relies greatly upon the feeling of satisfaction and delight with which the audience will greet the happy ending of the play and the punishment or reformation of the bad characters. In such plays the dramatist makes comparatively little use of satire; the audience is led to dislike certain characters not because they are satirized but because they are depicted as morally bad (not socially bad as in the intellectual types of comedy) and because they are trying to thwart the good characters or the characters with whom the audience has been led to sympathize.

Of course there are very few, if any, comedies based exclusively on one or the other of these two types of appeal; most plays combine the two. But in the combination one appeal is nearly always utilized much more extensively than the other. Congreve's *Way of the World* depends mostly upon the intellectual appeal and makes very little use of sympathy or hatred, or a strong interest in the outcome of the action. The same is true of Molière's *Misanthrope* and Jonson's *Alchemist* and *The Haunted House* of Plautus.

On the other hand, Shakespeare's *As You Like It,* though it contains a certain amount of satire and some very witty dialogue, depends primarily upon the interest of the audience in the outcome of the story and its strong sympathy for some characters, like Rosalind, and its dislike of others like Orlando's wicked brother, Oliver, and the usurping Duke Frederick. This same subordination of the intellectual to the emotional is characteristic of *Twelfth Night* and of Cumberland's *West Indian.*

The six general types which we have noted in our sketch of comedy from Roman to modern times are easily classified as depending primarily upon either the emotional or the intellectual type of appeal. Thus the Roman comedy of intrigue or situation, the Jacobean realistic or satiric comedy, Molière's high comedy or comedy of character, and the Restoration comedy of wit or comedy of manners depend chiefly upon the intellectual appeal. Shakespeare's romantic comedy and the eighteenth-century sentimental comedy depend chiefly upon the emotional appeal.

This discussion of the six main types of comedy and of the two fundamental types of appeal found in them has not brought us to a definition of the form. Many definitions might be quoted, but they would all be found to be either historic definitions referring to comedies of certain periods and inapplicable to others, or modern definitions which, in attempting to include all types, have been made too general to be helpful or have been made specific at the cost of the dogmatic exclusion of many plays which their authors have called comedies and which the audience has accepted as such. So long as so many different types of comedy continue to appear on our stage either in their historic forms or in modern combinations, it is unlikely that any satisfactory definition of the form will be framed.

If the student of the drama remembers that, in general, comedy makes a less exalted appeal and a less profound analysis of human emotions than tragedy, that it deals more honestly and less irresponsibly with its material than farce and melodrama, and if he becomes familiar with the fundamental characteristics and typical aims of the six general historic types of comedy and with the two fundamental types of comic appeal upon which they are based, he will probably have a fuller understanding of this form of drama than could be gained from any study of that ideal definition of comedy which no one has yet succeeded in formulating.

A. GREEK COMEDY

In comedy, as in tragedy, the drama of the ancient Greeks marks the beginning. The plays of Aristophanes bear much the same relationship to comic tradition that those of Æschylus, Sophocles, and Euripides bear to the tradition of tragedy. Long before the rest of Europe knew any recorded culture, the Greeks were watching the production of comedies which already made use of most of the comic devices known to the modern stage.

Greek comedy belongs to approximately the same period as

Greek tragedy,[4] although its chief poet, Aristophanes, was not born until after the death of Æschylus. Most of his comedies were written for the same audience which watched the plays of Euripides, and the physical theater and the general background of the production were much the same in the Athens of Aristophanes as in the Athens of Æschylus and Sophocles.

In its origin and in the circumstances of its production, Greek comedy, like tragedy, was religious. It grew out of and was always associated with the worship of Dionysus, or Bacchus. Like tragedy it was performed in the public theater about the altar of Dionysus; its production was organized and financed by the state; and it was given on the same occasions as tragedy, as part of the dramatic contests at the two annual festivals of Dionysus.[5]

Tragedy had its origins in the lamentations associated with the worship of Dionysus, but comedy sprang from the revels in his honor as god of wine, fruitfulness, and reproduction. We have seen how different the Greek conception of religion was from ours in its application to tragedy; in comedy the contrast is even more striking. It was from the drunken and licentious phase of the worship of Dionysus' pious devotees, from the boisterous phallic performances at his festivals that comedy developed, and the marks of this origin are on all the plays of Aristophanes. Phalluses were regularly worn, the figures of the actors were padded to make them appear grotesque, the action was sometimes of the broadest sort, and the lines were often gross and scurrilous. Not precisely what we should call religious, but we must remember that this was the tone of the Dionysiac festival. Without these features the comedies would have lost their appropriateness; they would have seemed flat and unseasonable to the audience.

All this must not be taken to mean that the plays of Aristophanes were simply dramatized orgies. Though traces of the orgy are undoubtedly to be found in them, other elements are much more important. Satire is perhaps the most prominent characteristic of

[4] In this discussion, we shall always use the term Greek comedy to refer to the plays of Aristophanes, the only comic dramatist of ancient Greece whose plays are extant. The times and conditions of production referred to are those of his plays. As a matter of fact, there were really three periods of Greek comedy, the Old Comedy (about 470–390 B. C.) of which Aristophanes was the chief exponent, the Middle Comedy (about 390–320 B. C.), and the New Comedy (about 320–250 B. C.). The Old Comedy is the only type of which complete plays have been preserved—those of Aristophanes. There are, however, references to and extant fragments of the work of many other writers of comedy, and from these records we know that the three types of comedy were different in purpose and structure. The only name, besides that of Aristophanes, of any significance in a brief survey like this, is Menander. He lived 342–291 B. C. and was the most important writer of the New Comedy. Though none of his plays is extant in its entirety, there are many fragments.

[5] See p. 23.

Greek comedy. The comic dramatist was allowed a freedom in ridicule which is unknown on the modern stage. He could attack anything he saw fit—the rulers of Athens, the education of the time and its leading exponents, the most cherished social customs of the people, the most essential policies of the state. Aristophanes attacked specifically and by name the most powerful men in Athens. In the midst of a war he protested against the conflict and ridiculed the generals and soldiers. Nations at war usually execute men for exercising such freedom, though nowadays we have attained a broad-mindedness which allows them to suffer nothing more than imprisonment and mob violence. In ancient Athens the state not only permitted such freedom of speech but financed the plays in which it was exercised.

This satiric indictment of individuals and institutions was the essence of the comedy of Aristophanes. In a way, it performed something of the critical functions of the best type of independent modern newspaper by exercising freely the right of criticism on any subject. But no newspaper article or cartoon can be so vivid or outspoken as Aristophanes' attack on the powerful demagogue, Cleon, in his *Knights*. Nearly any form of indictment or ridicule was open to the comic dramatist. He was handicapped scarcely at all by plot; his attack could be the keenest satire or the most ridiculous burlesque, or both; he could use violent action and comic songs; and, when he liked, he could drop his satiric attack and his buffoonery entirely and turn to lyric verse whose beauty was wholly unrelated to his attack.

In structure Greek comedy was, of course, utterly unlike modern drama. It had some elements in common with Greek tragedy—the chorus, the restrictions and advantages of the peculiar theater, the masks, the song and dance—but still its plan differed nearly as much as its tone. Though Aristophanes often varied the structure of his comedies to suit his particular purpose, the general outline was always the same. The plays began with a scene between two or three actors in which the setting and the general situation were outlined. (There were no programs, of course, and unlike the tragedies, Greek comedies were not based on familiar myths.) Then the chorus appeared, singing its entrance song. This chorus consisted of twenty-four men, and its conduct and appearance were quite different from those of the tragic chorus. It was boisterous and ridiculous, and its members were often dressed in outlandish costumes. In one play they represented men riding ostriches; in Aristophanes' *Frogs,* they were dressed to resemble frogs; and in his *Birds,* they were decked out in plumage. After the chorus had sung its entrance song, it remained in the orchestra until the end of the play.

In the third scene of the typical Greek comedy, two rival actors engaged in a contention (called the *agon*) upon some subject which was central to the play: war and peace, the government of the city, or the new type of education. At the close of this scene, in which one character was always victorious, the actors withdrew, and the chorus came forward to sing its chief song. In this song the comic poet often attacked members of the audience by name; it had little connection with the rest of the play, but was a personal appeal or attack by the dramatist. Following this song, called the *parabasis,* there were several short scenes separated by choral songs. These scenes developed further the subject which had been the basis of the argument between the two actors in the third part of the play. The final part of the comedy was the last song and the withdrawal of the chorus, generally accompanied by wild revelry.

This general plan indicates the characteristic lack of plot in Greek comedy. Aristophanes was usually concerned with attacking some individual, his ideas, and his works, or with showing the absurdities or advantages of certain policies. The looseness of the form allowed him to do this in almost any way he pleased. In *The Clouds,* in which he attacked Socrates, one scene showed the great teacher in his "Thinking Shop" with a would-be pupil. Socrates directs the pupil to lie on his couch and think out a theory, but the couch is so infested with fleas that the pupil can only toss about in misery while Socrates calls out, "Are you thinking?" In *The Frogs,* Æschylus and Euripides have a contest in hell to see which is the greater poet. They take turns spouting verses into a pair of scales. In *Lysistrata,* which was written while Athens was fighting the Peloponnesian War, Aristophanes attacks war. The women of Athens decide that the war must stop, and to enforce their decision on the men they go on what Gilbert Seldes called a "sex strike."

These scenes are broad farce, but Aristophanes could make equal use in his comedies of higher forms of art, like the magnificent poetry of the chorus in *The Birds,* the brilliant parodies of the style of Euripides' verse in *The Frogs,* or of the verse of Agathon in *Thesmophoriazusæ.* This free adaptation of various types of appeal is one of the most outstanding characteristics of Greek comedy. No modern dramatic type allows such freedom.

For the modern reader of Aristophanes, the great difficulty lies in his unfamiliarity with the contemporary events and contemporary personalities so important to the comedies. The allusions are so local and personal that footnotes are necessary for almost every verse. These references are not merely incidental, but, as we have seen, usually fundamental to the whole purpose of the play. The difficulty does not end with a multitude of footnotes, for many of the allusions are too subtle for brief explanation. Aristophanes often amused his audience by clever parodies of other poets, especially Euripides. No notes can adequately illuminate these passages; they demand a familiarity with the sound of the verse parodied; even Greek scholars do not always find their knowledge of Aristophanes' contemporaries quite adequate.

This unfamiliarity with the politics and the personalities of fourth-century Athens is usually too great a handicap for the modern reader who wants to find an adequate sample of Greek comedy in one play. It is only after some study of the times and the reading of several plays that the great comic genius of Aristophanes is revealed. Such a study is eminently worth while, but if the limits of a hasty survey make it impossible, the preëminence of Greek comedy must be accepted on the testimony of later ages.

After more than two thousand years the purifying laughter of Aristophanes can still be heard. Recently one of his plays, revised for the modern stage and the modern audience by Gilbert Seldes,[6] was a great success in the American theater. After one had seen this old play, the modern comedies of the season seemed petty and savorless, simple childish jokes or puny attacks on trivial affairs. Aristophanes seemed to have something more vital to say than our playwrights have; his attacks had an irresistible power; and better than any of his successors he knew that "laughter is man's greatest and most neglected weapon."

B. ROMAN COMEDY

Roman drama was a more or less slavish, more or less courageous adaptation of Greek tragedy and comedy to the low culture level of Latin audiences. In the case of tragedy, where numerous examples of Greek, and a relatively small number of tragedies in Latin survive, it is possible to study the exact relationships between the originals and the imitations and adaptations. In the case of comedy we are not so happily situated, since there is extant no complete Greek comedy later than those of Aristophanes.[7] It

[6] *Lysistrata,* produced first in Philadelphia and then in New York in 1930. Later it was performed in numerous other cities.

[7] In recent years, three plays of Menander, discovered in highly fragmentary condition, have added considerably to our knowledge of his art and style. For a translation of these lately discovered papyri, see *Menander; the Principal Fragments.* With a translation by F. G. Allinson. (London: Heinemann, 1921.)

is certain, however, that the extant Roman comedies of Plautus and Terence were deeply indebted to those of Menander, Philemon, and other writers of New Greek Comedy, and one of the reasons for the significance of Roman comedy is that it furnishes the material for a hypothetical reconstruction of Greek comedies which exist only in fragmentary form. On the other hand, since it was through the extant comedies of Plautus and Terence that the traditions of realistic comedy were transmitted to the Renaissance, a study of these plays and the type of theater in which they were produced is justifiable, quite aside from the crude but efficient nature of the plays themselves.

From what can be gleaned of the nature of New Greek Comedy from the rich fragmentary remains and adaptation and imitation of it by Plautus and Terence, it was a comedy which differed from the Old Greek Comedy of Aristophanes in its exclusion of fantasy and extravaganza, in its omission of personal satire and travesty, and in the minimizing of the element of literary satire. It was, in fact, something like realistic domestic comedy of contemporary Greek life. Its materials were found in events, common or uncommon, involving familiar current types,—fathers, wives, their children, their sweethearts and lovers, and such circumstantial figures as the braggart soldier, the parasite, the slave-owner, the panderess. The events were of the sort that might, with considerable assistance of coincidence and luck, conceivably have happened to one's next-door neighbors in Athens or Sparta. The models for Roman comedy, then, were fairly coherent, fairly adroit comedies of contemporary life, with considerable attention to characterization along pretty strictly typical lines.

The Theater

Like Roman comedy itself, the theater in which the plays of Plautus and Terence were performed was an adaptation of Greek or Hellenistic models. The stage had been thrust forward until the orchestra was no longer a full circle but a semicircle. In consequence, the auditorium itself had become semicircular in nature, probably to improve the sight-lines of the spectators. The stage was probably on a level with the seats in the first row of the auditorium, and the level of the orchestra had been sunk four or five feet. The stage was a long platform, deeper than that of the Greek theater, but still permitting much freer movement from side to side than from front to backstage. The back wall of the stage (the front wall of the actors' dressing-rooms) was, at least until the Roman theaters were roofed over, faced with ornamental pillars and pilasters, and studded with three doors for entrances and exits.

When the Roman theater was roofed over, either temporarily (with canvas awnings) or permanently, the back wall of the stage had to be carried up three or four stories to furnish a support for the roof, and the ornamentation of pillars and pilasters was extended to cover the necessary wall space. The stage, then, represented an elongated open space, somewhat like a street with three doors opening upon it, conceivably representing the entrances to the houses of close neighbors. The entrances at either end of the stage might be used by dramatists to suggest arrival or departure from important off-stage points like the market place or the harbor. But whatever action was represented had to be thought of as occurring, not inside a public building or a private dwelling, but in an open street or on the doorstep of one of the private dwellings, and this convention of staging frequently forced upon the dramatist varyingly ingenious explanations for the transactions of intimate business in the open street.

The production of Roman comedy in such a theater as we have described followed, it would seem, the lines established for the performance of New Greek Comedy. Since the Romans themselves classified their comedies as either *palliata* or *togata,* on the basis of whether the Greek *pallium* or the Roman *toga* was worn by the characters, it is obvious that Roman comedies in which there was some pretense that the locale and characters were Greek were garbed in what the Roman producers considered correct Greek attire. Another extremely important convention inherited from the Greek theater was the use of masks for all the characters. The New Greek Comedy had already developed an elaborate series of character-masks; there were, for instance, eleven types of masks for young men, and fourteen for young women. It is almost certain that this complicated equipment of masks was not taken over completely by the producers of Roman comedy, but it is certain that a considerable number of them was regarded as necessary for the proper presentation of Roman comedies of the *palliata* type.

The Audience

Conclusions as to the nature of Roman audiences have to be derived, in the main, from internal evidence in the plays that have come down to us. This evidence points, in general, to an audience infinitely less cultivated and subtle than that which listened to Athenian tragedy or Aristophanic comedy, or followed the subtle shadings of the comedies of Menander. In the first place, the elaborate prologues which accompany most of the comedies of Plautus, whether or not they are from his own hand, indicate that the audience could not be trusted completely to follow the main outlines of the plot without having them explained in advance. Moreover, the attempt to win the audience over to a friendly state of mind by means of crude and coarse jesting in the prologue and the willingness to interrupt the action with direct appeals from characters to the audience suggest a rather crude and insensitive audience. In the plays themselves the general coarsening of the devices and effects and the drawing out to an interminable length of a single comic situation seem to be appeals to an audience much less cultivated than that of Old or New Greek Comedy.

The Plays

Nevertheless, both for themselves and for their influence, the comedies of Plautus and Terence are worth some attention. Possibly the most significant of the characteristics of these plays is the constant and, on the whole, effective use of stock characters. From New Greek Comedy, Roman Comedy took over a fairly elaborate set of type characters, distinguished by simply emphasized traits of temperament, and differentiated, for the most inattentive theatergoer, by distinctive costumes and wigs and masks. The somewhat rough and ready adaptations of Plautus and Terence were seemingly negligent of the most subtle distinctions in Greek comic characterization, but the surviving plays furnish forth a goodly company of types that, since the Renaissance, have done duty again and again in realistic, satirical, or even sentimental comedy. Of these major types we may mention two types of fathers, respectively severe and indulgent, two types of wives (and mothers) shrewish and kindly, the amorous spendthrift hero, capable or incapable of reform in marriage, the witty resourceful servant, the lazy cowardly slave, the panderer or panderess, the parasite, the cook (native or foreign), and the boastful soldier.[8]

It is perhaps in the characterization of young heroines that the Roman borrowing from the storehouse of Greek types was most slavish. The convention that all the represented action in New Greek Comedy should take place in the street was a serious handicap in the depiction of feminine characters, since Greek *mores* discouraged the appearance on the street of young women of good character. The Greek playwright, then, had to circumvent this handicap in one of a number of ways; he frequently presented his heroine at first as a girl enslaved or in suspect circumstances, and,

[8] On the type of the boastful soldier are based the *Miles Gloriosis* of Plautus and the *Ralph Roister Doister* of Nicholas Udall. A reading of these plays illustrates vividly the impact of the Plautine tradition on English comedy in the sixteenth century. An even more accessible illustration of this influence is that of Plautus' *Menæchmi* on Shakespeare's *Comedy of Errors.*

then, by a series of revelations provided her with a good reputation and Greek parentage, and thus made possible her legal union with the hero. Even among women of bad reputation, the Greeks and their Roman adaptors made a distinction that has become time-honored in the drama, that between the mercenary evil woman and the woman whose kindliness of heart tends to redeem, for an indulgent or sentimental audience, the evil of her ways.

The plots of Roman comedy consist, in the main, of the permutations and combinations of such chess-like figures. If a certain conventionality of situation and plot is apparent, it is not surprising. The imbroglios of spendthrift sons with lively young women and stern parents; the machinations of clever servants to extricate their young masters from situations in which their passion or their stupidity has landed them; the adventures and recoveries of long-lost children; the incidental humors of rascally and stupid servants and kitchen-hire, or of the hangers-on of the wealthy: the parasite and the boastful soldier; the separation of lovers by well-meaning but narrow-minded parents—these themes recur almost monotonously in the Roman comedies of intrigue.

It is to the credit of Plautus and Terence that, despite the basic conventionality of their characters and situations, they should have been able to attain a considerable variety of effect. The most common mood of Roman comedy may truthfully be said to be harsh, insensitive, matter-of-fact and somewhat coarse-grained. But one encounters, even in Plautus, surprising incursions of sentimentality (as in the *Adelphi*) or of the paraphernalia and atmosphere of romanticism (as in his *Rudens,* The Rope).

The works of Plautus and Terence are not great or original enough to attract the attention or admiration of any but students of Roman life and literature. But, though their intrinsic values may not be great, these rather rough and ready comedies, these anachronistic transplantings of Greek life and culture, have proved tremendously important as influences and models for later comedy. Their urban domestic nature, their preoccupation with the fortunes of lovers, with the adjustments between parents and children, between wealthy men and their hangers-on, have directed the attention of writers of comedy away from the fantastic, satirical, bawdy, lyrical comedy of Aristophanes, to a type of comedy of a satirical or sentimental sort that approximates more or less closely the tone and manners of bourgeois existence.

In the Middle Ages, certain of the plays of Terence sank to the indignity of text-books. It was only with the Renaissance that there came to be any wide-spread interest in these plays as dramas to be acted and imitated. In the history of the drama of the Renaissance, no influence in the writing of comedy is perhaps so important as that revealed in the reading, presentation, and imitation of Roman comedy.[9] And even though sixteenth-century English Comedy, in the hands of Dekker, Robert Greene, and preëminently Shakespeare, was definitely romantic and not classical, the Roman tradition was manifest in the realistic satirical urban domestic comedy of Chapman and Jonson and their followers in the early seventeenth century, in French comedy of the seventeenth century and its imitations in Restoration England, and in high comedy of the eighteenth and nineteenth centuries. Characters and plots that stem from Menander and Plautus still move upon the stage of the world, and Farquhar's Archer and Aimwell and Goldsmith's Hastings and Young Marlow would not find themselves alien to the atmosphere of either New Greek or Roman Comedy.

C. MEDIEVAL COMEDY

We noted in our study of tragedy that the drama of the Greeks and Romans was completely stamped out by the barbarians and the early Christian Church, and that when drama appeared again —the drama from which ours has grown—it began as a part of the service of the Church and developed into those great cycles of plays which, in fourteenth- and fifteenth-century England, were presented by the gilds at Whitsuntide or on Corpus Christi Day. Though these plays were based on the biblical narrative (not noted for its humor) and presented on religious occasions, many of them contain episodes deliberately made humorous. A few of them are really well-developed short comedies.

This comic element is often a surprise if not a shock to the modern reader. The religion associated with Greek comedy is an unfamiliar one in which drunken revelry might well have a part; Latin comedy had no religious significance; but medieval comedy is associated with a religion which does not make much of revelry, a religion with which we are more or less familiar, but which we have never seen propagated by means of comic scenes. The explanation of this apparent irreverence does not lie in the peculiar presentation of the plays, or in the organization of life in the Middle Ages;[10] it lies primarily in the psychology of the medieval man, dramatist and spectator alike, and secondly in the concern of the early playwrights to bring the biblical events close home to the audience by expanding the stories to demonstrate that ancient

[9] Inquisitive students will find the details of this revival traced in Malcolm W. Wallace, *The Birthe of Hercules* (Chicago: Scott, Foresman and Company, 1903).

[10] See Chapter II, Section B.

Hebrews and Egyptians and Romans were not very different from fourteenth-century Englishmen.

Five hundred years ago religion and the Church were much more familiar everyday affairs to our ancestors in York and Chester than they are to us. We have seen how powerful and all-embracing the Church of the Middle Ages was. We could scarcely expect the medieval Christian to maintain a consistent attitude of reverent veneration toward an organization which was so familiar, so much a part of his daily life. A man may sustain a hushed reverence for an hour or two a week perhaps, but it cannot be done hour after hour and day after day—at least not if the man has a sense of humor—and medieval Englishmen certainly had. Furthermore, the Church, which usually had a pretty accurate idea of the capacity of its communicants, did not expect solemn, unwavering reverence. There might be a few who could maintain such an attitude, but the medieval church was a universal church, and the average communicant was the average citizen. Many examples of this broad tolerance have come down to us.

The hundreds of medieval cathedrals and parish churches which are still standing in England are full of them. These buildings are adorned with all the beautiful and endless detail which is one of the characteristics of Gothic architecture—carvings on capitals and screens and choir stalls, stained glass in the great windows, wrought iron in chapel gates. Most of this decoration, as we should expect, is sacred in character, depicting saints and angels, biblical scenes and martyrdoms. But not all of it. The thousands of medieval English workmen who spent so many years patiently creating the great beauty of the Gothic cathedrals *could* work with the utmost reverence, as when they produced the great windows of York Minster or the figures in the angel choir at Lincoln, but they could also forget their reverence and carve or paint with an hilarious abandon. On the end of a pew in one village church there is carved a cat playing a fiddle, while nearby a cow jumps over the moon. This certainly was not calculated to inspire reverence in any villager who gazed at it while mass was being said. In the cathedral at Ely is a wood-carving of Herodias before Herod, but Herodias is not dancing; she is turning a somersault. Within a few feet of the famous shrine in the cathedral at St. Albans is a carving of a milkmaid milking her cow. At Boston, in Lincolnshire, is a woodcarving of a fox dressed up in the vestments of a bishop, standing with his crozier in a pulpit and preaching to an audience of five hens and a cock. In a fourteenth-century stained glass window at Selby Abbey, two monkeys stand beside a table ready to cut up the body of a third monkey which lies on the table between them.

A carving at Worcester depicts an altar upon which a sheep's head lies, and beside it stands a fox, in vestments, saying grace.

All these little pleasantries of the medieval workman were tolerated by the Church. The churchmen watched them at their work and paid them when they had finished, as hundreds of accounts show. It is this same attitude of easy familiarity, this feeling that the commonest scenes of everyday life and even caricatures of churchmen and holy offices are not out of place in sacred surroundings, that we find in the comic scenes of the mystery plays. Side by side in medieval life we find the sacred and the profane, and we cannot escape the conclusion that these violent contrasts, sometimes shocking to us, gave a keen delight to the medieval Christian.

In the plays, the comic scenes which stand out so sharply from their pious background are often intended to do more than simply create merriment. Many of them obviously strive to make the Bible stories more vivid, more convincing, by adding details familiar to the unlettered audience. Such details may be touching in their naïve sincerity, as in the Wakefield *Second Shepherds' Play,* where the shepherds offer the new-born Christ child gifts of a bunch of cherries, a bird, and a tennis ball; but they are more likely to be amusing, as in the play of *The Deluge* at Chester, where the sons of Noah drag their mother, kicking and struggling, into the ark; or where one of the devils in hell proposes marriage to an unusually dishonest ale-woman who has just been damned, in the Chester *Harrowing of Hell.*

In common with all plays, the drama of the Middle Ages reflects the times in which it was written, the tastes and interests of the audience for which it was produced. Though this medieval audience was in many ways inferior to that for which Aristophanes and Shakespeare wrote, yet in many of the plays we can see the unknown dramatist groping for comic effects which Shakespeare was to achieve with masterly sureness.

D. ELIZABETHAN COMEDY

Elizabethan comedy, which was, of course, a product of the same times and written for the same theater and the same audience as Elizabethan tragedy,[11] was divided into two general types—romantic comedy and realistic comedy.

The realistic type presented a picture of everyday life in Elizabethan London, with particular emphasis, as in all realistic comedy, on the follies and fads, the foibles and vices of the day. It was a comedy of tricks and frauds, in which some one was always being

[11] See Chapter II, Section C.

relieved of his money or his wife. Comedies of this type are common enough on our own stage and they are as old as Menander. The problem lies not in comprehending the type or its aim but in understanding the background of everyday life well enough to appreciate the constant allusion and satire. The best beginning for a study of Elizabethan realistic comedies, like those of Jonson, Middleton, Chapman, and Brome, is a close examination of everyday life in the taverns, inns, and shops of seventeenth century London. Such an examination is out of place in a hasty survey of dramatic epochs; it belongs to a much fuller study of Elizabethan drama than this one.

It must be the romantic comedies of Elizabeth's time, then, to which we turn our attention, the type of comedy generally written by Shakespeare and Greene and Heywood. Romantic comedies are sometimes difficult for modern readers to understand because we have nothing quite like them in our theaters. The old-fashioned musical comedies are as near them as anything we have, but musical comedies are generally so badly, so almost illiterately written that the comparison is none too helpful. The most illuminating beginning for a study of romantic comedies is a glance at the sources from which they were usually taken.

The rapidly growing reading public of Elizabethan times had developed a taste for prose romances, tales of love and adventure in sylvan glades and Arcadian pastures. These stories were frankly unreal, set in fanciful realms and built upon highly improbable plots; they formed what we should call a literature of escape. In them a shipwrecked prince disguises himself and courts a pretty shepherdess who is really an exiled princess; or a king's daughter, abandoned in babyhood, is raised in the hut of a shepherd, where a wandering nobleman sees her and returns in disguise to woo her. Disguise is always an important element in the prose romances, and reunited kindred and hopeless affairs happily concluded are popular features. These stories, sometimes translated from the French or Italian, sometimes written by Englishmen, but generally with their roots in the long tradition of the classical and the medieval romance, formed a large part of the stock of the booksellers in the earliest days of the Elizabethan drama. Their popularity was well established.

During the height of this popularity, the number of London theaters and the demand for plays were increasing. The playwrights cast about for suitable subjects. (Elizabethan plays, like most great plays, nearly always took their plots from stories or histories or poems already current; they were seldom what we should call "strictly original.") What more promising material for a popular play than a prose romance which had already proved its power of catching the public! So the prose romance became a standard source for Elizabethan comedies.

These dramatized versions of popular literature, though retaining the essential romantic characteristics of the prose romances, were freely adapted by the playwrights. Often two or even three romances were worked into one play; new episodes were written or old ones cut out, as it suited the purpose of the dramatist; and original features, not suitable to fiction but highly effective on the stage, were added. Songs and instrumental music were made a regular part of these comedies. The romantic situation could be adroitly built up by off-stage music, or by serenades, hunting songs, or love songs on the stage. Elizabethan music, as we have noted, had reached a very high stage of development; the musicians of the theater were at hand to provide accompaniments or off-stage music, and singers were very common among Elizabethan actors, many of whom had had thorough training as choir boys. More than one romantic comedy owed part of its drawing power to the fine voice of the boy soprano who played the heroine.

From their sources in prose fiction, the romantic comedies retained a great deal of narrative interest, the story interest which, as we have seen,[12] was always demanded by an Elizabethan audience. The people were not particularly concerned with the credibility of these stories; they were willing to accept a great many impossible situations in the theater for the sake of entertainment. Therefore, the plots of many romantic comedies, like those of the prose romances, are highly improbable, to say the least. The more naïve of modern readers sometimes disdain this improbability in romantic comedies like *Twelfth Night.* They say, "But I don't believe that Viola and Sebastian would have been wearing identical clothes after their shipwreck and separate wanderings." Of course they wouldn't, but what has this to do with the essential charm of the play? Neither Elizabethan nor modern audiences have gone to romantic comedies to see a study of the superficial characteristics of dress and conduct. They have been perfectly willing to accept numerous improbabilities of plot if the characters were interesting and their adventures entertaining.

In fact, a large element of the charm of romantic comedy lies in its improbability and unreality—in disguised heroes and heroines and eternal love at first sight. The greatest of the writers of romantic comedy, Shakespeare, saw this so clearly that he set his comedies in some far-off place which, deliberately, he made as unreal as possible

[12] See Chapter II, Section 2.

—Illyria or ancient Athens or the forest of Arden. The strangeness of the background blends with the improbability of the events; only the people are real.

For in the best romantic comedies, the people are completely real. Greene's Margaret and Shakespeare's Rosalind and Viola and Sir Toby Belch are memorable characters. The unreality of their adventures makes them no less living personalities; on thousands of people, Shakespeare's captivating heroines, moving against the unreal background of Illyria or the forest of Arden, have exercised a charm which has made his romantic comedies successful on the stage of every country in the civilized world.

E. THE COMEDY OF MOLIÈRE

The comedies of Molière,[13] which many critics have thought the world's finest achievement in the field of comedy, are almost the complete antithesis of Shakespeare's comedies. Shakespeare was a romanticist, who set his comedies in distant, often fabulous places, who individualized his characters as completely as circumstances would allow. Molière was a classicist whose plays are usually set in contemporary Paris, and whose characters are types, generalized so that they represent a class and do not stand apart. To a certain extent this contrast is due, no doubt, to differences between the man Shakespeare and the man Molière, but more important than these personal dissimilarities are the differences between the national

[13] Since this section is devoted entirely to the plays of one man, the main facts of his life ought to be kept in mind. Molière, whose real name was Jean-Baptiste Poquelin, was born in Paris in 1622. His father was a prosperous upholsterer, and he had a good education. In 1643 he became an actor (not a very respected profession then), took the stage name of Molière, and helped to found a group of ten actors and actresses who called themselves *L'Illustre Théâtre*. For a time this troupe acted in Paris but they could not compete successfully with the older organizations, and after a few years they became a touring provincial company. For more than a decade they acted in the provinces with great success, and in these years Molière developed into a brilliant comic actor. He assumed responsibility as the manager and director of the company and he wrote several plays for them.

In 1658 the troupe returned to Paris, won the praise of Louis XIV, and were granted the privilege of establishing themselves in the royal theater in the Petit-Bourbon. For fifteen years Molière directed the affairs of this company in Paris, wrote his great plays for them, and attained recognition as the finest comic actor of his time. He was seized with a convulsion while acting Argan in his own play, *Le Malade Imaginaire,* and died the same night, February 17, 1673.

Molière wrote, in all, thirty plays: farces, burlesques, tragicomedies, comedy-ballets, pastorals, and comedies; but he is best known for his great comedies, *Le Misanthrope, Les Femmes Savantes, Tartuffe, L'École des Maris, L'École des Femmes, Les Precieuses Ridicules,* and *L'Avare*. It is these plays upon which this discussion of Molière as a great writer of comedy is based.

See Chapter II, Section D for an account of the theater and audience of Molière's time.

dramatic traditions in which the two great dramatists were working.

The Elizabethan stage was, in general, romantic; the French seventeenth-century stage was classic. These terms are indicative of fundamental differences between the interests of the two national groups in the theater. The English interest in individuality, adventure, and sentiment, as we see it in Shakespeare's comedies, is familiar to us; it is part of our own tradition and we take it for granted that such things are "interesting," as we say. The French tradition is not ours, and we find it necessary to make an effort to understand why the French audience is *not* interested in personal idiosyncrasy and in romantic adventure, and why it *is* interested in character types displayed with comparatively little action, as in the comedies of Molière.

Our first task then, in trying to appreciate the comedies of Molière, is to understand certain standards which Molière and the seventeenth-century Parisian audience held to be proper for comedy.

In the first place, the French thought of comedy more as a socializing force than the English did. Elizabethan comedy often dealt sympathetically with the opposition of an individual to recognized social authority. In *As You Like It* Shakespeare draws the sympathy of the audience toward the defiant Rosalind and Celia and makes the audience unsympathetic toward Duke Frederick, though the Duke is the father of one girl, the uncle of the other, and the political sovereign of both. Society in general says that the authority of parents and guardians and political rulers is a safeguard for social institutions and should be respected. Shakespeare would be one of the last to deny this; yet he writes a play in which recognized social authority is made tyrannical and ridiculous and the rebelling individual is given the complete sympathy of the audience. This tendency to sympathize with the individual and to defy social authority is typical of English and American comedy, whether in the sixteenth century or the twentieth. It does not mean that the English stage has made a persistent campaign of nearly four hundred years to tear down authority, or that the English think society is generally wrong. It does mean, and this is the important point, that the English audience has always been more interested in the individual than in the social group; in the theater this audience does not think much about society but simply watches the struggles and triumphs of a certain individual. The social implications of this justification of the rebelling individual and the condemnation of social authority and social conventions are seldom considered.

Just the opposite is true of the French audience. In the theater, as elsewhere, the French are more logical and more social minded than most other peoples, much more so than the English and Americans. And Molière is the most typical as he is the greatest of the French dramatists. In his plays he is interested in the truth *in general* about society in its relationships with the individual, not in the truth of a particular situation which may differ from the normal. While English comedy usually justifies the individual in his revolt against social conventions and social authority, Molière justifies society and ridicules the non-conforming individual. In *Le Misanthrope,* Alceste is made ridiculous because he attacks the petty dishonesty of ordinary social intercourse and thinks he can reform society; according to Molière society is right and Alceste is wrong. An English dramatist would have been much more likely to make of Alceste a glorious uncompromising hero who fearlessly attacks vicious social dishonesty. In fact, the English audience is so likely to take this attitude for granted, that they sometimes insist that Alceste is a tragic figure and fail to see that Molière clearly thinks him ridiculous.

The same conception of society as more important than the individual is found in Molière's other comedies. In *Les Précieuses Ridicules* he makes fun of a group which is trying to reform language and manners; in *Le Bourgeois Gentilhomme* he ridicules the attempts of a wealthy middle-class merchant to rise out of the social class into which he has been born. In his *L'École des Femmes* his butt is a man who thinks he can improve on the ordinary conduct of wives by defying social customs and developing a method of his own for educating his intended wife.

It follows logically from this conception of society as being more important than the individual that in his characterizations Molière is more interested in the traits of a character which make him *like* others of his type than in traits which make him *different*. In other words, Molière's characters are social types, not highly individualized creations.[14] Tartuffe is the hypocrite who uses religion for personal advancement; Armande is the prude who pretends to exclusively intellectual interests and makes a great parade of false

[14] See Chapter XIII, pp. 202–205 for a discussion of type characters and individual characters. In Molière's comedies, the pains which the dramatist takes to keep his characters typical and to avoid individuality are very evident. In all his plays only two leading characters have real names of their own. All the others are simply Alceste, Sganarelle, Henriette, Armande, names which had been used over and over again and which did not distinguish their bearers from dozens of other characters. Most of them have no surnames at all. Furthermore, Molière carefully refrains from giving any information about the character which is not strictly relevant to the particular situation. The audience is never given individualizing details such as Shakespeare gives: Hamlet's age, his schooling, his miscellaneous accomplishments; or as Ibsen gives scores of details about the past of Hedda Gabler and Mrs. Alving.

delicacy; Alceste is the humorless individual who is so anxious to exhibit his over-scrupulous personal honesty that he becomes a disruptive force in society.

Each of these character types is a menace, or at least a distraction to a well-ordered society, and this social implication of the action always interests Molière. To make it most evident, he must keep before his audience the representative traits, not the individual traits, of Tartuffe and Armande and Alceste; for every situation he must find the speech which most perfectly epitomizes the reaction of that type of character to that type of situation. It is his unsurpassed skill in selecting and in expressing these reactions that makes Molière one of the masters of characterization. Yet modern readers sometimes fail to see this mastery because they expect characterization of Shakespeare's individual type, and do not understand the fundamental differences between the aims of Shakespeare and of Molière.

These interests of Molière in the social significance of his action and in the representative function of his characters are part of his creed as a classic dramatist. Not that he made a studied attempt to follow the critical pronouncements of Castelvetro and Boileau for he was not a theorist but an eminently practical man of the theater. His practice follows the rules because his genius was essentially classic, and to Molière the classic standards are the reasonable requirements of stage effectiveness.[15]

Other classic standards which were accepted by this dramatist and his audience as requirements for the best comedy are to be seen in Molière's characteristically French admiration for the middle course, the reasonable conduct, the sensible avoidance of extremes and exaggerations. Molière's best comedies have less violent passion, fewer flights of unrestrained imagination, less buffoonery than Elizabethan comedies. In *As You Like It* Shakespeare and his audience admired the reckless independence, the vigorous imagination, the sudden infatuation, and the happy-go-lucky adventuring of Rosalind; in *Les Femmes Savantes* Molière and his Parisians admired the unaffected naturalness, the straightforward honesty, the practical common sense, and the easy charm of Henriette. This same reasonable common sense is a cardinal virtue in heroes as well as heroines. Even the style in which the dramatist sets forth his play is imbued with this careful avoidance of extremes. His vocabulary must be limited to words which are universally expressive; he must avoid slang and colloquialism on the one hand and highly imaginative or original phrases on the other. In his diction the classicist

[15] See Chapter VI for a fuller discussion of classicism.

is striving for accuracy, not for color or for a transcript of actual conversation.[16]

Finally the classic comedies of Molière are urban comedies. Not only are they usually set in Paris, but the interests are urban interests—intelligence and sophistication are more important virtues than honesty and good nature; naïveté is more likely to be made ridiculous than charming. Problems of life and death seldom arise; the elemental emotions are seen only in their more rarefied forms. Urbanity and intelligence are the ideals of Molière's characters, and their actions are set forth for the intelligent observation and for the amusement of the audience; little attempt is made to stir the emotions.

Molière's best comedies are thus primarily intellectual in their appeal. Their narrative and their emotional interest are slight. They make little use of overt action, but by the adroit revelation of character, the nicely planned clash of individuals of opposed ideas and motives, and by the skilful exposure of fundamental human weaknesses and absurdities, Molière hopes to provoke that "thoughtful laughter" which is the ideal response to high comedy.

F. RESTORATION COMEDY

In the comedy of the Restoration, the effect of the very limited audience for which it was written is much more evident than in the tragedy. Not only was its scene London and even the very streets and houses frequented by the wits of the audience, but its plots were based on tricks and intrigues in which these wits might well have been and sometimes actually were involved. The characters on the stage had their counterparts in the pit and the galleries; in fact, more than one comedy of the time was so explicit in its delineation that the original of a character was recognized by his friends and enemies in the audience, and on a few occasions the actor or the dramatist was beaten or even stabbed for his impudence.

All this means that an appreciation of the clever comedies of the Restoration demands a little more attention to the background of the times than was required by the tragedies. The ideals of the

[16] Though the English translations are usually in prose, Molière himself wrote most of his great comedies in rhymed verse. Apparently Molière's practice was to write his plays first in prose, and then, if it was not necessary for his company to act the play immediately, he turned the prose into verse. In one or two of his plays he had time to start writing the verse, but not time enough to finish it; so, in his *Princesse d'Élide,* the first act and part of the second are in verse, but the last three acts are still in prose. This is sufficient indication that Molière thought of his verse as a sort of polish for his lines—desirable, but not necessary. Here again Molière differs radically from Shakespeare whose verse is the very essence of his expression.

narrow court circle and especially its manners were reflected with little exaggeration in the comedies of the time.

We have seen in our study of Restoration tragedy something of the elegance of the courtly audience upon which the theater depended. Dress and manners, wit and compliment, were the constant study and the essential attributes of the gallant; they occupied almost the whole of his time, and it is little wonder that his elegant manner became his hall-mark. Such manners were, of course, highly artificial, as they are in any time. No courtier could consider frankness or simplicity or naturalness as anything but vulgar; these traits he assigned to the country folk, the lower classes, and the simple-minded. His own studied and elegant manner was constantly displayed in his conversation, his dress, his walk, his bow, his insistence on the superficial, and his neglect or disdain of what are often called the fundamental virtues.

It is not surprising that the finest dramatic achievement of such a time should be the comedy of manners, an aristocratic type of play in which the brilliance of wit, the elegance of manner, and the sophistication of the leading characters reflect most effectively the ideals of the Restoration audience. Such a type of comedy is, of course, narrow in its appeal; it is not written for the middle classes; to the naïve it appears stiff and unnatural; to the sentimental it is wicked and repulsive. A true comedy of manners could never be made to appeal to the average movie audience.

A further obstacle to the modern production of such comedy is the difficulty of finding actors sufficiently well-trained to take the parts. In general, the simpler a character is, the more easily he can be impersonated by an actor; the more intelligent and complicated the character becomes and the more he conceals his thoughts by polite conversation and a conscious manner, the more difficult the delineation. Comedies of manners are full of the latter type of character. The actors selected to take the leading rôles in a Restoration comedy like *The Way of the World* or *Love for Love* must be able to make the audience understand their true feelings when most of their words and most of their acts express precisely the opposite; they must be able to convince the audience that they are ladies and gentlemen of birth and breeding, wise in the ways of the world; they must be able to appear at ease in gorgeous costumes which demand a practised grace and rhythm of movement unknown in a modern drawing-room; they must be able to express highly improper sentiments in such a way as to make them sound discreet and charming; and, perhaps most difficult of all, they must be able to speak lines of flashing wit and perfect literary finish with such subtlety that the full beauty of the prose is revealed, although the audience seems to hear only the natural expression of a cultivated individual. This subtle and difficult art requires long training. Many a half-wit has been taught to say, "Sez you?" but only the most finished actress can get the full value of Millamant's famous "O ay, Letters—I had Letters—I am persecuted with Letters—I hate Letters—No Body knows how to write Letters; and yet one has 'em, one does not know why —They serve one to pin up one's Hair."

Something of the producer's difficulty in finding an actress finished enough to play Millamant in *The Way of the World* or an actor equal to Valentine in *Love for Love,* faces the reader who must stage these plays in his imagination. The elaborate manners and studied wit are confusing. In the background of our minds, of course, are the manners of our own times—the catch-as-catch-can, no-holds-barred type—by which we judge these people, and find their words and actions approaching the absurd. The best antidote for this confusion, and a great help in reading any type of play, is a constant reference to the costume of the time. Manners always depend on dress. Conduct that is ridiculous in a sweater and slacks appears more fitting in evening clothes, and may be quite appropriate in a gorgeous brocaded coat, with gold buttons, velvet knee-breeches, silk stockings, and high-heeled shoes with silver buckles. If we remember the elaborate splendor of a Restoration gallant's clothes, his affectations are easier to understand; and we certainly miss the full charm of a heroine like Angelica, in *Love for Love,* unless we imagine her in a gay satin dress, its voluminous skirt looped up to show the ruffled taffeta petticoat which covered her silken ankles, lace falling from her arms, and her bosom bare.

In the Restoration comedy of manners, the dramatists were not concerned, as Molière was, with fundamental human weaknesses or with social maladjustments; they wanted to make a gay and intelligent audience laugh at the vanities and affectations of its acquaintances. Certain character types were favorites, of course, and they appear again and again in the comedies. Their counterparts could be found in any audience of the time; their foibles and their difficulties were very familiar in the best society of the reign of Charles II. But since they are less familiar to the twentieth century, we sometimes puzzle over the characteristics which the Restoration audience took for granted.

Generally in these comedies the hero is the gay young rake, like Valentine in *Love for Love* or Dorimant in *The Man of Mode* or Mirabell in *The Way of the World.* He is a young man of good family who moves in the most exclusive circles. His attitude toward life is that of Bellmour in Congreve's comedy, *The Old Bachelor* who says, "Come, come, leave business to idlers, and wisdom to fools: they have need of 'em: wit be my faculty, and pleasure my occupation, and let father Time shake his glass."

Like all gentlemen of the time, this young rake lives on his income, or more usually, beyond his income, for he is almost always in serious financial difficulties, hounded by his creditors and desperate for money. Frequently he is also pestered by ex-mistresses of whom he cannot rid himself. The immorality of the Restoration is too notorious to require much discussion. It was taken for granted that all men of the court circle, from the King down, kept mistresses, and one of their chief concerns was to acquire new ones and get rid of the old. Mistresses and lovers, seductions and illicit love affairs were constant topics of conversation with both ladies and gentlemen in real life and on the stage. To our grandparents, and to some modern readers, this lamentable state of affairs was the most important fact about the Restoration; the scandals were bad enough, but the plays which actually referred to them in intelligible words were declared unfit for the eyes of decent people.

Usually the attempts of this young gallant to get the money he needs so desperately to carry on the extravagant life of a courtier, form a part of the plot. He tries to raise money by tricking or persuading some wealthy relative or by marrying a rich woman. He would no more have tried to *earn* the money than a modern business man would hold up his bank cashier at the point of a gun to raise capital; his code would not allow it.

With this attempt to secure money a love affair is usually involved, but it is utterly different from the love affairs of Elizabethan romantic comedies or of modern sentimental plays; the young people are too sophisticated for romance. They have no illusions about eternal love; moreover, good manners demanded that they conceal their emotions. In these urbane plays, a passionate declaration of love is likely to be thought either the outburst of an innocent from the country or the calculating approach of a young rake. And the girl in her replies is as unemotional as the man in his proposals. Millamant comes near to the Restoration ideal when she hears her lover's proposal in *The Way of the World*. She does not confess her love in beautiful poetry like the Elizabethan heroine, or blush and sigh like the Victorian miss, or even leap into her lover's arms like the modern young lady. She calmly enumerates a whole series of privileges which she must have as a wife, and finishes, "And lastly where-ever I am, you shall always knock at the Door before you come in. These Articles subscrib'd, if I continue to endure you a little longer, I may by degrees dwindle into a wife."

This heroine of the comedy of manners, as Millamant's speech indicates, is no innocent child. She is a woman of the world, not likely to be swept off her feet by any emotion, and well aware of the value of money. She is quite able to take care of herself, cool, witty, and free in her speech. She is sometimes shocked by the unmannerly but never by the immoral. She discusses the affairs of her acquaintances almost as frankly as the hero does; she is much more impressed by the humor of life than by its seriousness. A gay, reckless demeanor, clever tongue, cool head, perfect poise, and charm of manner are likely to be her most outstanding traits.

Often the hero or heroine has a clever servant, unscrupulous and quite the equal of master or mistress in intrigue; he is entirely capable of poking fun at callers, fooling creditors, and making witty speeches at the expense of any one. The liberties he takes are somewhat surprising, but the age was a tolerant one; even the King did not exact undue respect; some of his courtiers called him nicknames to his face, and his love affairs were common talk.

These characters and their intrigues are, on the whole, sympathetically treated, but with them in the plays appear others freely satirized. One is the woman, past the prime of life, who thinks she is still a gay young thing and is eager for a husband. Her illusions about herself, her suspicions of all women, and her scandalous over-eagerness were stock jokes of the time, frequently put into the comedies in characters like Lady Wishfort.

Perhaps the most commonly satirized character is the man who has position and wealth but not brains, and who is constantly making a fool of himself by carrying the vanities and fads of the time to excess. Such people are always with us but the playwrights of the Restoration found them especially ridiculous, with their extravagant affectation of the latest vanities in styles, their self-conscious display of a strained wit, their malicious gossip, and their frantic attempts to appear notorious lady-killers. The dramatists repeatedly pointed out the follies of the time (a perennial function of comedy) by means of these characters who pose and simper in play after play: Tattle in *Love for Love,* Sir Fopling Flutter in *The Man of Mode,* Lord Foppington in *The Relapse.*

All these characters, even the most foolish, speak with a wit that was characteristic of the time. Indeed, clever sophisticated dialogue was the real interest of the best of the Restoration dramatists. They consistently neglected the development of their characters and their plots in order to concentrate on the graceful turn of a phrase or the witty expression of a sarcastic speech. For this reason the same character types appear again and again in these comedies, and often the plots are obscure or inadequate. The playwrights cared little what the characters did so long as they spoke amusingly. In some of the best comedies of the time the audience is not quite sure what is happening, though it cannot miss the perfection of the lines. This polished wit sparkles through most of the Restoration comedies, especially those of Congreve.

Such consistently brilliant conversation is produced only for an audience capable of appreciating wit, and itself anxious to cultivate repartee. Some of the reported conversation of the Restoration courtiers almost equals that displayed on the stage. Sir Charles Sedley, one of the King's favorites, did, in fact, compete with the plays. Seated in the pit during a dull play, he is reported to have started talking himself, and to have so outshone the dramatist by his extemporaneous wit that those about him ignored the play and fastened upon the words of Sir Charles. Such stories help to account for the brilliant dialogue so characteristic of Restoration comedies. The best of it, in Congreve's masterpieces, has never been surpassed on the English-speaking stage.

G. EIGHTEENTH-CENTURY COMEDY

The eighteenth century is not one of the notable periods of fine comedy. Taken as a whole, the plays of this time are greatly inferior to Elizabethan, Restoration, and modern comedies. Furthermore, the best of the eighteenth-century plays, those of Sheridan and Goldsmith, are not characteristic; they are not the most perfect expression of the typical ideas and interests in eighteenth-century comedy, as Shakespeare's plays are the most perfect expression of the ideas and interests of Elizabethan romantic comedy, and Congreve's of the popular Restoration comedy of manners. The best eighteenth-century plays were written by men in open rebellion against the drama of their time, by men who felt that contemporary comedies were trash and who tried to bring back to the stage plays of a type popular almost a century before. Thus *The School for Scandal* and *The Rivals* and *She Stoops to Conquer* are not truly representative of the eighteenth century. In interest and in method they are more like the plays of Congreve and Wycherley and Etherege than they are like the comedies of the contemporaries of Sheridan and Goldsmith.

In choosing one or two comedies of the eighteenth century for study, then, one must select either good plays which still have an appeal on the modern stage, but which give a false impression of the time, or inferior comedies which are, however, typical of the popular theatrical fare of the eighteenth century. For several reasons it seems more profitable to study the inferior plays.

In the first place, a rapid survey of the drama which considers both Sheridan and Congreve involves a certain duplication, for Sheridan was deliberately imitating the comedy of manners of his great predecessor of the Restoration. Since we are interested here in noting different types of comic interest as well as different periods of comic development, it is better to study the inferior comedy of the eighteenth century and thus become familiar with a new type, sentimental comedy, than to study Sheridan's comedy of manners as well as Congreve's. In the second place, we are interested, in part, in the relationship of plays to the theater and audience for which they were written. This relationship is much more apparent in men like Cumberland and Kelly who were fairly typical products of their time than in Sheridan and Goldsmith who were attempting to rebuke and to reform the popular theater. Finally, there is great value in every survey in occasional study of poor plays; it offers a means of comparison. The adroitness of Ibsen's exposition is much easier to see after reading a clumsy attempt like Cumberland's in *The West Indian;* Shakespeare's subtle characterization is more fully appreciated after studying Hugh Kelly's *False Delicacy.*

For these reasons, therefore, we shall consider typical eighteenth-century comedies, even though they are inferior plays, rather than the superior plays which Goldsmith and Sheridan wrote in a vain attempt to raise the dramatic taste of the audience of their time.

The Audience

The most fundamental reason for the striking difference between the popular comedies of the Restoration and the popular comedies of the reign of George III is to be found in the great change which had taken place in the typical audience. The average audience of 1770 was much larger than that of 1670, and it differed sharply in character. As we have seen, the Restoration theater was dominated by the court circle and its taste; the eighteenth-century theater was not. By 1760 audiences were dominated by the middle classes as completely as the Restoration audiences had been by the aristocracy. The upper classes did not consistently avoid the theater in the days of David Garrick and of Mrs. Siddons, but they were greatly outnumbered by the crowds of merchants and tradesmen and their families, and it was to the taste of this middle class audience that the play must appeal if it was to be successful.

This middle class audience demanded not only that its plays be exceedingly proper in words and actions, but that the plays themselves should be moral tracts which displayed the rewards of virtue and the invariable punishment of evil. An amusing illustration of this demand is found in the indignant reproof of a dramatist who had failed to comply with it: "The hero of this play is a man who first deserts his country, and then seduces the object of his love; and the heroine is a woman who has not merely violated the purity of her sex, but has done it in defiance of a solemn vow. Yet, in contempt of every principle of morality, these characters are made happy, and that without their having shown the most trifling marks of contrition!"[17]

But it is not simply in plotting and in characterization that moral standards must be upheld. The playwrights of the late eighteenth century regularly pander to this taste for comedies which are illustrated sermons for the moral edification of the audience by larding their plays with moral sentiments. The pure and good characters repeatedly deliver themselves of smug speeches which are really copybook maxims set forth for the gratification of the audience. Frequently these pronouncements were applauded by the audience for their moral rectitude and not for any particular bearing which they had on the play. Thus in George Cumberland's comedy *The West Indian,* Belcour apologizes to Miss Dudley for having believed the false story that she was really the mistress and not the sister of Charles Dudley. Contritely he asks, "What reparation can I make to you and to virtue?" Miss Dudley replies with the gentle forgiveness and the moral admonition which the eighteenth-century audience so greatly admired: "To me there's nothing due, nor anything demanded of you but your more favourable opinion for the future, if you should chance to think of me: Upon the part of virtue I'm not empower'd to speak, but if hereafter, as you range thro' life you shou'd surprize her in the person of some wretched female, poor as myself and not so well protected, enforce not your advantage, compleat not your licentious triumph, but raise her, rescue her from shame and sorrow, and reconcile her to herself again."[18]

This speech illustrates another phase of the taste of the eighteenth-century audience—a strong preference for sentimentality. Sentimentalism can be found in the plays of many periods, but the late eighteenth-century audience was so fond of it that sentimental comedy came to be one of the most popular dramatic forms.[19] These comedies constantly sing the praises of the kind-hearted and the simple-minded. They are travesties of real life, because the evil characters are invariably defeated in spite of their shrewdness, and the good characters win out because of their compassionate love for their fellow men. Beauty and virtue in distress are repeatedly exhibited in order that the audience may indulge itself in the luxury of tears; pity and charity are regularly exalted as the chief virtues;

[17] Quoted in Nicoll's *A History of the Late Eighteenth Century Drama, 1750–1800* (Cambridge: The University Press, 1927) from *Biographia Dramatica,* III, 216.

[18] Act V, Scene 5.

[19] See Chapter IX for an extended discussion of the characteristics of sentimentalism and of sentimentality in the drama.

and repentance and forgiveness are displayed again and again as life's most edifying spectacles. Often characters in these sentimental comedies are quite explicit in stating their sentimental principles, as when Captain Dudley, in *The West Indian,* defends an admired author from a charge of looseness: "I hold him to be a moralist in the noblest sense; he plays indeed with the fancy, and sometimes perhaps too wantonly; but while he thus designedly masks his main attack, he comes at once upon the heart; refines, amends it, softens it; beats down each selfish barrier from about it, and opens every sluice of pity and benevolence." [20]

This demand of the large middle class audience for the triumph of virtue, the enunciation of moral sentiments, and the display of touching distress, virtuous poverty, tearful repentance, and sweet forgiveness, sets its mark on most of the plays of the eighteenth century and particularly on the sentimental comedies.

The Theater

The effect of the taste and character of the eighteenth-century audience on the plays of the time was modified, of course, by the conditions in the theaters in which these plays were presented.

The most notable characteristic of these playhouses, as distinguished from the Restoration theaters and the Elizabethan theaters, was their size. As the audience grew larger, the theater buildings were enlarged, until, by the last decade of the century, Drury Lane was estimated to hold an audience of 3,611, and its chief rival, Covent Garden, was nearly as large. These two, the most important, though by no means the only theaters of the time, were not only larger than any of the earlier London theaters, but much larger than the average modern theater.[21] When one recalls the difficulty of seeing and hearing from the top balcony of one of the larger theaters to-day, he is appalled to think of the strain the eighteenth-century audience must have experienced in trying to see a stage lighted not by carefully focused electric lights but by candles, and in trying to hear the voices of the distant actors above the minor disturbances in an audience much less well-behaved than the modern one.

The difficulty which the actors had in making themselves seen and heard in a large, ill-lit theater with bad acoustics is one of the important influences on the plays of the time. George Colman, the younger, one of the popular playwrights, points out the situation in a song which he wrote for his *New Hay at the Old Market,* performed in 1795.

[20] Act II, Scene 2.
[21] The average New York theater holds about 1,000.

Or if, tardily, the sound
Travels all the house around,
'Twixt the action and words there's a breach·
And it seems as if Macbeth,
Half a minute after death,
On his back, made his last dying speech,
Let your Shakespeares and Jonsons go hang, go hang!
Let your Otways and Drydens go drown! etc.[22]

Under conditions like these, it is apparent that effects could never be very subtle: the audience was too likely to fail to see the significant gesture or fail to hear the change in tone. The dramatist and the actor placed most reliance on the large gesture and on the oratorical speech delivered in ringing tones from the apron of the stage.[23] These declamatory speeches appear very frequently in the plays; they were, of course, much more effective in the huge, badly lighted theaters for which they were written than in the intimate modern drawing-room settings in which we are likely to imagine them.

A large theater of this type is well suited to spectacular displays, and the eighteenth-century audience was regaled with castles blowing up and ruins falling upon the stage, heroes rushing through fire to rescue fair ladies in burning towers, animated skeletons sinking beneath the earth in bursts of flame, and various types of sea pieces. These wonders, however, were generally displayed in melodramas, pantomimes, and the various minor dramatic forms which were an important part of the theatrical fare of the time. In the comedies, the staging did not differ greatly from Restoration staging, though somewhat more use was made of the proscenium curtain and though, sometimes, toward the end of the century, modern box sets with doors were used instead of the conventional wings and drops. In spite of these developments, the old opening and closing scenes were still in general use. Minor improvements on the stage have very little effect on eighteenth-century comedies; the important influence of the physical theater upon the plays of the time is to be found in the size of the huge playhouses.

H. MODERN COMEDY

Modern comedy, though it really developed somewhat later than modern tragedy, may be taken for the sake of uniformity to in-

[22] Quoted in Nicoll's *A History of the Late Eighteenth Century Drama, 1750–1800,* p. 24.

[23] Of course the Elizabethan platform stage had long since disappeared, and even the apron was less conspicuous than it had been in the Restoration theater, but still the stage bowed out beyond the proscenium arch far enough so that the actor who came down to the footlights was partly out of the stage picture and had a slight advantage in addressing the audience directly.

clude all the comedies written since 1880. These plays, since they are written for our own times, present none of those unfamiliar characteristics with which we have had to acquaint ourselves for all earlier periods. There are, of course, certain aspects of the modern theater and the modern audience whose significance or peculiarity we are likely to neglect because they seem normal or "natural" to us, but they have already been discussed in the chapter on modern tragedy, and they may be referred to there.

In type, modern comedies present for the most part adaptations and combinations of the six historic types of comedy which we have already surveyed: comedy of intrigue or situation, realistic or satiric comedy, romantic comedy, high comedy or comedy of character, comedy of wit or manners, and sentimental comedy. Certain modern plays are really combinations of two or more of these types, but many of them are just the old types slightly modified by modern stage conditions and modern prejudices.

The old Roman comedy of situation or intrigue which presents type characters in ludicrous or embarrassing predicaments, which is not dominantly satiric in purpose, and which does not descend quite to the level of violence and gross exaggeration characteristic of farce,[24] is to be seen on the modern stage in plays like Lady Gregory's *Workhouse Ward* and *Hyacinth Halvey* and Drinkwater's *Bird in Hand*.

Satiric or realistic comedy which attempts primarily to ridicule the foibles and petty vices of contemporary life is to be found ridiculing twentieth-century follies on the modern stage in much the same fashion that Jonson ridiculed the follies of Jacobean London, except that modern comic dramatists are seldom so virulent as Jonson was. Plays like Synge's *Playboy of the Western World* and Shaw's *The Doctor's Dilemma* and *Major Barbara* are comedies of this type.

Shakespeare's romantic comedy is not a popular type in our theaters; yet we occasionally have plays with the same idyllic background, the same strong interest in the final happy union of the lovers, and the same mixture of laughter and romance. One of the modern plays most like the Elizabethan romantic comedy in its general characteristics is *Prunella* by Harley Granville-Barker and Lawrence Housman. But on the modern stage we are accustomed to find the interests to which Shakespeare appealed in

[24] Not that the Roman comedy never descended to the level of farce, but, as we have noted in our chapter on the form comedy, we are arbitrarily considering farce as a separate form even in those periods of dramatic development which did not distinguish it from comedy.

the more romantic [25] of our musical comedies rather than in plays. At first glance this may seem surprising, because Shakespeare's romantic comedies are literary masterpieces while musical comedies are quite insignificant as literature. Yet different as the two are in the greatness of their achievement, the fact remains that they are designed to appeal to the same general type of interest in the audience. Though *As You Like It* is a classic, it is of the same comic type as *The Student Prince* and *The Cat and the Fiddle.*

Molière's high comedy, or comedy of character, which depends for its chief interest upon the inevitable clash between characters of opposed ideas and temperaments and which attempts to study in a half-humorous, half-serious fashion the fundamental relationships between certain eternal types of men and women, is fairly popular on the stage of to-day. There are not, of course, a great number of these comedies, for they are one of the highest types of dramatic achievement and consequently not to be found in every season. But Bernard Shaw's *Candida* and S. N. Behrman's *Biography* and perhaps his *Second Man* and St. John Ervine's *The Second Mrs. Fraser* are notable modern contributions to this type of comedy.

The comedy of wit or manners characteristic of the Restoration period in England which was written for a sophisticated audience, and which, though it did make fun of the pet vanities and affectations of high society, was intended to amuse the audience chiefly by the brilliance of its witty dialogue, occupies a prominent place in the modern theater. Such comedies, depending as they do on the ability of the dramatist to sustain the brilliant conversation for the length of the play, are almost as great an achievement as comedy of character, and are, therefore, never really common. Modern examples of the type include plays like Oscar Wilde's *Lady Windermere's Fan* and Somerset Maugham's *The Circle* and Philip Barry's *Paris Bound.*

Finally, there is the sentimental comedy of the eighteenth and early nineteenth centuries. Because of the modern reaction against sentimentality this type of comedy is not popular with the more sophisticated element of the audience in our theaters. Yet there are modern comedies which exploit the old interest in preaching

[25] Modern musical comedies are of two general classes: satiric, like *Of Thee I Sing, Stand Up and Cheer,* and *Let 'Em Eat Cake,* which poke fun at some aspect of American life—presidential elections or big business; and the more old-fashioned romantic musical comedies which tell a pretty love story, with songs and dances and a certain amount of miscellaneous nonsense by the comedians. It is this latter type, of course, which resembles Shakespeare's romantic comedy.

from the stage, the interest in the supposedly inevitable triumph of the soft-hearted and virtuous over the hard-headed and wicked, and the tearful delight in the pitiful and lugubrious for its own sake. Perhaps the closest modern approximations to this rather cheap type of comedy are Channing Pollock's *House Beautiful* and *The Fool*. But the most successful sentimental comedies on the modern stage are not so insistently moralizing or so naïve in character as these. Plays which combine sentiment and humor and fantasy are more admirable modern variations of the sentimental species. The greatest modern exponent of this type of comedy is Sir James M. Barrie, whose *Kiss for Cinderella* and *Quality Street* and *Alice-Sit-by-the-Fire* are really notable plays.

This survey of the historic types of comedy to be found on the modern stage has been misleading if it has given the impression that all modern comedies are easily classifiable as belonging to one or another of these types. In fact, one of the characteristics of modern drama is that it tends frequently to mix dramatic types and even dramatic forms. Plays like Shaw's *Androcles and the Lion* combine the wildest farce with keen satiric analysis, and Sean O'Casey's *Juno and the Paycock* even mixes hilarious comedy with stark tragedy in almost equal proportions. When such combinations of apparently incongruous appeals have been successful, it is not surprising that less startling mixtures of comedy of situation with comedy of wit, as in Kelly's *The Torch Bearers* and in Kaufman and Hart's *Once in a Lifetime* are popular in our theaters.

One of the reasons for this frequent mixture of types in modern comedy is the wide-spread interest among leading contemporary playwrights in the use of drama for the propagation of ideas. In comedy this interest traces back to Bernard Shaw, though Shaw derived it from Henrik Ibsen. Shaw's comedies nearly always have an idea or a doctrine to expound, and the dramatist concentrates on his idea, sometimes setting it forth through satire, sometimes through direct statement. The dramatist pounds in this idea as insistently as he dares, dropping it only at intervals in order to keep the audience in a good humor and a receptive state of mind by means of a little miscellaneous entertainment, generally farcical in character, and then returning to the idea again. In *Arms and the Man* Shaw proclaims that the romantic glamour of warfare and the heroic life of the soldier are all nonsense; in *Man and Superman* he preaches his doctrine of the life force and ridicules popular notions on the modesty of women and romantic love. These comedies and others like *Cæsar and Cleopatra, Getting Married,* and *The Apple Cart* have been so challenging to modern audiences and modern readers that the interest in ideas has come to characterize many of our best comedies.

In fact, the influence of Shaw and Ibsen has been so great that in some modern comedies the dramatist has dwelt upon his idea at the expense of his play. And certain modern theater-goers and critics have encouraged this by sneering at plays which do not have a thesis to set forth and lauding badly written plays just because they preach a favorite doctrine. Such critics forget that many of the greatest dramatists have had no controversial ideas to present in their comedies. Shakespeare had none, nor did Congreve, Sheridan or Wilde.

In spite of this occasional tendency to use the stage as a lecture platform, modern dramatists have made the comedy of our time a significant achievement. They have produced excellent comedies of nearly all the historic types, and they have combined the old types in effective new variations. Though it is always extremely difficult to be sure of the real value of the plays of one's own time, it seems not impossible that the comedies of Shaw and Barrie and Ervine and Behrman may some day be accorded an honorable place in the long development of comedy from the ancient masterpieces of Aristophanes.

CHAPTER IV

MELODRAMA AND FARCE

Melodrama and farce are less significant dramatic forms than tragedy and comedy. This does not mean that they are less popular, for a large number of stage successes are farces or melodramas; the majority of popular movies will be found to be one or another of these two forms. They are less significant because they are designed to make a more trivial and temporary appeal than the higher forms; no one is expected to carry anything away with him from these plays; they have no "inner meaning." We expect plays of these two dramatic forms to be more obvious in their appeal than tragedy and comedy; they depend upon action, and their fundamental conflict is an external one, like the fight between two men for a woman or the violent attempts of a debtor to fool his creditors; they do not depend upon more subtle conflicts like Hamlet's mental struggles or Alceste's fight against social conventions. In melodrama and farce the plot and the individual incidents are more important than the characters or the implications of the action as a whole. The highest aim of melodrama is a thrill; the highest aim of farce is a laugh.

In general it may be said that melodrama is a lower form of tragedy and farce a lower form of comedy. These resemblances, however, are only superficial. Melodrama, like tragedy, does deal with serious or painful elements in life—death, dishonor, and misfortune of various sorts. But the attitude of the dramatist and his treatment of his material are more important factors in a play than the subject matter. It is in these fundamentals that melodrama differs most sharply from tragedy.[1] The same is true of the similarities and differences between comedy and farce. They are alike in their interest in the less catastrophic phases of life, in the amusing and the ridiculous; but the difference between the keenly observant

[1] The casual observer sometimes says that the chief difference between melodrama and tragedy lies in the ending: a melodrama ends happily, a tragedy unhappily. This is not true. Although most tragedies do end unhappily, we have seen (p. 16) that happy endings are sometimes used; much more significant, we have seen that the character of the outcome is not of primary importance in a tragedy (p. 16). So it is with melodrama. Though most of them end with success for the sympathetic characters, not all do; and in either case the handling of the material and the aim of the dramatist are infinitely more significant than the concluding events.

method of comedy and the irresponsible, grossly exaggerated method of farce is almost as great as the difference between the methods of tragedy and melodrama.

MELODRAMA

Many theater-goers are inclined to think that melodrama is a form of play which was popular in the nineteenth century when our grandparents flocked to see *Uncle Tom's Cabin* and *The Girl of the Golden West,* but that it is seldom seen in our modern sophisticated theaters. This is far from the truth. Melodrama is just as popular now as it ever was. If we take into consideration the movies, it is more popular with the modern audience than it has ever been before. The change that has taken place is not so much in the taste of the audience as in the method of advertising the plays. Since so many people have a vague idea that melodrama is an old-fashioned unsophisticated type, slightly beneath them, the press-agents (who know what the public likes, whether it is willing to admit it or not) give new names to the same old type of play. The modern version of the old-fashioned "bad man" melodrama is advertised as "A thrilling drama of love in Chicago's gangland"; the antiquated virtue-in-distress melodrama is brought up-to-date as "A poignant tale of love amid the breathless life back stage"; and the old military melodrama becomes "Mud! Blood! Glory! As the Pursuit Planes Fly through Death in the Last Great Drive on the Western Front!" Only the names and places and the means of transportation are changed in these plays; the essential action is just the same as in the popular melodramas of fifty years ago.

The term melodrama was first used in English at the beginning of the nineteenth century, though the type of play is much older. Originally the word, as its etymology indicates, was applied to a serious play which was accompanied by music; but the musical accompaniment is no longer a necessity though it is still sometimes used to stir up the audience. The really essential elements in a melodrama are the thrills. The necessity of producing thrills at any cost is the root of most of the distinguishing traits of the form.

For this reason, the characters in a melodrama are usually only type figures, and frequently they are quite inconsistent; invariably the characters are dominated by the plot. This is almost inevitable if the thrills are to be frequent and easily experienced by every member of the audience. The playwright must expend his ingenuity in devising exciting situations—the sudden kidnapping of the heroine by the gangsters whose opium cache she has accidentally discovered; her clever escape just before the hide-out is shot up by rival gangsters; her quick work in saving her lover, the young state's attorney who couldn't be bought-off, just as he had started on his one-way ride; and finally the desperate gun battle in which the girl and the state's attorney out-shoot One-eyed Mulligan and Benito the Bomber. In manipulating such situations as these the dramatist has no time to spend in setting forth the subtleties of the character of the heroine. If he did stop for characterization, the audience would be annoyed at the delay in the exciting action and probably bored at being forced to consider the mind of a woman whose function was not to think but to act. It is enough that the audience be told that she is the usual melodrama type—brave, quick-witted, and virtuous, or, as the modern audience prefers to have it stated, "true to her man."

But there is a reason more fundamental than these for the sketchy or inconsistent characterization in a melodrama. The full development of a character would be not only unnecessary and distracting but it would also be positively disastrous to the plot. Well-developed characters have a way of taking the plot into their own hands; they cannot be made to do just anything the author may think exciting; they must do what their ideas and prejudices and character traits would have forced them to do in a given situation. This would never do in a melodrama. Honest and pains-taking characterization would force the author of the melodrama whose situations we have just outlined into all sorts of difficulties. For instance: If the young state's attorney were so honest, how did he happen to get elected in a city corrupt enough to be infested with gangs? This is not wholly impossible, but honest characterization demands some explanation of it, and the explanation of a peculiar local political set-up is not likely to be a very exciting prelude to a gang play. Again, if the heroine had enough brains to outwit the gangsters once, how did she happen to be so stupid that she was involved in a situation where desperate gun play was necessary? This also might be explained, but every step in outlining contradictory traits in the heroine's character would lead to greater difficulties in forcing her into the next exciting but highly improbable situation. Long ago writers of melodrama learned that it is best to give characters only the most obvious story book traits and then to keep things happening so fast that no one in the audience has time to wonder about the inconsistencies or notice that the heroine is only an old stock figure with no individuality whatever.

Even in an unusually clever and well developed melodrama like *The Green Goddess,* which George Arliss made so successful, the characters are never allowed to become real enough to get out of hand. Major Crespin is stupid when the plot requires that he insult the natives in spite of his long colonial experience, and he is quick-witted when the plot demands that he conceal his knowledge of wireless; he is a drunkard when it is necessary for the audience to sympathize with his wife, and a man of iron nerves when it is necessary for him to save the party. The heroine is a tender mother longing for her innocent babes when mother love is required to work up the Rajah's big seduction scene, but she is the ordinary love-sick heroine when she clings to her lover in order to inject the necessary pathos into the weird sacrificial scene. Even the Rajah, who looks somewhat like a well-developed character because he has a few vivid but superficial traits and is given a great many lines, acts as the plot and not as his own character dictates. He is sensitive and cultured when his civilization will appear most striking against the barbarous background; he is cruel and primitive when his blood lust will add to the excitement; he is cool and far-sighted when his intelligence will startle the audience, but childishly rash and impractical when it is necessary to stage a big finale.

The inconsistencies which we have noticed in melodramatic characterization should have called attention to the episodic character of these plays. More than other dramatic forms, melodramas are written not to present a logical sequence of events but to display a series of individual scenes. Each scene is exciting in and for itself and depends much less upon the preceding scenes for its effect than is the case in comedy and tragedy. In this regard a melodrama has much in common with a newspaper comic strip; this Sunday's paper displays the same characters as last week's and that of the week before, but there is usually no difficulty in understanding the situation, whether the earlier issues have been read or not. The old melodramatic movie serials took full advantage of this characteristic. Since the melodrama involves practically no character development and comparatively little evolution in the plot, the adventures of "Poor Pauline" on a runaway express train lose nothing if one missed last week's picture when "Poor Pauline" was carried off in a submarine. It would be inaccurate to say that any act of any melodrama could be fully appreciated by itself, but certainly there is much less interdependence of act upon act and scene upon scene in melodrama than in comedy or tragedy.

This discussion of the plot-dominated characters and of the episodic structure of melodrama has served to point out a third feature of the form—its essential dishonesty. In this respect melodrama is precisely the opposite of tragedy. The tragic dramatist asks himself, "What is the one thing which these people would do in these circumstances?" The writer of melodrama asks himself, "What is the most exciting thing these people might do?" and then, "How can I make it appear that they might actually have done such an improbable thing?" He is interested not at all in showing life as it actually is, but simply in writing an exciting entertainment, near enough to real life to keep the customers from walking out.

These features of melodrama—its simple inconsistent characterization, its episodic plot, and its dishonest portrayal of life—with its aim of mere excitement for the moment and nothing else, make it one of the most childish of the dramatic forms. The people and the events seen on the stage have no significance and only the most superficial resemblance to real life. No writer of melodrama expects to make his audience think;[2] in fact, the less thinking the spectators do the more they are likely to enjoy the play. A child of ten or twelve can appreciate the average melodrama as well as an adult. These are the reasons most good press agents refuse to admit that their sensational plays are melodramas; they are also the reasons that while the patrons of comedy and tragedy may number hundreds of thousands, devotees of melodrama number millions.

FARCE

Much of what has been said of melodrama will apply to farce, with the obvious difference that the first treats sensational events, the other ridiculous ones; that melodrama has for its highest aim a thrill, farce, for its end, a laugh.

The same reluctance of modern theater-goers to admit that they enjoy the cruder forms of drama is seen in farce as in melodrama. The theaters find it advisable to advertise their popular farces as "the hilarious comedy hit," "a drama of good clean fun for all the family," "the new laugh sensation." The short movies called "comedies" are invariably farces of the crudest type.

Though these advertisements are obviously written with the intent to deceive, they are not quite such bland attempts to pass off cheap entertainment for sincere dramatic writing as the advertisements of melodrama are. For the line of division between comedy and farce is not so sharply marked as that which divides tragedy from the lower form of serious drama. There are plays, like Goldsmith's *She Stoops to Conquer,* so close to this line that they are sometimes called comedies, sometimes farces, or even farce-comedies. Even plays on a higher intellectual level than *She Stoops to Con-*

[2] Occasionally we have a melodrama with a propaganda purpose in which the dramatist claims that he is trying to make the audience think about war or communism or fascism. As a matter of fact, such dramatists are not really asking the audience to be thoughtful; the real purpose is to make the audience *hate* war or communism or capitalism. There is a very interesting discussion of just this point in two articles by Joseph Wood Krutch on a play called *Stevedore.* (*The Nation,* Vol. 138, May 2 and 9, 1934.)

quer employ the technique of farce in certain scenes. In Shakespeare's *Twelfth Night* the duel between Viola and Sir Andrew Aguecheek is farce, and in Congreve's *Love for Love* Miss Prue's pursuit of Tattle is typical farce. Yet both these plays are rightly called comedies because the comedy scenes predominate and because the tone of the play as a whole is far above the exaggerated, irresponsible level of farce.

This occasional degeneracy of comedy into farce is evidence of the fact just mentioned, that the difference between the two forms is not so great as the difference between tragedy and melodrama. In fact, for many years in the history of the drama no distinction was made between the two types of humorous play. We have seen [3] that Aristophanes constantly mixed farce with satire and even literary parody, and Latin comedy, though unlike the Greek in many ways, resembled it in the mixture of comedy and farce. In fact, in the Restoration when the word farce was introduced, it was not used to refer to a special type of comic technique at all, but to the short humorous play which was coming into popularity at the time, a play of three acts instead of the customary five. These short plays usually dealt with highly exaggerated incidents and characters and were much less subtly and brilliantly written than the longer plays. Gradually these characteristics became more closely associated with the short plays until the word farce came to refer not to the length of the play but to its comparatively crude technique of exaggeration and slapstick. It is this meaning which we attach to farce to-day.

Probably the most distinguishing characteristics of farce technique are its exaggeration of incidents and character traits, and the consequent dominance of the plot over the characters. This exaggeration is more than the heightening of effects which is always a part of the method of the drama; it is a simplification of character and action to the point where there is very little character involved at all and the action derives chiefly from situation, involving only one simple meaning.

In the most obvious type of farce, physical action is most important; the dramatist is interested not in what people think and feel but in what they *do*. In *Charlie's Aunt* the young scapegrace dashes about Oxford dressed as an elderly lady and getting into all sorts of ridiculous difficulties; in the movie "comedy" the fat man steps on the soap and falls. Farce of this sort is easy enough to distinguish from comedy, but theater-goers are sometimes confused by plays which are equally typical of farce technique but which rely less on the purely physical. One of the best examples of this less violent type of farce is Oscar Wilde's *Importance of Being Earnest*,

[3] See p. 87.

a play which has none of the running about or the slapstick frequently associated with the form and which is full of clever witty lines. Yet when one examines the play, it becomes apparent that the fundamental humor of the piece is based on situation, not character, and that a large proportion of the comic scenes are the result of gross exaggerations. Lady Bracknell's absurd cross-questioning of her daughter's suitor—the amount of his income, the number of bedrooms in his country house, his politics—is typical of the essential exaggeration of farce; and the ridiculously improbable situation —a young man who knows nothing of his parents since he was found in a handbag at a railway station, but eventually finds that they were relatives of most of the rest of the cast—dominates the action of the play just as in more violent farces.

This exaggeration and the importance of situation in farce lead almost inevitably to the simplification of character. As in melodrama, the characters must be kept simple so that they will not interfere with the improbabilities of the plot. Furthermore, the usual exaggerations of certain traits for comic effect make the people of farces caricatures. In Lady Bracknell of *The Importance of Being Earnest,* Wilde so magnifies the domineering manner and the shameless mercenary interests of the society dowager that his character is utterly inhuman, though she is very amusing.

The episodic character of farce, like its simple characterizations, provides a further resemblance to melodrama. In both forms immediate entertainment is the sole aim. Since consistency of characterization and reality in action are of little importance, the scenes are conceived one at a time and the characters are forced into the situations, regardless of probabilities, to provide the laugh or the thrill as the case may be. This essential dishonesty of farce, however, is not so misleading as it is in melodrama, for the ridiculous character of the exaggerations in a farce prevents them from being taken seriously, as the improbabilities of melodrama often are.

Farce, then, is one of the simpler forms of drama, demanding no thought for its appreciation. It depends for its humorous effects upon the exaggeration of a few simple character traits and upon action which is frequently, though not always, physically violent. It makes no pretense to depict reality and it constantly resorts to gross improbabilities in action and in character. As with melodrama, the essential dishonesty of the form and the limitation of its aims to purely immediate effects have distinctly limited the number of farces of any permanent interest. Yet this very simplicity of the appeal of farce has made it, with melodrama, the most popular of the dramatic forms.

PART II

DRAMATIC MODES AND VALUES

CHAPTER V

DRAMATIC MODES AND VALUES

We have already considered the variety of forms—tragedy, comedy, melodrama, and farce—that the drama has assumed in various ages. It remains for us to indicate the even greater variety of modes that have, from time to time, influenced the drama. Obviously, these modes are not so easy to distinguish or to evaluate as the external characteristics that we designate as historical and technical. But they must be taken into consideration, since, in the long run, it is upon the soundness and subtlety of the values elicited from theme and technique that the significance of the drama depends. There are, to be sure, plays that hold our interest and inspire a kind of admiration by the appeal of technique alone. But such plays are never veritably great, since their appeal is technical and not æsthetic. They may have a peculiar interest to craftsmen; they may have a transitory interest for the audience in the theater; but they cannot hold and enthrall audiences for generation after generation; they are unlikely to come to be regarded as repositories of infinitely treasured values not merely technical.

Moreover, it is the dramatic mode that gives meaning to the treatment of the story. Subject matter in and by itself is not a source of enduring interest in the drama. Until a story has been given form and meaning from a particular point of view, it is in barest summary no more important than any other bit of raw material.

It is perhaps easier to illustrate the relative importance of subject and attitude in lyric poetry than in the drama. Poetry is admirable and treasurable, in part, of course, because of the essential beauty or interest of its subject—a cloud, a bird, a shipwreck, unhappiness or happiness in love. Even more notably is poetry treasurable for the beauty and adroitness of the technique the poet displays in his rendition of the subject. But above all it is treasurable because of the values that the poet finds in the subject; the values, perhaps hitherto unsuspected, that he communicates to his reader. As every worthy poet finds new values in the subjects that he chooses, he can afford to treat even hackneyed or time-worn subjects, provided he treats them with new feeling, with new meaning. The values vary from poet to poet, from reader to reader, but unless they are perceptible, the poem will not long be cherished.

The Personality of the Artist

The source of the meaning of a poem or play, that is, the source of its values, is the attitude of the poet or dramatist himself; the meaning is the consequence of the impact of a particular personality upon a chosen subject. But the personality from which meanings and values derive, is an entity of almost unimaginable complexity. Despite man's time-long interest in himself and curiosity concerning himself, we are by no means sure of the causes of the basic attitudes characteristic of the human individual. A key to an understanding of the causes of basic attitudes is the fact that every personality is the product of two forces of varying power and influence: heredity and environment. Without being dogmatic, we may assign to the influence of heredity the characteristics of the individual's physique: vitality or fragility, sensitivity or coarseness. Certain types of reaction to the world by means of which the personality develops seem to be a matter of the basic tone of the nervous system. The types of reaction which have come to be called introvert and extravert are so fundamental to the personality that they seem to depend ultimately on the quality, supersensitive or coarse-grained, of the nervous system the individual is born with. In any case, this basic bent of the individual conditions the whole system of values that he develops through his experience in the world. To an introvert, the world has an almost completely different meaning than to an extravert. To an extreme introvert, the world appears hostile, dangerous, and forbidding, and his impulse is to flee from it as from the plague. To an extreme extravert, the world seems sunny, alluring, and enticing, and he can hardly wait to throw himself into its arms. To heredity, perhaps, may also be attributed a capacity for emotion or a capacity for thought, which some environments discourage and others encourage, but which none can completely thwart. Whatever the personality's experience in the world, it is certainly in the basic trend and direction of that personality that we must find the sources of most of those values which he imposes upon his treatment of the subject, the sources of his interpretation of the universe itself.

Illustrations of the important influence of the artist's personality upon his representation and interpretation of life are easy to discover in almost any field of literary activity. Certainly one of the major reasons for Shakespeare's domination of the dramatic literature of all time is the basic soundness, wholesomeness, and serenity of the man. There is about him nothing namby-pamby, nothing sentimental. He faces with unflinching courage the utmost horrors and evils that the world and his imagination bring him; but in his most desperately tragic plays his judgment is unshaken, his soundness unimpaired. Shakespeare's greatest literary contemporary, Ben Jonson, illustrates in another way the significance of personality in literature. In him we feel qualities that Shakespeare never manifests: inexhaustible energy, tremendous intellectuality, personal and artistic integrity, scrupulous and fastidious craftsmanship. His self-assertiveness, his harsh and unfeeling judgments of his contemporaries illustrate to perfection the less attractive side of his nature. Thus, despite Jonson's very great power as a personality, it is very difficult to do him justice, for although almost everything about him is admirable, there is very little that is alluring or appealing or charming.[1]

But the personality, whatever its initial bent and trend, is the product of environment as well as of heredity. The artist's experience, intimate and public, intellectual and emotional, is of the greatest importance for its effect on the meanings he is to find in his chosen material. Modern advocates of analytical psychology maintain with considerable persuasiveness that it is the emotional experience of the individual that is of preëminent importance in his evolution. In any case, the dramatist's experience with people, in his own family group and outside it, in love and out of love, in business and out of business, has a tremendous weight in the evolution of his philosophy. If we follow Alfred Adler a little distance in his contention that the basic motive in human conduct is the desire for the feeling of superiority, whether in amatory, social, professional, or artistic relations, we can agree that the degree of success that the playwright has in one or all of these fields of human activity will make its contribution to his estimate of the world and the value it allows him to place upon himself and the world as he has found it.

We are not contending, of course, that all literature is autobiographical, although in one sense at least all great literature is. The insistence on the autobiographical element in literature was one of the major evidences of the degradation of romantic criticism into sentimentality. The combination of a sentimental attitude to the dramatist and ignorance of his time resulted in Edward Dowden's explanation of Shakespeare's artistic evolution in terms of his emotional experience. By this worthy Victorian, Shakespeare's career was divided into four periods: In the Workshop, In the World, Out of the Depths, and On the Heights.

According to this theory, Shakespeare wrote comedies when he was happy personally, tragedies when he was feeling tragic, and romances when he had arrived at the serenity of old age. Such a

[1] In other fields than the drama, likewise, the nature of the basic personality gives value to the most casual utterance of men like Goethe, Tolstoi, or Thomas Hardy.

sentimentalizing of Shakespeare's career is possible only when one ignores the history of the drama and of theatrical taste during the years in which Shakespeare was writing. From even a superficial study of the cycles of taste during those years, it becomes apparent that Shakespeare probably wrote tragedies because tragedies were extremely popular in the first decade of the seventeenth century, and wrote romances because younger men had succeeded with romances—not because he was following the dictates of a personal experience which he was too reticent to reveal to the vulgar world of the theater.[2]

The Artist and the Spirit of the Age

And yet, in a very important sense, all art is autobiographical, and one will not err widely if he remembers that a full consideration of all art upon which the stamp of individuality has been placed must involve a study of the emotional and intellectual life of the author. In such a study, apart from the elements already mentioned—the influence of heredity and of the personality's success in wresting the satisfaction of his desire from the refractory world—the contribution of the spirit of the age is not least in importance. His relationship to the spirit of his age may be close or remote, but, no matter how vigorously individualistic he may be, he must share, with certain reservations, at least some of the ideas and values of his age. These ideas reach him in a variety of ways. The most significant formal agency is education. From education, he is likely to acquire conceptions of man's nature and his duties, conceptions of the world and its significance that are slightly more conservative than the conceptions generated by the liveliest movements of thought and feeling of the time. Moreover, formal education has ever had a variable effect upon both the sluggish and the active minded. Its rigidity and conventionality, its emphasis on discipline and application are likely to prove offensive to the more creative personalities that are submitted to its influence. But formal education in its power to communicate essential information about the individual and his place in the universe has its unquestioned effect on even the most rebellious personalities.

In all probability, however, a personality comes into contact with

[2] A recrudescence of the narrowly autobiographical interpretation of Shakespeare's career appears in J. Dover Wilson's fantastic *Essential Shakespeare* (Cambridge: The University Press, 1932), where Shakespeare's change from comedy to tragedy and problematical comedies is made to hinge on the rise and decline of the Earl of Essex. Undoubtedly, Shakespeare was interested in Essex's fate, but it is extremely hazardous to make this relationship the most important influence in Shakespeare's career. The process by which experience is transmuted into art is a more indirect one than this narrowly autobiographical interpretation would allow.

the spirit of his age more directly through informal than through formal education. From his observation of his fellow man and his successful or unsuccessful adjustments to them he may acquire infinitely valuable concepts and materials for artistic treatment, provided he brings to experience unusual powers of insight and interpretation. And from the reading of books, whether systematic as in the case of Jonson and Milton, or unsystematic as in the case of Shakespeare, he can discover not merely raw material but rich and fructifying stimuli in the forms of ideas and artistic manifestations. But the significance of literary culture as a foundation for highly sophisticated forms of literary art varies from artist to artist. In so deeply learned an author as Milton, literary culture cannot be neglected in any real attempt to appreciate his own magnificent synthesis of the learning and ideas of his age. Similarly, Sir Philip Sidney's *Defence of Poesie* is revealed in its actual significance only when one realizes that it is a *cento* of most of the important ideas of the critics of the Italian Renaissance. In the case of Shakespeare, whose culture was not preëminently bookish, it is still of importance to attempt to determine the extent to which he was, and the extent to which he was not, a mirror-like reflection of the mind and spirit of his age.[3]

But the learning of the age in which the dramatist lives and works is of considerably less importance than those more elusive values of the age that comprise its spirit. No matter how complex an age may be (and it becomes increasingly complex the more one studies it), it is almost certain to have a dominant tone, a tone that may be created by the common man of the age or by a small but vocal group who succeed in imposing their spirit upon their more or less passive or complaisant contemporaries. For instance, although it may be questionable how actually characteristic of the post-war period is the spirit of cynicism and disillusionment rampant in the works of writers like Aldous Huxley and Ernest Hemingway, yet these writers have a sufficiently large following to give some weight to a characterization of this period as one of destructive despair and negative denial.

The values that enter into what we call the spirit of the age are the feeling-tones that invest the general conception of the value of existence. It is easy to exaggerate the enthusiasm and optimism, the sunny vitality of the Elizabethan age, for any open-eyed scrutiny of it will show dark and negative elements in it. However, there is no

[3] A gross misinterpretation of Shakespeare as the mirror of his age may be found in Burton Rascoe's *Titans of Literature* (New York: G. P. Putnam's Sons, 1933). A much more successful attempt to define Shakespeare's relationship to his age will be found in the concluding essay of C. F. Tucker Brooke's *Shakespeare of Stratford* (New Haven: Yale University Press, 1926).

question that there is a marked difference in the spirit of the late sixteenth and the early seventeenth centuries. Where the one is romantic, the other is either falsely heroic or cynical; where the one is exuberant, the other is critical and carping; most Elizabethans of importance, including Shakespeare, who lived on into the Stuart period were touched, and touched intimately, by the changed spirit of the age. And so, it is possible to characterize succeeding periods in history and literature with some degree of accuracy, if with necessary qualification, and this spirit, thus defined, must be taken into consideration in any thoroughgoing attempt to estimate the elements that enter into the values implicit in the dramatist's attitude toward his work and to life.

In the following pages, we shall attempt to define the major modes which in one age or another have attracted large or small groups of dramatic craftsmen. For, as we said at the beginning of the chapter, the critic must take into consideration, not merely the subject and form of a drama, but the mode the playwright adopts and the values implicit in his view of art and life.

CHAPTER VI

CLASSICISM

The term *classicism* as applied to the drama has come to mean not only a particular dramatic technique but also an attitude toward art and toward life. Since the classicist's attitude toward art is more specific and more tangible than his attitude toward life, it will, perhaps, be advisable to attempt first a definition and analysis of the æsthetic principles that have come to be regarded as classical.

Before we attempt such a definition, however, it should be said that classical æsthetic principles are the result of a long evolution of dramatic practice and critical discussion. The basic materials for this evolution are the dramas surviving from Greek and Roman antiquity and the critical theories primarily of Aristotle but secondarily of Horace. The history of the evolution of classical æsthetic principles is, by and large, the history of the critical discussion of the principles of classical tragedy and comedy as stated by Aristotle in the *Poetics*. That history has involved not only misunderstanding and misrepresentation but, on the side of growth, expansion and extension of the principles inherent in Aristotle. It has been the function of criticism, from the Renaissance almost to the present day, to analyze and debate the validity of Aristotelian and pseudo-Aristotelian principles.

The problems of the validity of the three unities, of the nature of the tragic hero, of the function of comedy, of the meaning and process of catharsis—all these and other aspects of Aristotle's observations and doctrines have provoked volumes of controversial criticism. In France, for instance, from the seventeenth to the nineteenth centuries, discussion of the æsthetics of the drama was confined almost entirely to a defense of, or an attack on, some real or pseudo-Aristotelian principle. It was in the eighteenth century, in particular, in both France and England, that the principles of classical æsthetics were held most rigidly and dogmatically. Since that time, the incursions of romanticism and realism have extended the discussion of the æsthetics of drama far beyond the limits fixed by Aristotle.

The Elements of Classicism

Classicism, like romanticism or realism, results from a particular emphasis on some of the elements present to a degree in all forms of art. It has been said that classical art is that sort in which the element of reason takes precedence over the element of emotion and of fidelity to fact. Even if this definition is not entirely sound, it is at least suggestive. If we regard reason as that element in personality that at its best controls and directs activity, then we can agree that in classical art the element of reason has tremendous force, since the classical artist desires above everything to control his material with the intention of securing certain qualities in his product. Perhaps the most striking characteristic of classical art is its orderliness; its shaping of rough and crude material into a form and pattern preëminently orderly may very well be regarded as the work primarily of reason.

Control and orderliness, which seem to constitute the essence of classical art, are reinforced by the classicist's conviction that order in art may be secured most certainly by adherence to the techniques and styles of great works in the past, in particular, the great works of classical antiquity. For, from the classical point of view, the imagination and the appetite for gross and unshaped fact need restraint, and that restraint can be learned and exemplified most satisfactorily by imitation of great works of art in which order and restraint are already manifested to perfection. From this point of view, then, uncontrolled imagination, free invention, and originality are qualities distinctly less admirable than faithful adherence to the practices of classical literature. The most dogmatic and conservative of the classicists is unwilling to admit any essential alteration in the principles he finds in the great art of classical antiquity. His gaze is turned eagerly, not to the future, but to the past where works have already been achieved which he can imitate, but hardly rival or outdo. In classical art, even at its best, there is a strongly conservative element. In its insistence on the unrivaled greatness of classical art, in its reprobation of free imagination or originality or freakishness, classicism stands for the preservation and defense of those values of which time has proved the importance. The classical hostility to change and experimentation has stood firmly in the way of the development of new art forms and new artistic principles. But, despite its sometimes slavish adherence to the past, its function in the preservation, interpretation, and exemplification of the traditional is particularly important in a period of transition or a period, like the present, of æsthetic chaos or nihilism.

The Classicist's View of Life

There is a marked interaction between the classicist's view of art and his view of life. In manifestations of both his thought and feeling, the classicist's love of order involves respect for authority and submission to it. That authority, the classicist finds embodied in the experience of mankind in politics, religion, economics, and social morality. If he is not a reactionary praiser of things past, he is bound to be basically conservative—a believer in the *status quo*. At his worst, he is a narrow and bitter defender of tradition; at his best, he is the major agent in the preservation of the best that the experience of the race has discovered. His view of human nature is less generous, less optimistic than that of the romanticist, less impartial than that of the realist. He is as acutely aware as the romanticist of the potentiality of human nature in the direction of evil as of good, but he is more willing than the romanticist to credit the depravity of human nature and its tremendous need for repressive and coercive influences. The repressive measures devised by authority are to be carried out through the essentially conservative agencies of the school, the church, and the court-room. In his most generous moods, the classicist acts steadily on the principle of *noblesse oblige*. In his more pessimistic moods, he washes his hands of the too pressing problems of the real world, and retires to the economically independent ivory tower of proud and disdainful isolation.

The Qualities of Classicism

But our concern is not so much with the philosophy of classicism as with the qualities common to classical art of whatever period. A discrimination of such qualities is especially important in a period like our own, when classicism is distinctly alien to the spirit of the time, and when such defenders of it as Irving Babbitt and Paul Elmer More have done it more harm than good by their stubborn narrowness and their violent hostility to all forms of art and thought except the classical.

Perhaps the essence of the classicist's position is his passion for order. This passion manifests itself in the classicist's handling of the subject as a whole and in the technique and style which he finds appropriate to his subject. The first manifestation of this passion for order is in the operation of the artist's intelligence upon the raw material history, literature, or imagination presents him, an operation of intelligence that involves the rejection of ideas and emotions irrelevant to the unified and coherent æsthetic effect he wishes to produce. In no other form of art is what is omitted of so much importance as in classical art. The raw material must be chosen or rejected until it promises to become a suitable medium for the expression of the unifying idea or concept which is the end-product of classical art. The quality of orderliness is manifested, perhaps most strikingly, in that dramatic technique which adheres more or less closely to the three unities, the most sharply exclusive of all dramatic forms. The classical artist frequently displays amazing ingenuity and dexterity in compelling refractory material into the set and unbreakable mould of the classical form. Finally, the quality of orderliness is manifested in the style considered most suitable to classical drama—a style that results from the most fastidious selection of words and figures and images, from the most painstaking shaping and polishing of diction and phrasing, and from the coercing of fancy and imagination to effects of the most appropriate lucidity and simplicity and directness.

A quality of classical art closely related to its orderliness is lucidity; a quality that, in a sense, arises out of orderliness, and that, like orderliness, is apparent in the whole design and in all the details of classical art. The strong emphasis on unity of theme and the more or less faithful adherence to the three unities both assist immeasurably in building up a total effect of lucidity. The quality of lucidity is especially apparent in the treatment of character and style in classical art. In the main, classicism in art necessitates a very considerable simplification of character, the elimination of petty individual qualities and habits, the reduction of character to its essential basic traits. Characters in classical drama tend to be built upon three or four major traits; they are almost always highly integrated; there is in them little of the divided purpose, the neurasthenic attractions and repulsions of characters viewed realistically. They tend to take on something of the simple grandeur of primitive sculpture; they are made universally intelligible by the suppression of individual traits, and the emphasis on typical traits. In the classical drama of France, indeed, the simplification seems occasionally to have progressed too far; the characters of Corneille seem sometimes to be personifications of a single emotion, such as love of country, or faithfulness to religion, although, even in this case, each character is rather more likely to display a conflict between two major opposing emotions, though usually not more than two. Lucidity appears again in the style of most varieties of classicism, a lucidity attained only by strenuous attention to all the devices by which ideas and emotions may attain their most perspicuous expression. Such a lucidity allows no possible divergence in understanding and interpretation; it achieves at its best a kind of pregnant gnomic utterance that embodies observations that have a universal, not to say proverbial, validity.

A somewhat more elusive characteristic of classical art is idealization. We have said that in the interests of order and lucidity the classicist tends to eliminate individual and contradictory traits in his characters. He goes further, however, and achieves a frank idealization in his representation of life by the suppressions of a great number of elements that we have come to call realistic. This suppression, whatever its origin, is apparent in the absence of details of appearance and costume, and, more particularly, in the elimination of references to eating, drinking, and the means of livelihood and subsistence. The conscientious elimination of the physiological and the mundane raises all the characters to a plane of existence far above life as the audience or the realist knows it, and gives a kind of elevation and remoteness to the whole drama that we find in no other form of dramatic art. In all probability, the classical convention that the major characters in tragedies should be members of noble or royal families is a kind of rule of thumb for investing the drama with that atmosphere of the heroic and super-mundane with which kings in most ages up to the present have been invested by the popular and the creative imagination.

This process of idealization results in another important quality of classical art—dignity. The dignity is, in part, a by-product of the idealization we have just discussed, and, in part, a product of the lucid and non-realistic style in which classical drama is written. But it proceeds ultimately from the desire of the dramatist to create in his treatment of the theme an impression of greatness that escapes and counterbalances the pettinesses of ordinary life. The dignity we have in mind is the dignity of character and conduct, the dignity of manner and of speech, and, what is more elusive, the dignity that derives from an essentially orderly and controlled attitude toward life and art.

From persons not of a classical turn of mind or taste come objections to classical art that cannot be overlooked. These objections, though in the main æsthetic, are really either intellectual or emotional in nature. The major intellectual objection to the classical point of view is its rigidity. The assumption that perfection lies in the past, the contention that success in art lies in the imitation of great models rather than in originality and innovation seem to the romanticist or the realist an essential negation of growth (which, of course, is not to be identified with progress, whether unintentional or controlled). The classicist position overrates the ideas and moral concepts, the æsthetic effects and principles of literature created in the remote past, and underestimates the necessity and the desirability of the artist's meeting the problems of representing and interpreting important alterations in man's ideas and problems and environment. In classicism at its most hidebound there is a kind of denial of the principle of life itself which means change and alterations and modification if not of actual renewal. And the intellectual rigidity of the classicist seems to his opponents to be reflected in his insistence on the inviolability of his creed as to the form and style of art. To the unclassical, the mould of form and style into which the classicist would have all artists pour their materials and ideas, seems unreasonably strict and formal. And this rigidity and formality have certain purely æsthetic consequences which to some critics seem limitations of the classical point of view. Rather superficial objections to the effect of classical art are its lack of variety and its monotony of tone, effects that inhere in the strict elimination of elements irrelevant to the unified effect desired by the classicist. This limitation of range in idea and feeling is an emotional counterpart of the technical limitations of the classical form. This limitation, too, gives ground for the objection of both the romanticist and the realist to the limited truthfulness of classical art. The romanticist objects that, if art is to represent and interpret life, it must represent the variety that is the very essence of life in the world. It is on this ground that the bitter controversy as to the presence of low or comic elements in tragedy was fought out. To the pure classicist, there is something abhorrent in the intrusion of vulgar characters or comic passages in the lofty, if not serene atmosphere of tragedy. To the romanticist, divergence in mood in itself is interesting, and the effects gained from the presentation of variety are, he feels, more faithful to life than is the conscientious uniformity of the classicist. The realist objects that the idealization of the classicist is actually a falsification, that the characters are by no means so simple or so sure of their motivation as the classicist would have one believe, and that the phenomena of physical and biological existence cannot be rejected in any complete representation of human nature and its problems. To this stricture, the classicist is likely to retort that, since art of a high kind involves, not merely representation but interpretation, interpretation is most lucid and most persuasive where the non-essentials of mundane existence are ignored or eliminated, and the essential elements in character and action and idea are emphasized.

But, despite its limitations, limitations which the open-minded classicist will acknowledge, the beauty of classical art is unique. It moves in an atmosphere, lucid and transparent; it moves with dignity and graciousness and serenity; it brings us humbly to the feet of great sculpturesque personalities moved by gigantic emotions and impulses to a catastrophe that is world-shaking. It brings us, through the turmoil of passions to a peace and serenity greater than comes from the contemplation of any other tragic art.

Classicism in the Drama

Something should be said, perhaps, of the part classicism has played in the dramatic literature of England and France. The influence of the dramatic classics of Greece and Rome was a not insignificant part of that revival of interest in the ancient world which is one of the most familiar aspects of the cultural movement known as the Renaissance. But English classicism and French classicism differ inevitably from the widely divergent classicisms of Greece and Rome. It is impossible to do more than outline the respective fortunes of the classical tradition in England and France. The influence of the classical tradition is apparent in both dramatic criticism and dramatic creation. It was the function of criticism during the Renaissance to consider, explain, and interpret the æsthetic principles expressed in Aristotle's *Poetics* and Horace's *Art of Poetry*. The earliest of the critics to recognize this duty were Italian, and the history of criticism during the Renaissance may very truly be regarded as the assimilation of Italian criticism by French and English critics and the determination of their own attitudes and principles toward problems suggested by Aristotle.

In England during the Renaissance there is a paucity of significant literature on dramatic æsthetics; as we have said, Sir Philip Sidney's *Defence of Poesie* is hardly more than a *cento,* a fusion and synthesis, of three generations of Italian and French critical discussion. Jonson's prologues to his plays are rich in critical material of a classical sort, but unfortunately he never made, not even in his critical note-book, *Timber,* a statement of his critical creed so systematic or so full as Sidney's. Most of the sixteenth-century critics in both England and France were almost slavishly Aristotelian. In the meantime, the application of Aristotelian principles had to make its way in the face of a very lively popular drama which, in both France and England, was the very antithesis of classical practice. In England, during the last half of the sixteenth century, valiant efforts were made to imitate with considerable strictness classical tragedy or comedy, but no such efforts as *Gorboduc* or *Ralph Roister Doister* or *The Comedy of Errors* were successes of the first rank. At the end of the century, the comedies and tragedies of Ben Jonson come nearest to the spirit and form of the classical drama. There was to be sure, in England, a strong infusion of the more obvious and violent elements of the drama of the Roman tragic writer, Seneca, into the popular drama, but the results were much more romantic than classical.

In the meantime there had been in France, as earlier there had been in Italy, a considerable imitation of classical tragedy in learned circles, an activity that is echoed by the unacted Senecan dramas written in England by the highbrow group of which the Countess of Pembroke was the social and artistic center. In France, however, it was not until the end of the first generation of the seventeenth century that classicism established itself firmly in favor with the tragedies of Corneille and Racine. From that time on, classicism in theory and practice was regnant in France, and it remained almost unchallenged until the belated outburst of romanticism in the first generation of the nineteenth century.

In the seventeenth century in England, Jonson's classicism found few imitators. For the appearance of classicism on the English stage it is necessary to wait for the cross-influence of French classicism, apparent before the close of the theaters in 1642, but not widely influential until after the Restoration (1660). From then on it had to struggle against a strong and complex native tradition, and its momentary triumph did not come in England until the eighteenth century. Even then its triumph was a hollow one, for, despite the conscientious imitation or adaptation of French models in Addison's *Cato* (1712), Ambrose Phillips' *The Distressed Mother* (1712), and Whitehead's *The Roman Father* (1750), English classicism was never perfectly acclimatized; in the last half of the eighteenth century strong trends toward romanticism, sentimentalism, and realism speedily undermined the affectation of classicism. There seems to be, and always has seemed to be something deeply repugnant to the English spirit in an art as formalistic as classical dramatic art.

Nevertheless, until well after the middle of the eighteenth century, the principles of Aristotle furnished the starting points for all critical discussion, and as they (or the Italian interpretation of them) had inspired the only important critical document of the sixteenth century in England, so they inspired in the seventeenth century perhaps the greatest of all English critical discussions of dramatic æsthetics, Dryden's *Essay of Dramatic Poesie,* the reflection in magnificent prose of a broad, tolerant, flexible mind upon the virtues and the defects of classical art and theory.

CHAPTER VII

ROMANTICISM

It is much simpler to point out the strictures of the romanticist upon the limitations of classical art than it is to achieve a definition of the elements essential to romanticism itself. Romantic theory, as distinct from romantic practice, came into being as a conscious reaction against the rigidity, the formality, and the constraint of classical dogma and practice. Accompanying this rebellion against classical restraint there were an enhancement of the freedom of the individual, an idealization of the instinctive and non-rational powers, a defiance of æsthetic and sometimes of moral authority, and an insistence on the artist's right to experiment with material and form to the end that the particular beauty for which he yearned might emanate from his work.

On the positive or creative side, it has been said that in romanticism the element of emotion takes precedence over the element of reason and the passion for fidelity to fact. Although such a statement is based upon a functional psychology now somewhat out of date, there is, nevertheless, considerable truth in it. The romanticist prizes above all else the existence and the creation of a particular kind of beauty—a beauty of a more complex sort than that of classical art, a beauty which, as Pater said, is mingled with strangeness. The difference may be illustrated most aptly by the difference between the eighteenth-century and the nineteenth-century treatment of Oriental material. In eighteenth-century drama, the Oriental setting has the allurement of strangeness and remoteness, but its representation is so strictly formalized, so deficient in detail, so unevocative that it has nothing of the complexity of effect that one finds, for instance, in the settings of Byron's Oriental romance. The quaint inappropriateness of eighteenth-century Chinese Chippendale illustrates the failure of the eighteenth century to appreciate soundly or to assimilate persuasively anything like the veritable spirit of the Orient.

Sources of Romantic Emotion

The strangeness that is an essential element of romantic art is attained by means many of which have become commonplace. Of this strangeness, a sense of remoteness is an almost indispensable element, and that remoteness may be the remoteness of time, place, or culture. So, from one point of view, romanticism is a cult of the past, and to this phase of romanticism belongs the rehabilitation of the Gothic Middle Ages which had been despised by classicists from the sixteenth to the eighteenth centuries. To it belongs as well the awakening of interest in the antiquities of Scandinavia, Wales, and Ireland, a movement which in the last instance forms the groundwork for the Irish Literary Renaissance. The emotion evoked by strangeness of place is apparent in the marked exoticism of most romantic literature, the exploitation of all parts of the earth remote from the life and manners of the author and his contemporaries.[1] It is also possible to find strange beauty in a culture remote from our own, not in time or place, but in the social scale. This cultural romanticism is illustrated by the interest cultivated persons take in the ballad and folk-song and in the arts and manners of primitive people.[2] Somewhat closer to cultivated contemporary experience is the life of the lower classes, and unquestionably in the humanitarianism to which romanticism made a not unimportant contribution, there is an element of the imagination that transforms the oppressed into admirable and glamorous creatures.

Of an æsthetic-moral sort is the strangeness associated with evil, whether physical or psychological. The romanticist found it possible to invest with something of glamour even the physically and morally deformed. In physical or moral ugliness, there was an element of strangeness which could, with all the other elements making for strangeness, be allied by some minds with the experience of romantic beauty. Such a union of opposites may be illustrated in the grotesqueries of medieval sculpture, the figure of the hunchback Quasimodo in Victor Hugo's *Notre Dame,* and the seductiveness of Byron's diabolic sin-smitten heroes. Allied to this infusion of the element of evil was the appeal of the irrational or superrational; madness, hallucination, magic, witchcraft, and ghosts became the common properties of romantic writers. When, at long last, the moral sanctions were lifted from romantic writers, there arose the decadents with their anti-moral representation of life in

[1] With the strongly Oriental quality of much eighteenth- and early nineteenth-century romanticism, the translation of the *Arabian Nights* into French in 1704–1712 had not a little to do.

[2] In this connection, the romantic idealization of the "noble savage" is at once one of the most touching and the most laughable of romantic phenomena. It has analogies, of course, with the classical idealization of the Golden Age, and the Christian myth of Paradise, from the blissful state of which all later human experience is a sad falling off.

which evil takes the place of good as the source of stimulus of desired emotion.[8]

The Technique of the Romantic Drama

Though the technique of romantic drama is far less rigorous than that of classical and neo-classical drama, it has come to have a number of fairly specific characteristics, primarily as a result of the persistent influence of the glorious outburst of dramatic writing in the reigns of Elizabeth and James I. Indeed, the technique characteristic of Shakespeare in most of his tragedies and comedies exemplifies most of the important elements of romantic technique. The essential characteristic of the structure of romantic drama is the substitution of the diversity of time, place, and action possible under the physical conditions of the Elizabethan and early Stuart stages, for the unities of time, place, and action.

The conception of the drama as a series of scenes occurring in a succession of times and places gave, and gives, the romantic dramatist a freedom in the selection and presentation of his material that is denied the strict classicist. From this basic structural principle derive most of the other technical and æsthetic characteristics of the romantic drama of the Elizabethan and succeeding periods.

From it derive, for instance, the tendency of the romantic drama to utilize a very considerable number of characters of major and minor importance, and, as a corollary, the necessity of adopting a descending scale of treatment for such characters, intensive for the major figures, typical for the secondary figures, and usually perfunctory for the minor figures. In its choice of characters, romantic tragedy follows the expected lines—it tends to choose characters of royal or noble blood, moving in an atmosphere and an environment markedly remote from the world of the dramatist's everyday life. In its conception of character, romanticism displays a greater complexity than classicism; the elimination is not so rigorous; there is some indication of a multiplicity of motives and impulses and purposes. But in romantic characterization, when the unity is not the easy one of a single impulse or at most of two conflicting impulses, a kind of unity is wrought out of multiplicity. In romantic drama, we shall not find, even in its rendition of psychotic states,

[8] An excellent illustration of the consequences in æsthetic theory of a thoroughgoing decadence is Arthur Machen's insistence that the qualities indispensable to great literature are "ecstasy and sin." In the work of Machen, ecstasy is almost always associated with sin, if not identified with it, but in an era in which sin tends to become unrecognizable in its complexity, Machen's methods of evoking the appropriate ecstasy become childish table-tipping.

that sense of the multiplicity of personalities within a single body that is one of the discoveries of modern psychology and one of the resources of the modern realistic dramatist.

On the whole, romantic characterization is more realistic than classical characterization. Characters are conceived, not as embodiments of one passion or the battlefield of two warring impulses but as a complex product of a rather considerable variety of impulses, moods, motives, and emotions. Moreover, there is a greater willingness on the part of most romantic dramatists to indicate the physical aspects of the lives of their characters, through description of their persons or their clothes, or through representation of such mundane processes as eating, drinking, fighting, and letter-writing.

Romantic style, too, is less rigorously selective in form and in substance than classical style. The variations, for example, upon the Alexandrine, the metrical norm for most neo-classical French dramas, do not begin to be so numerous or so audacious as the variations manifest in the development of Shakespeare's treatment of the unrimed iambic pentameter, or in the treatment of this national metrical norm by his successors, Fletcher and Ford. In diction and imagery as well, the romantic playwright allows himself a far wider range of observation and imagination than the classical dramatist permits himself. The difference can be illustrated easily by contrasting the size of the vocabulary and the range of imagery of Shakespeare and Corneille. The vocabulary of Corneille is notoriously small, and the imagery is limited. Moreover, the vocabulary and imagery of Corneille and the other neo-classical dramatists are more uniformly lofty and abstract than those of the Elizabethans or of the nineteenth-century romantic dramatists of England and France. The agitation caused in the French æsthetic breast by the use of the word *handkerchief* in Shakespeare's *Othello* or in the stout heart of Dr. Johnson by the phrase "peep through the blanket of the dark," in *Macbeth,* is extraordinarily revelatory of the æsthetic inhibitions of neo-classicism on style.

Not the least important divergence between classical and romantic art lies in tone. The tone of classical art is uniform; the tone of romantic art is various. The cleavage between the two is apparent in the opposed attitudes of classicist and romanticist to the problem of the comic passages in tragedy. To the classicist, the appearance of comic passages in tragedy is a hideous violation of the principle of unity of tone. He argues, with some rightness, that an interruption of the cumulative tragic mood is ineffective and tasteless. The romanticist retorts that the comic element in tragedy heightens the tragic emotion by relieving it, gives a truer picture of human existence, and furnishes a sounder representation of character and life. The problem is a purely æsthetic one; the solution of it is ultimately a matter of taste. But the divergent solutions of the problem explain to a large extent the uniform, sustained, elevated, grandiose tone of classical and neo-classical tragedy, and the diverse, now lofty, now humble, now playful, now overpowering, mood and tone of romantic tragedy.

In justice to classical as distinct from neo-classical drama, it should be said that the former permitted a rather greater diversity of mood than the latter. It not only regarded as tragedy what is actually tragicomedy, but permitted, even in tragedies of majestic dignity touches of comedy or realistic touches in minor figures like those of the herdsman and the messenger. But, within the limits of serious or tragic emotions, classical drama presents a narrower range of feeling than romantic drama. In classical drama, there is nothing like the tempestuous insanity of Lear or the corrupt diabolism of *The Revenger's Tragedy.*

The Romantic Attitude toward Life

The varieties of romanticism are so numerous that it would be absurd to expect to discover an attitude toward life common to them all. The range, from the robust moral sense of Shakespeare, the pruriency of Fletcher, the preposterous code of honor of the heroic play, to the impassioned social zeal of Shelley, the ecstatic sins of Byron, and the amorality of D'Annunzio, indicates the logical impossibility of a common romantic attitude to life. And yet, certain attitudes may be designated which have in one or another period been associated with romanticism. Romanticism in the main tends to be idealistic and optimistic and liberal. It sees life in general as glamorous, exciting, and admirable. Whether it emphasizes or ignores the conflict between good and evil in the universe, it feels that the conflict is an enthralling one, and that there is a possibility of an admirable and happy destiny for mankind. To the romantic, man is a complex being with great powers in the direction of either good or evil; at his worst, he is neither ignoble or petty; at his best, he is heroic and inspiring.

The sources of the romantic's moral sanctions lie much more definitely in the realm of feeling than of reason, in subjectivity rather than objectivity. On the one hand, the extremely individualistic romantic will find the sanction for his conduct in what he believes is his own capacity to distinguish between right and wrong; in this respect, the romantic shows himself to be independent of, and sometimes hostile to, the conventional morality of his time. The more definitely socialized romantic finds the sanction for his ethics, the highest values in existence, in the feelings and emotions stirred by the sense of the good of the social order he would promote. The romantic of this sort is likely to be vaguely or specifically revolutionary; his revolt is not personal but social, and his end, not the satisfaction of his egocentric desires and passions, but the achievement of a new society characterized by a greater degree of justice, freedom, and human kindliness than the one to which he is accustomed. But whether in law, theology, morality, or politics, the romanticist brings creed and practice to the test of an inner sanction of good or evil. To him the spirit of law stands high above the word of laws. From the creed of the romanticist spring prophets and fanatics, saviors and social workers.

The Qualities of Romanticism

Enough has been said of the characteristics of romantic art to indicate its most significant attractions: its variety and resourcefulness in structure and material, its range in mood, emotions, characters, and style, and its own strange beauty. It has given us not only the supreme masterpieces of English drama—*Hamlet, Lear, Othello,* and *Antony and Cleopatra,* but such minor masterpieces as Maeterlinck's eerie *Pélléas and Mélisande,* D'Annunzio's hectic *Francesca da Rimini,* the grandiose melodramas of Victor Hugo, the dexterous theatricality of Rostand's *Cyrano de Bergerac,* and the sultry morbidities of Wilde's *Salomé.*

To English students at least, the weaknesses of romanticism are likely to be less apparent than its virtues. The weaknesses have their origin in the lack of control inevitable in individualistic æsthetics. This lack of control is apparent on the technical side in the looseness and absence of focus of many romantic plays and the substitution of a variety of situations and motifs for a controlling unity of theme. It is apparent emotionally in the tendency of some romantic plays to attain an extravagant unreality in character, emotions, and motivation and to allow an indulgence in the preposterous false idealism of the English heroic drama.[4] It is revealed in the tastelessness which attempts to combine comic and tragic moods that defy combination.[5] This tastelessness is not merely an error of feeling

[4] All that the elementary student need know of the English heroic play can be gleaned from a reading of Dryden's *The Conquest of Granada* and Henry Fielding's *Tom Thumb the Great.* To the more advanced or determined student, Lewis N. Chase's *The English Heroic Play* (New York: Columbia University Press, 1903) is recommended.

[5] Examples of tasteless combinations of the comic and tragic are numerous in the drama of the early Stuart period. One of the best examples is Thomas Dekker's *The Honest Whore,* Parts I and II, which, to judge from the advertising title-page, endeared itself to popular audiences by the tediously farcical humors of the sub-plot rather than by the serious study of the reformation of a woman with a past. In the earlier Elizabethan period such a tasteless combination is well illustrated in *Dr. Faustus.*

but of form. The romantic drama furnishes splendid examples of the adroit interweaving of variously toned plots and emotions and ideas; *The Merchant of Venice* and *Lear* are convenient examples. But there are also dozens of instances of makeshift and clumsy or merely formal and mechanical combinations of discordant plots and themes.

A more subtle weakness of romantic dramatic art derives from the supremacy it assigns to feeling and emotion. For feeling may easily become confused with sensation, and sensation and sensationalism may become the means and end of the dramatist's effort. The result is the substitution for drama of melodrama, which in its quest for excitement sacrifices probability and that insistence on a serious representation of human character without which drama cannot exist in health. Melodrama is a legitimate form of entertainment, but it attains its effects only by deviating from the equal seriousness of comedy and tragedy. A more insidious weakness of romanticism is its proneness to deteriorate into sentimentality, a tendency so persistent that it requires separate consideration.

But, despite its weaknesses, romantic art has a profound, if disturbing beauty. It gratifies the imagination; it satisfies the human longing for heroic action and character. Above all, it invests its substance, whether remote or familiar, grotesque or mundane, with a glamour which we have defined as the infusion of beauty with strangeness, whether the strangeness be that of the Orient, the Forest of Arden, the grotesquerie of Quasimodo, or the perversity of Salomé.

CHAPTER VIII

REALISM AND NATURALISM

Though both classical art and romantic art contain elements of realism, realism as a mode permeating the whole of a work of art was attained in fiction only with the eighteenth century, and in the drama, only in the late nineteenth century. The theory of realism, not fully stated until the second half of the nineteenth century, is thus the youngest of the major dramatic modes.

Both historically and theoretically, realism is a more or less conscious reaction to romanticism. The realist objects to the limitations on subject-matter imposed by the romantic point of view. He objects to the amount of idealization inherent in the process of investing the chosen subject-matter with glamour. The extravagances and extremities of the romantic spirit he dismisses with the charge that they are untrue to life, or at least to his conception of life. To the technique of the romantic drama he brings the charge of infidelity to the interpretation of character, the representation of dialogue, and the course of existence as he has experienced it. In sentimentalism, he objects to the prettification of a harsh and unfeeling existence, the over-indulgent view of human character, the disparagement of fact, the exaltation of the more generous and kindly feelings, the prudishness, and the soft-headedness.

On the positive side, literary realism is actually a by-product of the scientific movement which is the dominant influence in the age in which it appeared. Realism apes the impartiality and impersonality of the scientist; it imitates the scientist's freedom from prejudice, his lack of conventional intellectual or moral inhibitions. Its aim, at its clearest, is to represent life as nearly as possible as the scientist sees it.

It is inevitable that there should be a great deal in common between the world-view of the modern scientist and that of the realist. Freed from the trammels of theology and of morality, the realist, with the scientist, sees the universe as a mechanism of unimaginable grandeur and complexity, in the operation of which he is unable to discover purpose, intention, or morality. To the realist, as to the scientist not only the universe but man also is a mechanism: his personality, an inevitable product of the forces of heredity and environment; his physique, a psycho-physical organism; and his conduct, not the product of character and free will but of chemical and physical processes over which he has no control. The realist who follows his theory to its logical conclusion does not concern himself with morality. His rendition of life has the objectivity of science.

Varieties of Realism

But, as there are varieties of romanticists, so there are varieties of realists. It is not always possible to distinguish easily between a right-wing realist and a left-wing sentimentalist. Indeed, fashions in realism alter so rapidly that what seems the ultimate boundary of realism to one generation seems perilously like sentimentalism to another. The right-wing realist, who grasps only partially the implications of the scientific point of view, is likely to share a fairly hard-headed sentimentalist's views of human character, to judge his characters and their behavior unconsciously in accordance with the *mores* of his own social group. There is, besides, an important type of realist (represented in the drama by such figures as Galsworthy and Brieux) that not only does not attempt the objectivity of the scientist but earnestly espouses a particular standard of morals and philosophy, and uses the drama to express his social purpose and his social criticism. So we have, in the realistic field, the phenomenon of the social or "useful" dramatist, who, while utilizing the technique and sharing some of the views of the objective dramatist, brings modern life sternly to the bar of his moral and ethical judgment. The left-wing realist is the type of artist who in continental criticism is usually called a naturalist.

The difference between realism and naturalism is one of degree, and not of kind. The naturalist is the variety of realist who accepts, without qualification, all the implications of the scientific view of life. Like the scientist, he stands for complete freedom in the choice of the subjects of his study, complete objectivity in the rendition of his subject, the thorough elimination of the ideal and sentimental element, and a minimization of the traditional technique of the drama. Even though absolutely naturalistic art is, as we shall see, practically impossible, the naturalist is, theoretically, on safer ground than his less logical fellow-realists.

We have already hinted at some of the realist's precepts concerning subject-matter and technique. It remains to illustrate the application of these precepts in some detail. The principle that the artist should be free to choose any sort of subject for his drama (or novel or poem) has led to a very great extension of the subject-matter of the modern drama. It has, above all, encouraged the selection of subjects which the inclination of the classical toward grandeur and the inclination of the romantic toward the strange and remote had previously debarred from artistic treatment. The lives of the humble, the characters and manners of the middle classes, the struggles of the oppressed, the life of common people in places remote from the centers of civilization, the sexual dilemmas of men in modern society—all these subjects have been exploited by the realistic dramatists. There has grown up a considerable body of plays dealing with social conflicts: between the artist and society (Sudermann's *Magda*); between the single-standard and the double-standard in morality (Björnsen's *A Gauntlet*); between the various economic classes (Hauptmann's *The Weavers,* Galsworthy's *Strife,* Toller's *The Machine-Wreckers* and *Man and the Masses*). There have been dramatic discussions of sexual psychology and sexual hygiene, topics which, in earlier forms of the drama, were idealized or romanticized beyond recognition.

The Technique of Realism

Both realists and naturalists strive for the elimination of the artificial elements in the techniques of the classical and the romantic drama. But, since the drama in any form is an art and since technique is artifice, the complete elimination of artificiality is impossible; yet realists and naturalists with their absorbing desire to write plays that approximate the effect of life as it is lived strive for the minimization of the theatrical. To this end, there is a strong tendency in realistic drama to simplify the treatment of plot, to substitute the interest of careful characterization and the accurate representation of speech, manners, and setting for the excitements of elaborate and contrived events.

In realistic drama, then, we are likely to find exposition, development, climax, and dénouement, treated with a simplicity and lack of emphasis unknown to classical and romantic drama. In the earlier stages of the realistic movement, in the plays of Ibsen for example, the exposition was handled with a care and ingenuity perhaps unequaled in the history of the drama. And the social dramas of Dumas *fils* and his English imitators, Sir Arthur Pinero and Henry Arthur Jones, exhibited a mechanical elaboration in the treatment of all the technical elements concerned which now seems distinctly outmoded. In plays of a more distinctly naturalistic sort—plays like Gorki's *Lower Depths* and Chekhov's *The Cherry Orchard* and *Uncle Vanya*—these inevitable technical elements are treated with the utmost simplicity; technique has been minimized until it is sometimes impossible to be aware of it as technique. Similarly in realistic plays, development, climax, and dénouement are toned down and understated. The complications of plot dear to the older drama are omitted, and, climaxes in particular, where they are not avoided, are treated with little emphasis on the potentialities of the "big scene." This avoidance of the "big scene" is in line with the realist's contention that drama, significant action, is as likely to be apparent in scenes of quiet and inaction as in striking scenes of conflict and controversy. In Chekhov's *Cherry Orchard,* for instance, it is not too easy to decide which scene is the climactic one. It is in all probability the scene in which Lopakhin announces that he has purchased the estate, but this announcement is made so incidentally and is received so quietly that the effect is not that of the theatrical "big scene."

Just as climax is minimized, so is the dramatic "curtain," the short sharp shock at the termination of each act. The curtain falls, to be sure, but it does not fall on an elaborately arranged tableau in which the characters are represented in unresolved and spectacular conflict like *tableaux-vivants.* Instead, the termination of the act is likely to be sudden, quiet, indeterminate; there is a sense of a veil falling not over action or emotion sharply emphasized but upon action or emotion continuing—but continuing problematically, since even the realistic dramatist must sustain the interest of his audience until the conclusion of the piece. Similarly, the final curtain, the one that terminates the dénouement, is likely to be much less decisive than that of the romantic and classical drama. Here is no divine ministration to the woes of the tragic victims; here is no Elizabethan judgment-seat at which all or nearly all the characters are sentenced to death or matrimony. Here life goes unemphatically on. There is no definite framing of the pictures, no sharp edge to the design of the play. Whether tragedy or comedy is the lot of the major characters, there is no termination to the life of the group. Sometimes, an indeterminate ending illustrates and reinforces the view of life implicit in the play. The sense of the drabness and hopelessness of existence, the necessity of losing oneself in pleasure or work are created powerfully by the termination of Chekhov's plays, *The Three Sisters* and *Uncle Vanya,* and there is no end in sight to the miseries of the wretches in the cesspools of society depicted in Gorki's *Lower Depths.*

The realist brings to his representation of character all or most of the resources of the modern scientist or psychologist. Instead of heroic souls acting freely though in conflict with the conceptions of society or of the universe, the realistic dramatist sees human personalities as products of heredity and environment, sees his characters as helpless and futile victims of impulses and powers which they cannot control. It is no wonder then that the realistic drama has frequently found its heroes in weaklings whom the classical and the romantic dramatist would reject as impossible subjects for heroic or glamorous treatment. Even the son of Napoleon is shown as the victim of heredity in Rostand's *L'Aiglon*. In him the spirit of the unscrupulous conqueror is in conflict with the degenerate self-indulgent Hapsburg strain, and his failure and death come about as the consequences of this conflict. Tragedies or tragi-comedies of the realistic sort tend to find their heroes and heroines in the middle and lower ranges of society, in creatures sentenced to life-long obscurity, incapable of masterful ambitions and emotions, and doomed or almost certainly doomed by social forces against which their impotence beats itself out in vain.

In the delineation of character the realist differs very considerably from the classicist and the romanticist. With him, character tends to become more complex than it is in the older drama; characters are composites of a large number of varying and contradictory impulses; they fail frequently to attain the integration marked in the figures of classical drama. The conception of character as an unresolved conflict is one that is peculiar to the realistic drama.

Moreover the realist, in his effort to represent life as it is, is driven to an exacting study of the surface manifestations of character. In neither the classical or the romantic drama is much attention given to the description of the clothes or physiques or manners of the persons concerned. The necessity for creating a complete and detailed picture imposes upon the dramatist a heavy burden of observation or creation.[1]

There are also problems of dialogue for the realist from which the classicist and the romanticist are free. Upon the older dramatists there was no necessity for approximating the effect of actual conversation in stage dialogue. This necessity affects, first of all, the movement of the dialogue, and encourages discursiveness and lack of sharp focus. It also requires the elimination from the dialogue of rhetorical and inflated elements, and the cultivation of exact and sometimes dialectal, or at least of markedly colloquial utterance. The subtle, poetic, imaginative discourse of the classical and romantic drama is distinctly beyond the province of the realistic drama.

A somewhat similar divergence is apparent in the handling of setting. The classical drama pays little or no attention to the depiction of setting; the problem of setting is solved by the simple con-

[1] Frequently in the realistic drama the playwright, impatient of the inevitable limitations of his medium, exceeds the logical functions of the stage-direction, and includes in it, as a means of characterization, facts that the dialogue and setting do not reveal and bits of analysis which the actor can only attempt to convey. This is an indication, at once, of a confusion of the novelistic and dramatic genres, and of the importance that the publication and reading of plays have attained in modern times.

vention of a permanent set. But the realist's passion for facts, his fidelity to them, and his belief in the significance of environment for the nature and fates of his characters necessitate a meticulously detailed description and representation of setting that is paralleled by a similar minuteness of treatment of setting in the modern novel, and was foreshadowed by the realism of seventeenth-century Dutch painting. This realistic treatment of setting has assisted considerably in creating a lively illusion of actuality. It has likewise been an important stimulus to the stage-producer and manager, and has trained all persons concerned with the theater to an awareness of the importance of accurate detail. A corollary of the realistic treatment of setting has been the rise of realism in stage-costume. Stage-costume until the contemporary period has always been a conventionalized treatment of contemporary costume; until the middle of the nineteenth century almost no effort was made in the major theaters of Europe to achieve historically accurate costuming for the great dramas of classical antiquity and the Renaissance. With the advent of realism, however, attention naturally turned toward the problems of setting and costuming presented by the classical repertory, and endless pains and study were devoted to the archaeologically accurate production of early plays.

The objectionable element in this movement to present plays from the classical repertory realistically was, first of all, that such plays were not written for realistic presentation, and, consequently, realistic production was sometimes seriously out of tone with the plays. In the second place, and more seriously, there are limits (very distinct limits) to the effectiveness of realistic setting and costuming in the theater. There is the primary difficulty of the transmission of the effect from the stage to the audience. A realistic painting can be studied over and over again microscopically; a stage-picture can be studied only fleetingly, and it cannot be studied minutely from the middle of the auditorium or from the last row in the gallery. Unquestionably, a tremendous amount of ingenuity and money has been expended in building up effects that are inappropriate to the theater. True realism in the theater aims at giving the effect of reality, and not reality itself.[2]

The Qualities of Realism

The values of realism in the drama are so familiar that they do not require elaborate statement or exemplification. Realism performs one of its services in the faithful and accurate rendition of life and character. Since nothing human is beyond the limits of

[2] From this point of view, the efforts of David Belasco to secure stage-realism seem in general to have been ill-considered.

human interest and curiosity, there is always a certain attractiveness about an untouched photograph of local customs, mannerisms of speech, and details of milieux. Realistic art trains both artist's and audience's eyes in the close and unflinching observation of human beings and emotions and environments. And such painstaking observation and rendition, and the appreciation of such rendition, are assuredly values that art can render in extending our experience by drawing attention to what we have been too casual or too ill-trained to observe. Similarly, realism has rendered art and humanity a great service in its deliberate extension of the subject-matter of art to include the humble, the despised, and the rejected, to allow the representation of all phases of modern industrial and agricultural life, and to describe the manners and customs of all levels of human society. And, finally, although objectivity proves a blind alley for art, objectivity has its lesson for both artist and audience. The spectacle of life, viewed dispassionately and without prejudice, with accuracy and without falsification, may be disturbing or even horrifying, but it is salutary in its truth and honesty.

But, though realism is the dominant literary influence of the artistic era in which the modern drama has been created, it is possible to escape sufficiently long from the spirit of the age to see very serious limitations and weaknesses in the theory and practice of realism. The weaknesses of realism arise, we believe, from two basic confusions—the confusion of art and science and the confusion of art and life. The first confusion is basic to realism because, as we have seen, the realist has been attempting, whether or not he was quite aware of it, to turn art into a science; to become in his own person an impartial and objective observer, unswayed by intellectual preconceptions or emotional preferences, and, consequently, to give his art the permanent validity of conclusions established by the application of the scientific method. But it is logically and practically impossible for the artist to become as impersonal and unselective in his observation as a camera or a microscope. Personality will creep in, and, if it does not creep in, the work suffers accordingly. For, though art is never at its greatest when it is merely emotional and subjective, it derives an essential value from the fact that it has been selected, shaped, and transmuted by a creative personality. To banish personality in this sense from art is to attempt to banish art.

Similarly, the realist tends to confuse the basic distinction between art and life. Again, he is attempting to make his art-product as much like life as possible. This process has sharper practical than logical limits. In the most vital respects, art and life differ enormously: art is sharply limited, life is illimitable; art is focused and shaped, life tends to lack purpose and design; art is coherent and intelligible, life is incoherent and (observed objectively) meaningless. Practically, even the artist who gets nearest to an effect of life must practise a selectiveness, a formalization, an abstraction that prevent its being, at its most life-like, any more than an extremely clever rendition of the effect of life. It can never be life itself.

Moreover, by making itself more or less frankly photographic, realism runs the chance of reducing itself to a skilled and ingenious representation of surfaces, omitting those complexities of feeling and meaning that art distils best. Even the realist with a social thesis suffers as an artist in the coercion of his material to the establishment of a social thesis of doubtful or narrow validity. The realist who denies himself a thesis becomes a photographer; the realist with a thesis becomes, what is worse, a preacher, not an artist.

A further limitation has been charged to realism; namely, that it exorcises the spirit of tragedy. In the main, it is true, the realist is hostile to grand and idealistic emotions and intentions; he feels, and rightly, that, in fidelity to facts he must eschew the idealizing and romantic elements in traditional art. From the strictest realistic point of view, objectivity permits neither a tragic nor a comic effect. The realist contents himself with accurate representation; meaning, if there is any, must be contributed by the audience. Practically, too, the realist tends to discard as a tragic device the greatness of birth or person in which classical and romantic drama found one of the easiest means to an effect of grandeur and nobility. If grandeur, either actual or intellectual or emotional, is the essential and indispensable element in tragedy, then it must be acknowledged that many realistic plays that end disastrously cannot be called tragedies. It is doubtful if Galsworthy's *Justice* can seriously be called a tragedy. The protagonist is too weak, too pitiable a creature to be an impressive tragic figure, and even the remorseless grandeur of the law that helped him to destruction is not enough to elevate this painful play to the dignity of tragedy. In the case of Galsworthy's Falder, none of the forces which link the victim to catastrophe is of sufficient magnitude to communicate a sense of great issues. Falder's fate is regrettable, but it is not genuinely tragic as is Hamlet's or Lear's or even the preposterous but magnificent Hernani's.

But there are ways in which the realist can evoke through his drama the sense of great issues at stake. For instance, if he is able to convince us that great social forces are involved, or if we get (as in Hauptmann's *The Weavers*) the sense of terrific social forces in conflict, the atmosphere of greatness, and, in the catastrophe, the atmosphere of tragedy is evoked through the climactic crash of tremendous forces. It is possible, too, for the realist to attain an effect of intellectual grandeur in his presentation of the philosophic implications of the modern view of man and the world. In this way, Thomas Hardy was able to give an effect of tragedy, not merely in his poetic closet-drama, *The Dynasts,* but in almost the slightest of his prose or poetic interpretations of human experience from the deterministic point of view. Similarly, in such a play as *Mourning Becomes Electra,* Eugene O'Neill has exhibited the tragic significance of a world in which character has given way to the powers of subconscious mechanisms, complexes, and compulsions which give human fate the cruel significance of animals trapped by forces within themselves over which they have no control. It is not only the multiplicity of his instances but the courageous acceptance of the implications of the scientific world-view that give O'Neill's tragedy its effect of tremendous tragedy.

But, as we have hinted, the essential weakness of realism arises from its insistence that art is representation and not interpretation. Art in essence is creative, and the weakness of most realistic art is that it does not create beauty, power, significance, or meaning greater than the representation of mediocrity and triviality permits. The spirit of man turns to art not merely because it is prettier or pleasanter than life, but because, even at its most illusive, it is other than life, a creation out of the material furnished by life, wrought to a significance greater than mere life can have unless it is meditated upon and shaped into an ethical and philosophical system.

CHAPTER IX

SENTIMENTALISM

Sentimentalism is perhaps the most difficult of the modes of drama to define and illustrate not merely because its values are the most elusive, but also because it is at the present moment beset by such violent misapprehensions and prejudices that it is difficult to secure calm consideration for it. The spirit of the twentieth century is, on its conscious and sophisticated levels, definitely anti-sentimental. This anti-sentimentalism, disguising itself as cynicism or objectivity, as brutality or candor, is a by-product of a cumulative revolt against the weaker elements in the Victorian way of feeling. This revolt has been furthered by the incursion of scientific attitudes into the realms of even the intimate emotions and by the destruction of social standards and inhibitions incidental to the World War. On the other hand, sentimentalism is still so tremendously popular on the lower levels of culture and education that to attack it seems to indict the taste and judgment of millions of one's contemporaries.

Historically, sentimentalism has deeply rooted connections with the romanticism which we have already discussed. Like romanticism, for example, it gives primacy to feeling rather than to reason or the sense of fact. But the feeling cultivated by the sentimentalist differs from that cultivated by the romanicist, chiefly in its object. Unlike romanticism, sentimentalism is not associated with the strange and remote but with the immediate and the familiar. Sentimentalism is a kind of domesticated romanticism that results from the discovery of the possibility of evoking agreeable emotions in the treatment of familiar social and domestic life. Such an investiture involves an idealization of the familiar and domestic which makes for a falsification of the values that derive from a realistic view of life.

The Sentimental View of Life

The process of idealization appears in some of the major assumptions of sentimental art. Of human nature itself, sentimentalism tends to take the rosiest view. It invests with roseate light, not the grandiose heroes and heroines of romance but the figures of common life. So, mother and child offer themselves as the handiest objects for false idealization. Motherhood itself, it is assumed, produces, not only in the sensitive spectator but in the biological entity herself, a kind of purification and spiritualization, infrequent, to say the least, among common or garden varieties of biological organisms. Similarly, sentimentality falsifies its representation of childhood by stressing its innocence, physical grace, and helplessness, and by ignoring the anti-social, animalistic, and vicious potentialities of human infancy. Almost inevitably, sin to the sentimentalist is not sin against self but against domesticity; so, the errant husband and the anti-domestic female become, the one, the object of missionary zeal on the part of mother and child; the other, an object of abuse and condemnation. As the flood of sentimentality rose, toward the end of the nineteenth century, the unmarried mother became an object of pity and compassion rather than scorn; similarly, the wayward woman, the brazen courtesan, was sentimentalized through the astonishing discovery that however reprehensible her behavior, at least she had a good heart. To this sentimentalizing of the courtesan, Dumas' *Camille* was an epoch-making contribution.

Outside the domestic sphere, sentimentalism found objects worthy of emotion in the alleged simplicity and purity of primitive man and in the socially down-trodden—the negro and the shop-girl—and thus contributed not only in art, but also in life, toward the movement for the improvement of society that has come to be called humanitarianism. Corollaries to the exaltation of the socially depressed were the condemnation of the aristocratic way of life and hostility to great wealth as making grace and dignity possible only at the cost of grinding down the poor.

The sentimentalist's cult of delicate feeling and his repugnance to harsh fact tempt him to interpret life not in accordance with the complexities of contradictory and baffling experience, but in accordance with his wishful thinking, his inordinate capacity for rationalization. So, life itself becomes a conflict between the soft-hearted and the hard-hearted, a conflict in which, however, the soft-hearted believe that they must win out, because after all the power behind the universe must share the tender-heartedness of the sentimentalist, and must therefore appreciate the desirability of giving them the reward they feel they shall, in the long run, eminently deserve. To the attainment of this victory, the chief means is not intelligence or respect for fact or the application of reason to human affairs, but the cultivation of the right kind and quality of feeling.[1] In the

[1] Despite Galsworthy's legal training and his attempts to be judicial, he belongs with the sentimentalists in his insistence that the social end which he holds to be desirable will be attained not by alteration of the forms of society or modification of

sentimentalist's battle with evil, the only weapons necessary are a kindly nature, a soft head, and an easy effusion of tears.

The Themes of Sentimentalism

Sentimental dramatists have found certain themes especially attractive and congenial. Some of these are perennial; the struggle of young womanhood to preserve her virginity, the struggle of young manhood against the sexual and economic temptations by which he is assailed. Another popular sentimental theme is that of the rehabilitation of drunkards, gamblers, libertines, courtesans, and wayward women. A theme closely allied to the rehabilitation-motif is that of the transformation of the hard-hearted into the soft-hearted by the power of kindliness and love, frequently through the agency of an infant or personable ward. Here belong the villainous or merely crusty curmudgeons or the socially snobbish or ambitious who are converted through the influence of simple innocence and virtue. The transformation of the worldly into the unworldly is frequently brought about through a trick of plot. A lost fortune is one of the surest means for bringing out in the selfish and corrupt the generosity and nobility that, according to the sentimentalist, are buried in the most callous breast. A social theme is often found in the road to riches, the successful struggle against tremendous odds of the poor but honest youth to the attainment of economic security, social esteem, and domestic bliss.

Related to the theme of the road to riches is the Cinderella theme, one of the most obvious among tried sentimental themes, of wish-fulfilment. The plain but kind-hearted heroine, depressed by economic or social circumstance, is given what she wants, sometimes without trying, sometimes with the expenditure of a surprising amount of ingenuity and intelligence. So, in Barrie's *A Kiss for Cinderella,* the oppressed heroine achieves her heart's desire, first in a delirium brought on by exposure to stage snow, and then in actuality in the person of an obliging policeman. The same writer's *What Every Woman Knows* is a much more adroit treatment of the Cinderella theme. Here the heroine is not merely plain but also intelligent, and her intelligence triumphs over the blindness of her egotistic husband and the wiles of a beautiful high-society adventuress. Sentimentalism is frequently combined with attacks on selfishness and worldliness in the celestial visitant theme, illus-

its laws, but by the development in modern men of the right feelings towards themselves, their own classes, and other classes in the current social order. The feeling which his plays in the main tend to evoke is effective enough as a social-æsthetic emotion; it hardly furnishes an adequate solution for the inordinately complex problems of modern political and industrial society.

trated by Charles Rann Kennedy's *The Servant in the House,* Jerome K. Jerome's *Passing of the Third Floor Back,* Knoblauch's *The Fawn,* and the dramatization of H. G. Wells' *The Wonderful Visit.* The nucleus of this situation is the assumption of the contagious and redemptive power of good; incidental is the exposure of social vices and shortcomings and their disappearance under the searching light of goodness.

The Technique of Sentimentalism

Sentimental dramatists have made no noteworthy contributions to dramatic technique, but they have had to face some problems more or less peculiar to themselves. On the one hand, in its representation of middle-class and lower-class characters, sentimentalism has been faced with the necessity of working out a dialogue-technique appropriate to such a milieu, since the elevated and urbane dialogue of upper-class drama was out of the question. The attempt to meet this situation was praiseworthy, but the results are distressing. The dialogue of eighteenth-century sentimental tragedy and comedy strikes the modern reader as painfully stilted and rhetorical; shopkeepers, apprentices, and the virtuous daughters of grocers speak with the rotundity of a Sunday-school tract, pregnant with moral platitudes. A few of these would seem not more offensive than the "sentences," the terse philosophical maxims of the Elizabethan drama, but, to the eighteenth-century sentimentalist there could not be too much of a good thing; [2] in consequence, speeches are distended with the most obvious commonplaces evolved from the sentimental point of view, smooth round generalizations that strike the modern reader not only as untrue, but as undramatic. But, despite the crudities of dialogue in early sentimental drama, sentimentalism made, in the long run, a very important contribution to the evolution of a prose dialogue that would have the effect of realism. Moreover, it prepared the way for the extremely adroit teary-smiley dialogue of a past master of sentimentality like Sir James Barrie.

A further problem that faced many sentimentalists was that of combining reality and fantasy persuasively. For sentimental themes frequently involve some use of the supernatural for the complete exemplification of their themes. The fantasy may be incidental, as in Barrie's *A Kiss for Cinderella,* or integral as in David Belasco's *The Return of Peter Grimm.* The problem is that of making the fantasy imaginatively persuasive, or, when the fantasy is incidental, of making the transition from the world of fact to the

[2] Cf., for example, the inordinate lengths of Richardson's histories of prurient but technically virtuous heroines.

world of fancy without a shock. The first case demands imagination; the second, imagination and tact. In a completely fantastic piece like Barrie's *Peter Pan,* the imaginative effort involved is tremendous, since it is necessary to create a dominant tone, and then to sustain it by the creation of details no one of which shall seem incongruous, no one of which shall bring the audience down to earth with a thud.[8] In the sentimental play in which the fantasy is only incidental, the difficulty is, as we have said, primarily that of building a bridge from the world of fact to the world of fancy. The transition may be made gradually, or it may be made abruptly, but in either case it must strike us as congruous, if not plausible. So, in Belasco's *The Return of Peter Grimm,* the return of the dead man is prepared for, rather elaborately in the first act, by the discussion of spiritualism; it is prepared for more subtly by the atmospheric and psychological details of the scene immediately preceding Peter Grimm's return in the second act. Once that difficult transition is made, Belasco is free to wring every ounce of pathos possible from the contrast between Peter's desire to communicate with his friends and his seeming inability to do so, and to exploit the irony of the contrast between his actual presence and his seeming absence. Where the transition is made more abruptly, as in *A Kiss for Cinderella* or Hauptmann's *Hannele,* the transition is frequently rationalized, in these cases by the device of a delirium, in others by the device of a dream.

The Values of Sentimentalism

The weaknesses of the sentimental attitude toward life and drama have, perhaps, never been so obvious as they are to the present age. The root of the weakness of sentimentalism is the falsification of fact that arises from the preference of the sentimentalist for pleasant feeling to harsh reality. There is, to be sure, a kind of falsification in romanticism; but romanticism, although it introduces an element of idealization into its representation of life, retains its grasp, at least in its more robust forms, upon the cruel and ugly aspects of human nature and existence. The soft-hearted sentimentalist, on the other hand, suppresses or minimizes those elements in human experience that are hostile to the emotion he cherishes. A further consequence of sentimentality, especially objectionable in modern eyes, is its encouragement of prudery in the treatment of sexual and physical functions. The harsh and cruel facts of the human love experience must be denied or re-

[8] The perennial appeal of so fantastic a play as *Peter Pan* to old and young alike says a great deal for the deeply rooted nature of sentimentalism.

pressed for the sake of the sweetness and prettiness dear to the sentimentalist. This prudishness frequently goes so far as to result in an absurdly false representation of human experience. To no form of art is the objection, "But life isn't like that" so logically relevant.

At its worst, sentimentalism is more insidiously immoral than coarseness or vulgarity or cynicism, since its falsification and lack of balance are less obvious, since its suppressions of unpleasant aspects of experience blind one to its falsity. If all art involves, implicitly or explicitly, some criticism of life, sentimentalism, with its stress on feeling and its underestimation of logic and the sense of fact, is likely to offer the least trustworthy guide to a sound interpretation of the meaning and the value of human experience.

But sentimentalism under control has its values which not even the most coldly intellectual age should underestimate. Its specialty is the tender emotions, and the touching appeal of the tender emotions is a valuable corrective to too purely intellectual or scientific an interpretation of human existence. Moreover, one of the particular effects of the sentimental is charm, an elusive winsomeness that is almost entirely absent from much classical or realistic art. Another of its particular values is pathos, which may almost be said to be the painful counterpart of irony, since, like irony, it depends usually on the contrast between the actual and the desirable. The difference is that this contrast is exploited by the sentimentalist for its touching quality, by the ironist for a consummately sublimated comic effect.

CHAPTER X

SYMBOLISM AND EXPRESSIONISM

SYMBOLISM

Symbolism in the drama is a less elusive and more reputable variety of romanticism than sentimentalism. Like romanticism, it does not aim at the mere representation of superficial aspects of reality. In its less lofty flights, it adds imaginative or poetic elements to the superficial manifestations of reality. In its most extravagant forms, it is distinguishable from romanticism only in the fact that it does not confine itself to the creation of a merely glamorous picture, but builds up a more or less specific indication of the intellectual or ethical or emotional significance of the work of art concerned. To be sure, the most rhapsodically romantic play is likely to offer some sort of comment on the meaning of human destiny, but symbolism differs from romanticism in the definiteness of its indication of meanings or values.

For a symbol is an object or act which has not merely an intrinsic but also an extrinsic value. The most obvious of symbols, a flag, intrinsically and objectively no more than a piece of colored bunting, acquires by experience and association a tremendous burden of extrinsic and subjective values, and thus, though tattered and maimed, is capable of rousing the most violent responses in the nature of admiration, self-sacrifice, and sacredness. A symbol, then, in life or in art, is a nexus of values, and the dramatist who indulges in symbolism is attempting to indicate a series of meanings or values which he feels that he could not express satisfactorily or compellingly without recourse to such short cuts to profound levels of feelings and emotions.

There is, of course, a very wide range in the appeal of symbols. Some, like the flag, are racial and national; some, like a wedding ring, are invested with strong social and personal values. The insignia of a lodge or fraternity vary in significance and validity with the allegiance and loyalty of the individual members of the order. Religion, which is forced to represent abstract or subtle theological concepts in tangible forms, is peculiarly rich in symbols; the cross, the altar, and the sacraments are all illustrations of the tremendously compelling power of symbols to evoke profound emotions and ideas, and to influence thought and conduct. In the face of almost universally accepted symbols, the poet or dramatist of any distinction is likely to feel himself dissatisfied, for the time-worn symbol will seem to him too stale a device for the adumbration of his personal set of values. The poetic dramatist feels driven to create his own set of symbols and to endow them with the significance that he has attached to them himself.

The appeals of symbolism are as varied as the appeals of romanticism. Symbolism satisfies the craving to escape from the banal and the mundane; it satisfies the desire for a meaning that may not be apparent in a strictly objective presentation of chaotic reality; it delights the person who, with a strong ethical or moral bent, feels that his time in the theater has been wasted if he cannot carry away an ethical or philosophical memory-gem from his evening's entertainment. It delights the poetic and the imaginative, since it is a stimulus to the activity of the connotative aspect of mentality. At its best and at its worst, it stimulates the mind and the imagination by encouraging the quest for values that do not lie casually on the surface of the work of art. Such a quest is justified if it does not go too boldly beyond the meanings that the poet or dramatist has indubitably indicated or suggested. At its worst the quest of values becomes a sort of re-creation of the work of art by the reader, a kind of creative criticism which may have validity for the creator-critic, but which can have little or no validity as a critical evaluation of the actual work of art under scrutiny.

It is necessary to distinguish between the dramatist who is veritably symbolical and the dramatist who uses the dramatic form to project, either specifically or vaguely, a "criticism of life," or a comment on social modes and practices. The distinction can be made on the ground of the presence in the play, or absence from it, of definite objects or acts that embody the meanings of the whole play or a part of it. The social drama, the problem play, might seem at first thought to be symbolical in nature since its plot and characters not only have the values of the specific action and the individual characters, but also carry the weight of the play's critical comment on the life of a particular period or social class or on life as a whole. But such a play is symbolical only in a loose sense, since it does not contain acts or objects or images which convey in concentrated form the values the playwright is engaged in communicating. Thus, Paula Tanqueray might be thought to be a symbol of all women with a past, but, more strictly speaking, she is not symbolic in the sense of Hedda Gabler's fondness for playing with pistols or her favorite phrase about "vine-leaves in his hair."

Even among dramas definitely symbolical in nature, the amount of symbolism varies enormously. In most dramas of this sort, the symbolism is usually incidental to a theme treated in a generally romantic or generally realistic manner. As we have already suggested, dramatists are inclined to resort to symbolical devices in order to project values that do not seem to emerge with sufficient distinctness or force from a merely realistic representation of human existence. Such incidental symbolism may be so elusive as to have no more value than a figure of speech in its suggestion of an analogical meaning; on the other hand, it may be so essential an element in the structure of the piece that it usurps the position of the superficial significance.

In the work of Ibsen, it is possible to observe a steadily increasing incursion of symbolism into the bourgeois realistic drama of his maturity. In *A Doll's House,* the talk concerning the masquerade costume and the tarantella has its significance in the prosaic interpretation of the plot, but it also suggests evocatively the deeper meanings of Nora's situation and her distress. So, the slamming of the door at the conclusion of the drama has come to be regarded, not only as an effective termination of the conflict in this particular play, but as a striking symbolic representation of modern woman's departure on the road to economic and emotional independence. In *The Wild Duck,* Ibsen was not content merely to use the figure of speech of the wild duck to suggest to the imagination the ironic plight of the Ekdal family. He felt it necessary actually to introduce a wild duck as an important element in the development of the plot, an attempt at symbolic representation which may be admired for its boldness rather than for its plausibility. It would certainly seem to be a more subtle use of symbolism to eliminate the wounded duck from the attic and to emphasize through repetition the analogy suggested by it.

In *Hedda Gabler* and *Rosmersholm,* however, the symbolism is kept beautifully under control. Despite the drabness of the settings, the dialogue, and the action, the symbols help lift these plays into the realms of imaginative tragedy. But in *The Master Builder,* symbolism of the most complex sort so overruns the play that it loses any coherent surface meaning, and in the meaning-mongering to which its incessant and conflicting symbolism drives us, it becomes, as F. W. Chandler says, a sort of intellectual blind man's bluff.

Another play in which the incidental symbolism tends to cloud and confuse the meaning of the surface drama is William Butler Yeats' *Cathleen ni Houlihan.* The surface action of the play has no intelligible meaning. It offers no explanation as to why the young hero, on the eve of his marriage, should sever his ties with his betrothed and his family, and depart at the call of a mysterious wandering old woman. It is only when we realize that the old woman is Ireland herself that the play takes on any plausible meaning. Here, as in *The Master Builder,* the superficial meaning of the play has been sacrificed to the symbolic meaning. The two planes of meaning have not been kept distinct. Instead, one plane of meaning is deserted for the other, and the result, from the point of view of logic, is chaos.[1]

The wholly symbolic play is the play written with the two planes of meaning kept steadily in mind and with no confusion of the planes. The best examples of the wholly symbolic play is the type of medieval drama known as the morality. In plays like *The Castle of Perseverance, Everyman,* or *Mankind,* the characters are either personified virtues or universalized types. In other words, what we are witnessing is not only a specific figure, named Wit or Everyman or Mankind, undergoing certain experiences, but a presentation in dramatic form of an abstract idea, such as the conflict between the virtues and vices for the soul of man or the difficulty of the mind's attaining to wisdom. In the more steadily abstract morality play, the awareness of the two planes of meaning is never entirely lost. It is interesting, however, to note that even in the morality play, some authors exhibited a tendency to treat the surface meaning so concretely that the abstract meaning is likely to be lost sight of. For instance, in the vulgarized morality, *Mankind,* the lack of sympathy with the virtues, the feebleness with which they are portrayed, and the gusto and realism of the depiction of the knaves must have made it very easy for an inn-yard audience to forget the moral lesson in their delight in the dramatic presentation of specific deviltries.

It is indeed difficult, in the case of the completely symbolic play as in the case of the incidentally symbolic play, to preserve a proper balance between the surface and the overhanging meaning. So, in Maeterlinck's symbolic drama, *The Blind,* the underlying meaning is only hinted at, not made directly manifest, and in his *Seven Princesses* the surface meaning is almost nil and the underlying meaning is hinted at rather than made manifest. Maeterlinck's only incidentally symbolical plays, *The Intruder* and *Interior,* are vastly more successful in their preservation of surface plausibility and in their suggestion of more than realistic values.

If we were to attempt to classify the themes and subjects dear to the symbolical dramatist, we should find that the themes tend to

[1] Yeats managed the symbolism more adroitly in *The Land of Heart's Desire,* which is and pretends to be no more than a fairy-play and is consequently written on a single, instead of a duplex plane of meaning.

be those to which in the course of experience human beings have tended to attach the greatest values. So, for instance, patriotism, religion, love, and, in a vaguer field, ethics and morality furnish the emotional-intellectual groundwork for most symbolic dramas. It is almost inevitable that this should be the case since the artist is likely to concern himself with subjects of almost universal human interest, because he himself is indubitably human and sees and feels more deeply than the common mortal the validity or unreality of human values. The values, of course, the genuinely creative artist will re-interpret in accordance with his own individual scheme of meanings. If he diverges too widely from themes of universal interest and significance, if his own symbolism is too arbitrary and too individual, he runs the risk of becoming not merely unintelligible but unimportant.

The dramatic symbolist, moreover, is handicapped in a way in which the poet or the novelist is not. His drama must submit itself to the conditions of actual presentation in the theater, and while both romanticism and realism impose their special obligations on the producer, the symbolist imposes an additional and peculiar burden. He requires the producer to create not merely the world of romance or the world of realism but a double world, one part of which may be sordid or picturesque but the other of which is inevitably abstract. So, in that curious blend of paint and canvas, light and human beings, which is stage-production, symbolism is likely to fare badly. As in play-writing, so in production, the world of appearance is likely to suffer in comparison with the world of inner reality, or the vision of the world of inner reality is likely to be lost in our preoccupation with the vividly realized concrete representation of surfaces. Both the conditions of creation and the conditions of production tend to make symbolism a minor though a baffling and intriguing form.

EXPRESSIONISM

Though the mode of drama to which German critics have given the name *expressionism* is likely to prove no more than an eddy in the current of dramatic history, it perhaps deserves brief analysis. The movement seems to have arisen as a kind of protest against the mutual exclusiveness of romanticism and realism. As its name suggests, it is an attempt to discover a technique and a method which will express what the dramatist conceives the inner reality of his drama to be, more perfectly and impressively than any of the older dramatic modes were capable of doing. Viewed broadly, it is another illustration of the tendency in the contemporary arts to permit or encourage a mixture of *genres* or modes distasteful to more formal periods of art and literature. It is a protest, on the one hand, against the sentimental unrealities of romanticism and, on the other, against the tendency of realism (or naturalism) to content itself with a scrupulous representation of the surfaces of life, the speech-habits, milieux, manners, emotions, and ideas of one or another class in society. To the expressionist, romanticism seems to substitute falsification for faithful interpretation of human experience; realism seems to miss the inner psychological realities through its preoccupation with the accurate reproduction of surfaces. More narrowly, expressionism reveals the influence on the drama of the contemporary preoccupation with the rich and complex, conscious and subconscious experience of modern personalities, and at the same time it betrays the impatience of dramatist and producer with the limitations of late nineteenth-century naturalistic staging, and an eagerness to exploit to the full the tremendous resources of modern theatrical mechanics and lighting, and to project through vigorously imaginative means the philosophical or psychical concepts of an experimental drama.

Expressionism encourages the freest possible handling of styles or tones or technical means. In the same play we are likely to find sudden and sometimes inexplicable shifts from verse to prose, from objective realism to highly subjective monologue, from conventional realistic dialogue to monosyllabic or telegraphic utterance. Since the emphasis is on the essential experiences of individuals or masses, there is in expressionistic drama a tendency to simplify plot, to minimize objective action, lest attention be diverted from the major issues. In Elmer Rice's *The Adding Machine* or Eugene O'Neill's *The Hairy Ape,* the actual sequence of occurrences is devoid of what we have called complication. Moreover, the effect of consecutive action is minimized by the representation of the high points of the plot in abrupt scenes which seem adaptations of the technique of the modern moving picture. In Andreyev's *The Life of Man,* which may be regarded as a kind of precursor of expressionism, the schematization of an average man's career has an essential simplicity which the elaborateness of the detailed treatment tends to conceal, and in Georg Kaiser's expressionistic trilogy, *Gas,* there is little actual complication but, instead, a heightening of the rather simple situation through mass-effects and adroit tricks of lighting and crowd-movement. To emphasize the general significance of the themes developed, characters are likely to be represented as types in order to minimize individuality and to emphasize typicality. The conviction that the machine age has ironed out individual differences undoubtedly accounts for the representation of character in the simplest and most abstract terms. Sometimes, as in *The Adding Machine,* subordinate characters do not have names but numbers; again, the unreality of characters is suggested, as in *The Hairy Ape,* by their wearing masks and jittering in doll-like or puppet-like movements. In Kaiser's *From Morn to Midnight* the profoundly conventional nature of some of the characters is indicated by their repetition of the most banal sentiments or observations, a kind of meaningless reiteration of the completely hackneyed. Expressionistic dialogue approaches, especially in the hands of Georg Kaiser, a sort of telegraphic tone and style, apparently intended to give the impression that everything except the absolute essentials of human speech has been pared away. The sentence disappears, and phrases or iterated words serve for communication. There has been, likewise, a reëmergence of the monologue, which is obviously of great assistance in projecting subconscious or semi-conscious material, but the expressionistic monologue is more broken, incoherent, and illogical than the traditional monologue.

But it is perhaps on the element of setting that expressionism has had the strongest influence. Here, too, there is a tendency to minimize setting until it shall indicate only the absolute essentials of form and feature. A room may be indicated by a chair or two, a hippodrome by the corner of the judges' stand. The strain that the rapid succession of scenes imposes upon even the complex mechanisms of continental stages explains a part of this simplification, but, at least from the playwright's point of view, such simplification would seem to be an attempt by omission to stress the essential, or to give the play the atmosphere of abstraction. In addition, the desire of the expressionistic playwright to objectify as tellingly as possible complex psychological states, particularly of an abnormal sort, has driven him to utilize stage-devices, akin in their super-rationality to the devices of romantic staging, but dependent on the elaborate mechanical resources of the modern theater for realization. For instance, various mechanisms for projecting whirling figures or forms on screens have been utilized in Rice's *The Adding Machine* and Kaiser's *From Morn to Midnight* to indicate the distorted mental processes of characters suffering great mental confusion and distress.

The best that can be said for expressionism is that it has helped to break down the rather artificial boundaries between dramatic types and genres. It has encouraged experimentation, not so much with material as with form. It has freed the dramatist from the rather hampering limitations of pure romanticism or pure realism. But much of the experimentation has been thoroughly unsuccessful. In Germany, where expressionism has flourished most vigorously, most of the plays written under its influence are no longer interesting except as dramatic curiosities.

In general, it may probably be said with justice that while expressionistic drama has furnished some admirable and powerful technical effects, the expressionistic dramatists have not found material fresh or significant enough to justify their experimentation with strange or grotesque forms. Usually the ideas which these dramatists attempt to convey expressionistically have already been treated effectively in the older recognized forms. Along with other evidences of simplification, the intellectual content of the expressionistic drama is often simplified to such an extent as hardly to justify the elaboration of the technical means of projection. Furthermore, the minimization of the elements of characterization and plot narrows the appeal of the expressionistic drama not only for the ordinary theater-goer but for the serious student of the drama and the theater.

PART III

DRAMATIC TECHNIQUE

CHAPTER XI

SUBSTANCE AND FORM

Every work of art has two indispensable elements: substance and form. Although certain æstheticians contend that these elements are, in any individual work of art, inseparable, it is possible theoretically to distinguish between them, and to evaluate them separately. Certainly, it is reasonable to maintain that Shakespeare's *Antony and Cleopatra* and Dryden's *All for Love* dramatize the same subject, despite the significant differences in their forms, just as Euripides' *Hippolytus* and Racine's *Phèdre* both present, with whatever noteworthy distinctions, the story of the guilty love of Phædra for her stepson Hippolytus.

The link between subject and form is technique. That is to say, technique is the art and craft by which substance is given a certain form. Since a literary work is a work of art, whatever its perfection or mediocrity, it is therefore a piece of craftsmanship, and the craftsmanship is technique.

Technique is the whole body of means and devices to which a writer has recourse in order to objectify his subject in the form of a work of art. Certain elements in dramatic technique are universal; they are means and devices common to playwrights of all ages. The technique of representing action through characters by pantomime or by speech is the very essence of the drama, and in the main the basic technical resources of the playwright have not increased tremendously since the dawn of dramatic art. But there are also elements of technique that are not universal but local—means and devices originated by a particular age or culture and broadly characteristic of all or most of the playwrights influenced by that culture. Certain playwrights, moreover, have originated bits of technique which may be called individual. But the drama is so imitative an art that, even when we can distinguish the originator of a particular technical device, we usually find that it has been adopted widely by the contemporaries and successors of the originator.

It is extraordinarily easy for the modern student of the drama to exaggerate the importance of the study of technique, since there has probably never been a period in the history of the drama when so much attention has been given to it. Such an over-emphasis on the study of technique has the unfortunate effect of encouraging in the student of the drama (whether as spectator or playwright) the conviction that technique is the most important element in the drama, and that he need give little or no attention to any other element. The fallacy in this conviction is the elementary one of confusing means and ends. The technique by which the playwright achieves his end, the satisfying and impressive treatment of his subject, is of the very greatest interest, but that interest is only incidental to the nature of the effect that he has created, and the values, implicit or explicit, in that effect. To exalt technique above all the other elements that contribute to our pleasure or illumination is to confuse technical with veritably æsthetic considerations.

The study of technique, to be sure, has its values: it can reveal to us, sometimes in amazing detail, the way in which a playwright secured a particular or a total effect; it may serve as an highly important guide in rationalizing the spectator's judgment of the work with which he is confronted; but the study of technique should not be permitted to usurp the place of a broadly æsthetic consideration of the art of the drama. Of distinctly greater importance than a study of the technique of a play is the consideration of its subject, the form that it has achieved through the use of a particular technique, and the values that arise from the happy union of subject and form.

The Choice of a Subject

Logically, it is true that the playwright is perfectly free to choose and to treat any subject he chooses in dramatic form; practically, it is to be observed that there are both moral and æsthetic limitations on the subjects available for dramatic treatment. Of these limitations, the moral are of far less consequence than the æsthetic, though historically, the former must be taken into consideration. Most students of the history of the drama and most serious playgoers have come to believe in the desirability of the complete freedom of the playwright to choose his subject without the censorship of contemporary morality. But this belief in the desirability of complete freedom of choice in dramatic material is but a part of the hard-won battle for intellectual and moral toleration, and it would be absurd to insist that the battle is yet over. Especially in a definitely socialized art like the drama, prejudice, fear, ignorance, and prudishness are likely at any moment to interfere with at least the performance of a drama that affronts some vocal section of the community. In European countries, such censorship, whether formal or informal, is likely to find its source in hostility to certain political or economic ideas. At the moment, dramas applauding the virtues of the bourgeoisie fail to reach audiences in Soviet Russia; in Italy under Mussolini, democratic and libertarian literature is sharply repressed. In countries in which the Catholic Church is powerful, censorship is likely to be of a theological or moralistic nature. In Anglo-Saxon countries, suffering from the unenlightened impulses of a degenerate Puritan tradition, the censorship is almost inevitably on the ground of sexual morality.[1]

But, despite these irrational sporadic efforts to censor drama on political or moral grounds, most serious æstheticians are fully convinced that no moral censorship should be inflicted upon the serious dramatist. All that the contemporary student feels justified in insisting on is that the theme, whatever it is, should be treated seriously. This demand for seriousness is not to be identified with an insistence that all themes should be treated tragically. It is simply the demand that a theme, whether given tragic, comic, or tragicomic treatment, should not have a merely sensual or prurient appeal. For the open-minded student, the problem of discrimination between the merely prurient and the serious treatment is not a difficult one to make, and unless he allows himself and the playwright a freedom as unlimited as that we have suggested, he will find himself in a position that is æsthetically untenable.

It is an insufficiently recognized fact that many of the greatest tragedies have dealt with subjects that are traditionally repellent to normal people. The most notable instance is perhaps *Œdipus Rex*. This is, of course, one of the most horrible stories ever dramatized, and yet the treatment given the theme by Sophocles is so serious, so powerful that there has never been any question as to the moral acceptability of the play. Perhaps, some light on the general acceptance of such themes in the serious drama is thrown by the psycho-analytical theory that one of the values of dramas that present anti-social emotions is that the drama objectifies similar unconscious elements in the minds of the audience, cleanses the bosom of its perilous stuff, or acts, in Aristotle's metaphor, as a cathartic.

A similar case may be made out for comedies that contain gross or morally shocking elements. The representation of such elements on the stage, from Aristophanes to the current Palais Royal farce, may be said to have its justification in its objectifying of the sensual or anti-social impulses of the audience. The mechanism of identification makes it possible for the audience to appreciate and enjoy, at almost the same moment, the plight or pleasure of lover

[1] Examples of Puritanic censorship are the enforced withdrawal of Bourdet's *The Captive* in New York, and the prohibition of performances of O'Neill's *Strange Interlude* in Boston. An example of political censorship is the banning (1932) of the Russian film, *Ten Days that Shook the World,* by the chief of police of Provincetown, Massachusetts, a summer colony notorious for its Greenwich Village morality.

and mistress, of deceiving wife or deceived husband. Moreover, since the audience never quite loses consciousness of the abyss between life and drama, it is possible for it to "enjoy" situations in drama which it would be immoral to enjoy or condone in real life.

But, as we have said, the æsthetic limitations upon the playwright's choice of a subject are of much greater significance than the moral limitations. For it is his painful, if fascinating task, to give appropriate form to the subject that he has chosen, and, in consequence, awareness of the limitations of the form will enter into the problem of his choice of a subject.

It is obvious, for instance, that the form of the novel (however staid or experimental) and the form of the drama impose different limitations upon the artist's choice of a subject. It is unquestionable that certain subjects lend themselves to more effective treatment in the novelistic than in the dramatic form. For instance, a subject involving a prolonged process of development or deterioration of character is better suited to the leisureliness of the novel than to the compression of the drama. It *is* possible to represent on the stage the changes that a long period of time brings to the bodies and characters of a group of persons, but, except in very loosely constructed dramas, such a representation is not likely to be very convincing. There are also spatial elements involved in some subjects that discourage their treatment in dramatic form. The Elizabethan stage, to be sure, took its geographical obligations lightly, but both the classical and the modern theater fail to give the playwright an inexhaustible range of scenes and climes. Furthermore, a theme involving a meticulous and microscopic representation of milieu is, in the main, better suited to treatment in the novel than in the drama since the limits on the kind and the amount of detail that can be communicated by means of setting in the theater are very strict.

Yet, despite the fact that there may be moral and that there are inevitable æsthetic limitations on the playwright's choice of a subject, the amazing resourcefulness of dramatists and their skill in overcoming apparently insuperable obstacles has brought it about that no important subject, no important human experience or emotion has been denied treatment on the stage, from the most violent of external events, the rise and fall of nations and dynasties, the world adventures of a picaresque hero, to the quietest of analytical or psychological dramas.

The Statement of the Theme

In the transformation of a dimly seen and diffusely imagined subject into a complete and integrated drama, an almost inevitable preliminary step is the focusing of the subject in the *theme*. The theme is the idea that gives the drama unity, that furnishes the dramatist's controlling purpose, that determines for him what is relevant and what is irrelevant to his purpose. The playwright is perfectly free to decide whether his statement of the theme to the audience shall be explicit or implicit but, unless he is able to conceive of his subject as a theme, he will run the risk of violating that impression of unity of subject, which is, when all is said and done, of infinitely greater importance to the success of his work than unity of time, place, or action.

From the point of view of the audience, however, there is a certain risk in the dramatist's making the statement of the theme too explicit, the risk of obviousness and over-simplification. Writers of social drama, dramatists with a passion for reform, are particularly likely to err in this direction. If they are veritably serious, if they are persuaded of the importance of what they have to preach, it is natural that they should feel that the theme cannot be stated too explicitly, too emphatically. But though a round and telling enunciation of the theme may, at first encounter, strike the audience a body-blow, the play with a directly stated message is likely, upon further acquaintance, to seem to be a Sunday-school fable rather than either representation or transmutation of life. If the playwright concerns himself with his message too exclusively, the play is likely to seem an over-simplification of life, or, at the worst, the reduction of life to an almost geometrical demonstration of a formula. Such is the case with many of the plays of Paul Hervieu, notably *The Torch-Race,* and *Know Thyself,* plays which, despite their enviable clarity and force, represent characters and conduct not in complexity but in specious though logical simplicity.

If we turn to dramas which have interested and attracted audiences for centuries, we shall find that it is not often very easy to state the theme satisfactorily in perfectly simple language. To be sure, the lines

> Vaulting ambition which o'erleaps itself
> And falls on the other. . .

might be judged to be a sufficiently explicit statement of the theme of *Macbeth,* but the theme of neither *Hamlet* nor *Antony and Cleopatra* can be stated simply, without falsification. To designate the theme of *Hamlet* as the revenge of Hamlet is to disregard most of the elements that make the play not merely a revenge tragedy, but one of the most complex dramas of all time. What Shakespeare would seem to be doing is to attempt to dramatize the whole of Hamlet's relationship to life, and not merely a single facet of it.

And in *Lear* and *Antony and Cleopatra,* a critic would be rash who insisted that one motif rather than another is the major one; these plays are dramatic symphonies rather than dramatic ballads. Dryden's title for his dramatization of the story of Antony and Cleopatra, *All for Love, or the World Well Lost,* is a sufficiently clear statement of his theme; it is also a clue to the impression of tidy simplicity that distinguishes his play from the lavish complexities of Shakespeare's.

The Choice of a Form

Whether the playwright indicates his theme implicitly or explicitly, he must decide which of a variety of dramatic forms he shall use, in order to give the most telling and appropriate expression to his subject. In early periods in the history of the drama, the decision seems to have been made for him. At least, in appearance, the writer of Greek tragedy had no choice; the form was given, and, if there was no reason why he should not modify that form or invent one of his own, convention and tradition were against him, and consequently his task was, not that of deciding which of a variety of forms he should choose, but how most effectively he could pour his subject into the mould set by tradition and convention. To be sure, even in this rather inflexible form, a rebellious playwright like Euripides was able to make considerable modifications.

Since the period of the English Renaissance, which witnessed the development of a technique that usually violated the unities of time, place, and action, writers of tragedy have had at least two major forms from which to choose. But, again, unless one was a particularly vigorous individual, like Ben Jonson for example, he was likely to follow the mode prevalent at the moment. The power of such an accepted and admired mode is apparent in the history of French tragedy during most of the seventeenth and eighteenth centuries. The domination of French classicism, which was far more restrictive than Greek classicism, was so complete that no major dramatist had the courage to depart very widely from the form given him by the taste and judgment of the age.

The evolution of modern tragedy has, in turn, offered the playwright a form which is a kind of compromise between the classical and the Elizabethan forms of tragedy. On the one hand, although modern tragedy does not always or even frequently adhere exactly to the three unities, it tends to limit the number of distinct milieux to no more than three or four; it is likewise built up into a series of acts that resemble the episodes of classical tragedy more closely than the scattered scenes of Elizabethan tragedy. Moreover while modern tragedy does not limit itself to the paucity of personages characteristic of classical tragedy, it eschews the multiplicity of supernumeraries encountered in Elizabethan drama. Modern tragedy, then, tends to be a freer form than the classical, a stricter form than the Elizabethan.

The Choice of a Mode

But the major difference between modern and earlier forms of tragedy is a difference in tone, arising from the dramatic modes, classical, romantic, and realistic. Of almost equal importance as the dramatic form into which the playwright moulds his subject is the feeling-tone with which he attempts to invest his treatment of the subject. This tone, to be sure, is in some respects closely related to the form which he chooses, but it is also dependent in part upon the playwright's personal response to the subject, in part upon the taste of the time, and in part upon that view of life held by the dramatist, which is sometimes implicit, sometimes explicit, in his rendition of the theme. It is obvious that the same material for drama, the same plot, may be regarded romantically or cynically, tragically or comically, seriously or trivially. The same theme may be used to illustrate, through one treatment, the capacity for heroism and beauty in human nature, and in another treatment, the capacity for evil and ugliness.

Any great storehouse of legend will furnish familiar instances of the varieties of effect that can be wrought out of the same basic material. The materials furnished by classical antiquity, for instance, have been seen differently by every successive creative age. Every genuine movement in creative art involves a re-valuation of some or all of the significant bodies of material furnished by the past. Thus the material of classical antiquity has been submitted to authentically classical treatment by the ancients themselves, to realistic treatment in Chaucer's *Troilus and Criseyde* and Jonson's *Sejanus* and *Catiline,* to cynical treatment in Shakespeare's *Troilus and Cressida,* to neo-classical treatment by Racine, Corneille, and Voltaire, and to romantic treatment by Goethe and Keats. The possibilities are tremendous, and the playwright, especially the modern playwright, must be as fastidious in his decision as to the tone with which he invests his subject as he is in the selection of the form most appropriate to his subject-matter.

We have discussed the major dramatic forms—tragedy, comedy, melodrama, and farce. We have sketched the chief periods in the history of the drama. We have attempted to distinguish the characteristics and values of the modes of drama—classical, romantic, realistic, sentimental, symbolic, and expressionistic. In the following pages, we shall attempt a consideration of the problems of technique—plot, characterization, dialogue, and setting.

CHAPTER XII

PLOT

Plot is that element in the technique of the drama which imparts form to the action represented. It is, therefore, imperative that we consider the major problems that confront the dramatist in his attempt to shape his material into that form that we call plot.

The distinction between plotless and plotted narrative is really a simple one. In the plotless narrative, events are related to each other only through the fact of their occurrence in consecutive time. The formula for plotless narrative is—this happened, and then something else happened, and then something else happened, and so on. The plotted narrative is one in which a number of events occur, not only in temporal but in logical sequence. The formula for plotted narrative is thus—this event occurred, and, therefore, this event occurred, and therefore this event occurred. It should not be inferred that the plotless narrative is incapable of arousing interest, but the interest that such a narrative can arouse is different from that stimulated by narrative with plot. The interest aroused by narrative-without-plot is an interest in separate events; if these events involve the same character, as in the picaresque novel, there may be a certain cumulation of interest, although the omission of any one of the events would hardly be noticed. The problem faced by the writer of narrative-without-plot is, then, to arouse the reader's attention as much as possible in each event. In a sense, he must make a fresh start with each successive event, and he cannot count very heavily on the interest already aroused by the initiation, but already allayed by the conclusion, of a particular incident. The problem of the writer of narrative-with-plot, whether or not he uses the dramatic form, is primarily that of logical construction.[1] He must shape and modify the raw material of his story until it exhibits a logical sequence of relationships between events A, B, C, and D. Not only must he interest his audience in the separate events, but he must relate each of the events to the preceding and following

[1] It should perhaps be said that the logic in question is not the logic of abstract thought but the logic of human psychology. Logical action is motivated consecutive conduct. The nature of the motivation in a particular play will depend ultimately on the conception of human nature entertained by the author as that conception is modified by the conception of human nature common to the age in which he lives.

events so that we shall regard the plot-structure, when finally revealed in its entirety, as plausible and logical. But despite his heavier burden, he has an advantage over the writer of narrative-without-plot. For once interest is aroused in a logical sequence of events, that interest tends to become cumulative; the dramatist can count on a more or less steady rise of interest as the play moves to its crises, climax, and solution. In other words, in narrative-with-plot, interest takes on the added intensity of suspense, and the task of the dramatist, even more conspicuously than that of the novelist, is to arouse interest, to intensify suspense, and to sustain suspense until he is ready to allay it.

Plot may be said to be of more importance to the drama than to any of the other literary forms since drama is, as we have said, basically and fundamentally, the representation of action. And although Aristotle's dictum, that of the two elements, character and plot, plot is the one indispensable to drama, may seem at first sight untenable, a little consideration will persuade the objector that a drama without character is possible, but that a drama without action is impossible.

And the great æsthetician was equally sound, though more obvious, in his assertion that a play must have a beginning, a middle, and an end. At first thought, this dictum seems too obvious to deserve utterance, but unquestionably Aristotle was using these familiar terms with certain technical implications. Though every piece of narrative must start somewhere, go on, and ultimately stop, in a sense, narrative-without-plot may start anywhere, may or may not go on, and may stop whenever writer or audience is weary. But a play, the representation of a logical sequence of events, must obviously begin at some point in the logical sequence. It must then follow out the consequences arising from the initial action without omitting any action of vital importance to the sequence. And it must not stop without at least indicating the terminal consequences of the sequence of events initiated by the first events in the series. In a very real sense then, the problem of the beginning, the middle, and the end is an unavoidable one for the playwright.

The initial technical problem of the playwright is that of deciding at what point his play should begin. Having arranged the events of his play in logical sequence, he must decide with what event the play should open. It might be thought that the reasonable playwright would begin his play with the first event in his logical sequence of events, and it is true that a great many plays have such beginnings. But whether or not the playwright opens his play with a dramatization of the initial event in the logical sequence of his plot will depend not merely on his own taste and judgment, but on the technical conventions of his contemporaries, which in turn depend, in the long run, upon the type of theater available for the production of plays. For instance, the problem of beginning a Greek tragedy is an utterly different (and infinitely more difficult) one from that of beginning an Elizabethan tragedy, because the conventions of the tragic form of these periods vary widely, and because the Greek theater was, structurally, a different sort of place from the Elizabethan theater, and it was customary to use it differently. The problem of beginning a play was particularly acute to the Greek playwright, because the drama of his time was expected to conform to the principle of unity of time. However elastic the conception of time might be, however non-realistically time might be treated in the drama, nevertheless, it was an almost iron-bound convention of Greek tragedy that the action represented should be continuous. In the Elizabethan theater where no such principle as continuous action was maintained, where indeed the whole influence of the native tradition favored anything but unity of time in the representation of action, the playwright was free to begin his play with the first significant event in the logical sequence of the plot. In the Greek drama the action is initiated at a point much nearer the climax and catastrophe of the play than is usually the case in Elizabethan dramas.

Exposition

The problem of exposition, then, varies widely for classical and for romantic dramatists. For the former, there is frequently a great deal of preliminary action to be introduced, a great deal of information concerning the characters and their actions that must be communicated to the audience before the represented action can really get under way. For the romantic dramatist, at least if he were writing for a theater as flexible as the Elizabethan, the opportunity for him to begin with the first significant action in his series lifts from him the burden of introducing into the exposition a considerable amount of pre-history.

For the playwright of any period, the exposition offers a number of constant problems: he must catch the interest of the audience at the earliest possible moment; he must introduce the characters and elucidate their relationships; he must indicate the theme and problem of the play before very much time has elapsed. The exposition is a very real test of the playwright's ability to build a sound foundation for the dramatic structure he hopes to raise.

Writers of various periods or of various plays of the same period have taken the problem of arousing interest at the earliest possible moment with varying seriousness. Interest may be aroused in one of a number of ways—by a striking bit of action, by the appearance of a lively or alluring character, or by the adroit indication of an interesting atmosphere or setting. Of the first sort is the street fight that occupies most of the first scene of *Romeo and Juliet;* of the second sort is the apparition of the ghost within a few minutes after the opening of *Hamlet;* and a combination of the first and third devices to secure interest is the scene of the shipwreck that initiates the action of *The Tempest.* But not even Shakespeare was always fortunate enough to hit upon action or character or atmosphere that arouses immediately an interested response from the audience.

Exposition in Classical Drama

The Greeks were sometimes content to open their dramas with a dramatic monologue. This at its worst was a perfunctory summary of the events preceding the first represented action with which it was necessary for the audience to be acquainted. At best it could indicate the nature of the drama that was to follow, establish the atmosphere, suggest the conflict out of which the plot was to rise, and the lines which the conflict was likely to take. An excellent example of classical exposition is the opening soliloquy of Aphrodite in Euripides' *Hippolytus.* This splendidly poetic opening serves at one and the same time to introduce the audience to the elevated atmosphere of the world of gods and goddesses, to indicate the conflict between the affronted Aphrodite and Hippolytus (the devotee of Artemis), and to sketch the lines of action that are to result from this conflict.

It is interesting to contrast the exposition in Racine's *Phèdre* with that of Euripides' *Hippolytus.* In the opening scene of Racine's tragedy, three bids for interest are made: the question as to whether or not Theseus is dead or alive, raised by Hippolytus' announced intention of going to seek him; the problem of Hippolytus' love for his father's captive and enemy, Aricia; the apparently minor problem of the consequences of Phèdre's enmity to Hippolytus. Of these three problems, the first is solved before the end of the first act, the second turns out to be the initiation of the sub-plot of the drama, and the third, as we learn from the expository material in the second scene, is to furnish the major conflict and the disaster of the tragedy. An exposition of this type is certainly more "modern" than the dramatic monologue of Euripides, but it is a question whether it is more effective.

The problem of exposition was complicated for the Greek playwright when he found it desirable to keep back essential facts in the pre-history of the drama until a later stage of the drama than the exposition. In this case, it was necessary for him to arouse the interest of the audience at the beginning of the play, reveal the situation and characters in part, and introduce the essential bits of pre-history at the most effective points in the later development of the drama. Such a delayed exposition has its disadvantages; the pre-history, if only partly revealed, may not give the audience a sufficiently lucid account of past events, or the delayed exposition may seem dull, lifeless, and destructive of interest when at last it is revealed to the audience.

The supreme example of delayed exposition in classical drama, perhaps in the drama of all time, is Sophocles' *Œdipus Rex*. In a very real sense the exposition of pre-history in this play is not complete until the play is more than two-thirds over, and yet the play is one of the most perfectly constructed of all dramas. It is interesting to observe the simplicity of the early exposition and the means by which Sophocles made it possible to delay the presentation of essential facts until well along in the play. It opens with a scene of communal lamentation: Thebes has been direly smitten by a plague, and seeks relief from it. This situation in itself is one to stir interest and sympathetic emotions, especially as the terrible inroads of the plague are described in language of great vividness and power. The plague-smitten citizens have turned to their king as the most probable source of succor. In the opening lines of the play, Œdipus introduces himself, describes the plague-ridden city, and announces that he has sent his wife's kinsman, Creon, to the oracle at Delphi for the answer to the riddle of the kingdom's miseries. The return of Creon with a riddling oracle provokes from Œdipus the oath that he will use every means in his power to discover the man whose presence within the kingdom is the source of the plague. The play takes on then the interest of a detective story in which the audience's curiosity is aroused by the problem of the discovery and capture of the guilty person, and Œdipus' quest of the guilty man motivates the gathering and examining of witnesses who may have something to reveal of the pre-history of the case. Here again the audience is placed in a position of manifest superiority—it is given reason to suspect (as Œdipus is the last person to do) that Œdipus himself is the guilty man, and it watches with fascinated and helpless horror the king spinning the web that is to bring his own destruction.

Exposition in Elizabethan Drama

As we have already indicated, the problem of exposition did not bear so heavily upon playwrights of the romantic tradition as it did on playwrights of the classical mode. In fact, Elizabethan playwrights cannot be said to have taken the problem of exposition very seriously. Almost any kind of opening would serve to initiate the complicated series of events that the Elizabethan playwright was free to present before his audience. The least laborious type of exposition was the introduction of indispensable information through the speeches of minor characters of whom the playwright could create as many as he pleased and of whom he need make no use, once the exposition was out of the way.[2] This was, perhaps, a more obvious and less artistic method of exposition than the opening dramatic monologue. Shakespeare's *Richard III* offers perhaps as fine an example as the Elizabethan drama contains of this time-honored device. We are introduced immediately and vividly to the major character of the drama; we learn something of his personal appearance, history, and motives; we are given the needed facts about the situation in which his malignity is to operate.

But the Elizabethan playwright was not unaware of the necessity of attracting attention or arousing interest as early in the drama as possible. *Romeo and Juliet* furnishes an excellent example, in its opening street-brawl, of a scene that begins stirringly, builds up to a swift climax, creates atmosphere, and lays the preparation for the drama that is to follow. Perhaps the most subtle type of exposition to which the Elizabethans sometimes resorted was the opening scene calculated to indicate the atmosphere and tone of the play to follow. Superb illustrations of this device from the skilled hands of Shakespeare are the opening scenes of *Macbeth* and *Hamlet.*

Exposition Since the Renaissance

The eighteenth century contributed little to either the classical or the romantic handling of exposition, but the practitioners of the well-made play in the nineteenth century took this problem more seriously than the playwrights of any period before or since. Their preoccupation with this technical problem was only a part of their constant consideration of the more mechanical elements in the drama, and although some of the effects they achieved were unquestionably ingenious, to modern taste they seem over-elaborate and slightly silly. A convenient illustration of the exposition of the well-made play is the much admired opening of Sir Arthur Pinero's *The Second Mrs. Tanqueray.* Of this exposition no less popular a critic than Clayton Hamilton has said, "The first act of *The Second Mrs. Tanqueray* has never been surpassed in technical efficiency; and it stands as a monument of exposition that must be studied by

[2] For an instance of this type of exposition, see the opening scene of Shakespeare's *King Lear.* This type of exposition has been parodied once and for all in the opening scene of Sheridan's *Critic,* and yet it is the ancestor of the parlormaid-butler dialogue of many a "realistic" play.

all future playwrights." [3] And even William Archer (who should have read enough Ibsen to know better) defends the exposition in these words: "The technical manipulation of all this seems to me above reproach—dramatically effective and yet life-like in every detail . . . it is hyper-criticism that objects to an exposition so natural and probable as that of *The Second Mrs. Tanqueray* simply on the ground that certain characters are introduced for the purpose of conveying certain information." [4]

Let us see wherein the ingenuity of this brilliant exposition lies. In order to announce his marriage to Paula Jermyn, Aubrey Tanqueray gives a dinner in his apartment to three old friends. To make it possible for the audience to learn what it needs to know of the previous history of Mrs. Jermyn, Pinero allows Tanqueray, after the announcement of his impending marriage has been made, to excuse himself to his guests thus: "As we're going to turn out by-and-bye, let me scribble a couple of notes now while I think of them."

Was there ever a host, in or out of the drama, who seized the occasion of an engagement dinner to catch up with his correspondence? But Tanqueray's considerate withdrawal to a desk in a corner of the dining-room makes it possible for the guests to retail Paula's wretched past at the top of their voices and for Aubrey to throw in an apposite remark now and then. If this is technique, then the less we have of it the better. Fortunately the significant drama of the modern period has not found it necessary to resort to such obvious artifices as this.

On the whole, the modern drama has tended to simplify to the very furthest extent the process by which the pre-history of the play is presented. In audience and playwright alike, there has developed a great sensitivity to the artificiality of exposition in drama, and in consequence the emphasis now is on the least ostentatious and unelaborate means of conveying the necessary information to the audience. Indeed, in the more experimental dramas of the expressionists, there is an inclination to throw the burden of interpretation on the audience, to plunge it into the midst of a situation and to allow the audience to make what can be made of it.

Aside from the retrospective function of the exposition, it has another equally important function—that of laying the foundation for the developing plot. Structurally, it is absolutely necessary that the exposition should point the way to some interesting development that is to follow. Emotionally, it is absolutely necessary that

[3] *The Social Plays of Arthur Wing Pinero,* ed. by Clayton Hamilton (New York: E. P. Dutton and Company, Inc., 1917), I, 39.

[4] *Play-Making* (Boston: Small, Maynard & Company, 1912), pp. 121–122.

the interest aroused in the opening scenes should be quickened and deepened so that the line of emotion should be definitely rising at the end of the exposition.

Exposition and Interest

The question of the interest that can be aroused and stimulated in an audience is not a simple one; indeed, it embraces the whole relationship of the audience to the play. But, without analyzing in its entirety the nature of interest, it may be possible to point out the elements in the interest involved particularly in exposition. Although the feeling of interest is by no means the same for all plays, the interest aroused by exposition will usually be found to consist of four elements in various proportions: attentiveness in the broadest and vaguest sense, curiosity, suspense, and sympathetic or unsympathetic feeling. As we have already said, it is enormously important that the playwright should catch the attention of the audience at the very beginning of the play, and this feat may be accomplished, as we have seen, by a variety of devices. But since attention is extremely difficult to hold unless it is supplemented by strong motives, most playwrights attempt to reinforce the immediate attention by an appeal to a more persistent feeling. Of these feelings, curiosity is perhaps the one that is likely to put in an appearance early in the exposition of a well-built play. Curiosity, in fact, is one of the strongest forward-looking feelings on which the playwright can count.

Exposition and the Problem of the Play

Curiosity, like the attention attracted by the very opening of a play, may in its turn be stimulated in a variety of ways. It is usually stimulated by the appearance of a problem early in the piece. The problem may be extremely simple, even hackneyed, but it is usually present. It is frequently the problem of the results of the relationship between two or more of the major persons of the plays; the relationship of this sort most certain of arousing curiosity is the love-relationship. But the love-relationship is only one of dozens of problems in relationship that may arouse curiosity. Those playwrights and æstheticians who believe that the essence of drama is conflict, attempt to find in every play some basic conflict the progress of which the plot dramatizes. The conflict may be that of rival suitors for the hand of the heroine, or of rival claimants for a throne; it may be a subjective conflict within the complex nature of the hero, a conflict between love and one's duty to one's father, as in Corneille's *Cid;* or between love of woman and love of country, as in Corneille's *Horace*. The problem may have the nature of the protagonist's quest of a particular objective: a lady, a crown, reputation, fortune, and so on. In the more philosophical drama, it may be a study of the consequences of an act, whether hasty or premeditated. Thus Marlowe's *Dr. Faustus* shows little evidence of being a drama of conflict or a drama of a goal passionately desired and sought; it is rather the drama of the consequences of an act, in this case thoughtfully and rationally performed. In the case of *Lear,* although there are elements of conflict, the play (from the point of view of the King, in whom the audience is chiefly interested) is largely a representation of the consequences of Lear's rash and selfish decision to divide his kingdom.

But whether the problem is that of attainment of a goal, of conflict between opposing forces, without or within, or of the consequences of an act, it is the function of the exposition to indicate clearly the problem with which the play is to deal. In the simpler forms of drama, the conflict may be indicated early in the play, and with considerable directness. In Plautus' *The Haunted House,* for instance, we are first shown the hero's spendthrift conduct. Then, upon the news of the father's unexpected return, the problem of how he is to escape the consequences of his misbehavior is immediately presented. In Molière's *L'École des Maris* a problem of a rather subtler sort is suggested in the opening quarrel between the two brothers, in which their theories of female education are brought into sharp opposition. Curiosity is immediately aroused as to which of the theories is to work out satisfactorily for the brother who maintains it, and the rest of the play shows the results of the application of the theories that have been expounded to us.

Even in the serious drama of modern times, the curiosity-arousing problem is often of a very simple sort. In Galsworthy's *Loyalties,* the problem stated at almost the beginning of the play is not the real problem of the play, as indeed the title suggests. The first problem presented in this play concerns the theft of De Levis' money, a question of a type that could be paralleled in thousands of mystery plays. But it is to be noticed that, for certain characters in the play, this problem is solved before the end of the first act. De Levis himself, on not very good evidence, and two of Dancy's friends, on better evidence, come to the conclusion that Dancy is the guilty man. It then becomes apparent that Galsworthy's interest is not in who is the guilty man, but how the various characters with their degrees of knowledge and their class and racial sympathies will react to the problem raised by the theft. This larger social problem is the one in which Galsworthy himself is interested, as his title suggests almost too obviously and as one of his characters points out near the climax of the play.

But in dramas with any depth or persistency of appeal, it is not enough that the exposition should attract attention and arouse curiosity, however indispensable these appeals must be. The exposition must also excite feeling, either sympathetic or hostile for some or other of the major characters concerned. In dramas of any real consequence, the feelings aroused are sometimes of almost incredible complexity, but even in plays of an elementary nature, they are present. In melodrama, for instance, where the appeal to curiosity is very important, there is an unabashed attempt to arouse sympathy for the purity and sweetness of the harassed heroine and the manliness, decency, and courage of the hero, and hostility to the machinations of the complete villain. But these distinct, black and white responses are only caricatures of the subtle feelings of sympathy, pity, concern, compassion, admiration, repulsion, anger, and detestation, over which the practised playwright has command.

It is out of this complex web of emotions that suspense arises, suspense that means the pointing forward of emotion and the sustaining of interest until the problem of the play is solved. Suspense may be taken, in this connection, to mean curiosity supplemented by feeling, positive or negative. As in the case of curiosity, it may be of an elementary or a complicated sort. The suspense may be as simple as the anxiety as to whether the pure heroine will escape the clutches of the villain; it may be as complex as the concern as to whether or not Hamlet will succeed in his task of revenge; it may be as subjective as the concern as to whether or not a character racked by conflict will end in integration or disintegration. But in all plays that succeed in holding the attention of the audience, suspense is an inevitable element.

Foreshadowing

A not unimportant function of the exposition is what has been called *foreshadowing*. The term *foreshadowing,* as a special aspect of exposition, may be said to concern, not the larger issues of plot, characterization, and mood, but specific instances of objects, elements, or motifs that are essential to the subsequent development and dénouement of the piece. In the slang of the contemporary theater, such foreshadowing is called "planting." Very frequently in dramas intricate of plot, a considerable number of objects, circumstances, or motifs are required for the complication and solution of the problem of the play. These objects and circumstances must be "planted" definitely but not too obtrusively in the early part of the play so that they will be ready when they are needed. In plays built on the mystery story model, these instances of foreshadowing involve the clues, false or sound, which in the long run will be necessary to an intelligible and plausible solution of the problem. In dramas less plot-ridden than mystery plays, foreshadowing is likewise necessary. In Brieux's *The Red Robe,* for instance, the dramatist takes pains, fairly early in the play, to fix the audience's attention for a moment on the paper-knife which, in the play's dénouement, is to do such damage to the villain of the piece. In Sidney Howard's *The Silver Cord,* it is necessary to indicate the presence of a pond near the house where the action takes place, in order that it may be available for the attempted drowning that precipitates the dénouement of the play. The function of foreshadowing may even be considered to include the stressing of semi-prophetic ideas or concepts that the development of the play is to corroborate. For instance, the remark of Desdemona's father to Othello, "She has deceived her father, and may thee," is a device of ominous foreshadowing. Greek tragedy, in particular, is rich in such prophetic warnings. Foreshadowing, then, may furnish a basis for some specific turn of the developing plot; it may provide the basis for some ideational or emotional development; it may include the indicating of the thesis idea, as in George Kelly's *Craig's Wife,* which the play is intended to illustrate. But foreshadowing of whatever sort is one of the devices by which an effect of coherence may be given to the structure of the developing drama.

Complication

That portion of a play that Aristotle designated as the middle is perhaps the least easily distinguishable portion of the play, but it is an essential portion. It is that portion of the play devoted to the development of the elements that have been presented to the audience in the exposition. Structurally, the elements essential to the development of a plot are complication and crisis; in some forms of the drama, the climax may also fall within the limits of the development of the play; in others, it is delayed until it becomes a part of the dénouement.[5] Both elements, complication and crisis,

[5] The notion that the climax, the turning-point in the protagonist's fortunes, is to be sought somewhere in the middle of the play is due in large measure to the influence of Freytag's *Technique of the Drama.* Freytag found that a considerable number of Shakespearian tragedies could be described in terms of an isosceles triangle, resting upon its base, with the exposition represented by a portion of one of the sides of the triangle, the climax or turning-point by the apex of the triangle, and the dénouement by the side opposite the expository side. From this analogy come the common conceptions of the action as rising or falling. For instance, in *Macbeth,* his swelling fortune is the rising action, the failure to kill Banquo's son is the climax, the turning-point in the action, and his declining fortunes occupy the rest of the play. A similar analysis, perhaps, might be made of *Othello,* but *Hamlet* and *Lear* fit into this scheme with difficulty, and Freytag's schematization is profoundly inappropriate to many classical dramas and to most modern ones.

are essential; climax is not. Complication is a basic element in plot structure; in the simpler forms of drama, it consists in the introduction of persons or events that delay the arrival of the hero at his goal or that intensify the conflict between opposing forces; it may involve the introduction from the pre-history of hitherto unexpected elements. In the simple love plot, the complication may take the form of a rival, of parental opposition, or of one of those misunderstandings (objective or subjective) to which lovers in drama (and life) seem particularly prone. It is true of drama, even more conspicuously than it is of life, that the course of true love never does run smooth; if it did, there would be no drama. Even in so serious a comedy as Rostand's *Cyrano de Bergerac,* the complications are not of a very subtle sort. The major complication is the length of Cyrano's nose, on which comedy, even pathos, but certainly not tragedy, can be made to depend. The further complication, Christian, one of the stupidest of romantic heroes, would be an utterly insignificant obstacle to the resourceful Cyrano if he had not discovered to his distress that Roxane loves the booby. The conflict, then, becomes a subjective one, between Cyrano's love for Roxane and his desire for her happiness. But not content with this complication of the relationship between Cyrano and Roxane, Rostand felt it necessary to invent another rival for Roxane's favors, De Guiche, a painfully stagey figure, who, however, motivates the marriage that is brought about with Cyrano's assistance, the departure for battle that ends with Christian's death, and Cyrano's self-administered oath of secrecy.

In dramas of a more serious type, the complications are likely to be both subjective and objective in nature. In Galsworthy's *Loyalties,* a complication of the objective sort is the discovery by Dancy's friends that his coat-sleeve is wet with rain, evidence that he is guilty of the crime with which he is charged. A further complication as the play moves to its climax in the black-balling of De Levis by the club which he aspires to join, is the discovery of the stolen notes in the hands of the persons to whom Dancy has given them. But these objective complications would have comparatively little meaning, if they were not given weight by the feeling aroused by them. In the first instance, De Levis' discovery that he has been black-balled angers him so deeply that he breaks his promise not to reveal his suspicions about Dancy. The discovery of the notes causes Dancy's lawyer to give up his case, at the moment when it seemed to be progressing toward a judgment favorable to Dancy.

In a purely subjective drama like Ibsen's *Rosmersholm,* the complications naturally are of a very different sort from those in a play of external plot and action. The play begins apparently very close to the point where a satisfactory relationship between Rosmer and Rebecca West is to be established. The complications that arise and that ultimately bring both hero and heroine to suicide are events and ideas and emotions in the pre-history of these characters, not apparent at the opening of the play, which, as they are brought to light in the unfolding of the past, make it more and more certain that this alliance which seemed promising must end in disaster.

Along with the complication that is necessary to the development of the plot, there must also be an increasing and deepening of interest, curiosity, and suspense. This effect is an almost inevitable accompaniment of the complications we have been considering; it is, in a way, the audience's contribution to these events, the repercussions of these complications upon the feelings and emotions of the audience.

Crises

It will usually be found that the development of the play is such that it produces a series of foci for emotions, which we may call crises. These crises are situations usually involving a clash of interests and emotions and a number of possible reactions to the specific situation. Such a crisis, even though it is a minor one, involves like the exposition the attraction of interest, the deepening of suspense, and an increase in the number and variety of the emotions felt by the characters and shared by the audience.

Take, for instance, the scene of Othello's appearance before the Senate in answer to the complaint of Desdemona's father. The marriage has already taken place, but the audience has had no opportunity to observe the emotions evoked by this occasion in the persons most involved. Brabantio's complaint concerning Othello's behavior makes evident the complex emotions aroused in him by this distasteful event. Then Shakespeare seizes the occasion to permit Othello to trace with natural pride and great dignity his own history and the history of his courtship, and thus to sketch in his own character and that of Desdemona. But even this elaboration of the emotions incidental to this crisis is not enough. Desdemona must speak for herself, and, with assurance and courage and modesty, she reveals her love for Othello, for which she has been willing to sacrifice her father's love and defy convention. This is, of course, only a minor crisis in the play, but it illustrates sufficiently the contribution of a minor crisis to the development of character and the intensification and complication of emotions.

Another aspect of the technique of both minor and major crises in drama is the effective exploitation of the crisis. The playwright who has learned the principles of æsthetic economy will see to it that he gets and that his audience will get, the maximum possible effect out of each crisis as it develops and wanes. To skimp his treatment, to hurry over even a scene of minor crisis, is to fail to exploit fully the potentialities of the situation and the characters. To this end, there is observable in the skilful handling of almost every sizable crisis, a definite building up of incident and the emotions each incident produces in each beholder or participant, a definite heightening of the tension on the stage and in the audience. But none of the characters concerned gives all his effective responses at once; just as in the larger structure of the play there is a constant bidding for suspense, so, in the gradual revealing of incident and feeling and emotion, there will be seen to rise a carefully and efficiently wrought structure of incident on the objective and of feeling on the subjective side.

There is need, however, for discretion in this matter; a situation held too long is more fatal to the interest of the audience than a scene hurried over and unexploited. Probably the need for discretion is greater in comedy than in tragedy, for it is perhaps easier to sustain increasingly painful and sympathetic emotions than purely pleasant and diverting emotions. Certainly, the writer of comedy, no less than the writer of tragedy, must know when to stop. If the tragic writer persists too long, his audience is likely to react in self-defense against what comes to seem an exaggeration and extremity of painful emotion. If the comic writer persists too long, he risks the chance of being tedious, and tediousness is the unpardonable sin in the comic playwright. Probably, the best examples of minor crises too long sustained can be found in comedy written in periods when audiences had not lost the power to laugh endlessly over the simplest and most obvious of jokes. Plautus, who was writing for an audience with a modest degree of sophistication, errs again and again in this respect. In scene after scene of *The Haunted House,* for instance, the modern reader feels that Plautus is attempting to get far more out of the situation than it really contains. The sixteenth-century comedy, *Ralph Roister Doister,* modelled closely on Roman comedy, errs in the same direction. The cowardice and vanity of Ralph are illustrated in over-elaborate scenes that drive the point home again and again and again. So, somewhere between under-statement and over-elaboration, the playwright in comedy or tragedy must aim to get the maximum effect out of the situation that he has constructed.

Climax

As we have indicated, the climax of the play may come within the portion of the plot that we have called the development or within the final portion of the play, the dénouement. The climax is best regarded as the crisis of maximum emotion and tension.[6] It is the scene in the drama after which there is a tendency for the emotion to abate to the despair or the happiness of the finale. Structurally, it may also be the turning-point of the drama—in tragedy, the point at which the protagonist first catches sight of his inevitable but unwillingly accepted defeat; in comedy, the scene in which the protagonist begins to have reason to hope for his ultimate success. Since the climax in tragedy is likely to be the point where the fortunes of the hero turn from their favorable to their unfavorable aspect, it is usual to find it earlier in the structure of tragedy than in comedy. For, in tragedy, as we shall see, the dramatist has the difficult task of persuading us that the catastrophe is inevitable, that disaster could not be escaped. If the disaster comes too precipitately, we shall feel that it is as incredible as the cluttered and hurried happy endings of some comedies. The comic playwright, on the other hand, is likely to postpone the climax, the hero's sighting of success, until very late in the play; otherwise, since the affairs at stake are usually of less consequence than those in tragedy, the audience tends to lose interest in the hero's fortune very soon after he is assured of his ultimate success.

It would, then, be a mistake to assume that in every play of every sort there is a turning-point or climax in the middle of the play, as Freytag's *Technique of the Drama* has encouraged generations of docile teachers and students to believe. Sometimes, indeed, the turning-point is hardly a moment of conscious climax. In *Macbeth,* for instance, we can see, as we think back over the structure of the play, that Macbeth's failure to kill Banquo's son Fleance is the incident that leads ultimately to his own downfall. But surely neither audience nor reader will feel this scene to be the climax of the play. If the climax scene occurs near the middle of this play, it would seem rather to be the banquet scene, in which the appearance of Banquo's ghost sends Macbeth into a fit of insane terror. In Galworthy's *Loyalties* the turning-point and the climax are almost coincident. Our curiosity in this play is focused chiefly on whether

[6] The trial scene in *The Merchant of Venice,* the revelation of Magda's past in Sudermann's *Heimat,* the appearance of Captain Ardale in *The Second Mrs. Tanqueray,* the scene of the cross-examination in Jones's *Mrs. Dane's Defense,* and the disputation scene in *Candida* (close to the dénouement of that play) are examples of climax scenes cited by Richard Burton. *How to See a Play* (New York: The Macmillan Company, 1914), p. 172.

or not Dancy will escape punishment for his crime. There seems a very real chance of his doing so, up to the point where the lawyer, confronted with certain evidence of his guilt, decides that professional ethics will force him to give up the case that Dancy had seemed to be on the point of winning. It is in this scene surely that the emotional tension of characters and audience is greatest; after this scene we are still curious as to Dancy's behavior when he learns that he is trapped; there is further complication through the efforts of his wife and his friends to help him escape; there is suspense as to Dancy's escape almost up to the last moment of the play. But the tension is surely less great, the emotions that accompany his disaster are less complex than those inspired by the exposition and developed to the point of greatest variety and subtlety in the scene in the lawyer's office.

In *King Lear,* the mad scenes on the stormy heath are surely the scenes of greatest emotional intensity and complexity; they are a world symphony of varied and terrifying emotions, but they hardly furnish the turning point of the plot, since in them Lear definitely loses his mind and from then on is buffeted unconsciously between hostile and friendly forces. Perhaps the turning-point of the plot is the quiet and unobtrusive scene in which the audience learns that Cordelia is planning to come to the rescue of the mad King.

But, wherever the climax may be felt to be, whether it falls within the development or the dénouement, the playwright is under the necessity of constantly or almost constantly (since it may be desirable to furnish intervals for the relaxation of tension) building up interest, tensity, suspense, and more and more deeply sympathetic and anti-pathetic emotions, until his play is well nigh done. In the cruder forms of drama, this effect may be wrought by greater and greater complication of incident; in drama of the psychological variety the effect is that of multiplying and intensifying the emotions of the characters, and, by reflection, those of the audience.

Dénouement

The particular function of that portion of the plot we designate as the dénouement is that of solving the problem which the plot initiated and developed. A satisfactory solution or dénouement in whatever type of drama will be found to have certain characteristics: clarity, plausibility, and interest. The first of these characteristics would seem to be the easiest of attainment, but it offers its own particular difficulties. It is obvious that the playwright must not consciously leave his audience in doubt as to the outcome of the problem he has dramatized. On the other hand, he must not indicate too early in the dénouement the precise nature of the solution; if he is too immediately clear, he will sacrifice the interest of his audience. Something, of course, depends upon the nature of the solution in a particular play; in older forms of the drama, the ending was usually specifically tragic or specifically comic. But even among the Greeks, the term *tragedy* was applied to all plays of a serious nature, and *comedy* to plays, whether fantastic, satirical, or realistic, of a light and amusing nature. So, among the works of the Greek tragic writers, we find classified as tragedies plays which end happily, at least for the protagonists; of this type of tragedy, Æschylus' *Œdipus at Colonnus* and Euripides' *Iphigenia in Tauris* are notable examples. It is obvious that in such plays we have prototypes of what the Renaissance came to call *tragicomedy*.

The solutions of these various sorts of plays present to the playwright a variety of problems involving plot structure, characterization, motivation, and interest. In tragedy, the chief requirement perhaps is that the catastrophe should seem to have come about as a result of a series of external and subjective events the sequence of which is logical and credible. This "inevitability" is in part a matter of time, in part a matter of situation, but more especially a matter of character. The clash of elements within the hero himself, the conflict between his interests and those of his opponents must seem to explain and justify his final defeat. The death of Hamlet is an excellent case in point. He dies as a result of a wound received in a duel with Laertes, a duel that, it would seem, might have ended as easily in victory as in defeat and death for Hamlet. But throughout the play, there has been a steady accumulation of tragic emotion, of motivation on the part of Hamlet's opponents, the King and Laertes, and of motivation within Hamlet himself, which makes his death in the moment of his success seem particularly appropriate and "inevitable."

Of course, not all violent conclusions in tragedy can be made to seem plausible. Many minor playwrights eager for a definite and thrilling conclusion to their plays have slaughtered their heroes unceremoniously. In such instances, the audience is likely to feel that the disaster has been wilfully contrived by the playwright, that it is improperly motivated, and the dignity and significance of the play suffer accordingly. The conclusion of the play with the suicide of the hero or heroine furnishes especial difficulties. Whether or not one regards suicide, in the abstract, as an act of cowardice or an act of courage, in tragedy it must be made to seem not only inevitable but admirable. The inevitability must rise out of one's sense that there was no other possible solution of the hero's difficulties, since the character of the particular hero would allow of no other conclusion. Such appropriateness, such inevitability, one feels in the suicides of Antony and Cleopatra, in both Shakespeare's version of their history and in Dryden's *All for Love*. In Shakespeare's very considerably greater success in making complex characters of this superb pair of lovers are to be found the greater meaning and poignancy of their suicides. To these colossi, anything less than suicide would seem ignominious; in Dryden's Cleopatra, the wanton is so conspicuous that one doubts the appropriateness of her heroic ending.

In modern drama, suicide has all too frequently been an easy way out of the dilemma the dramatist has created for himself. Even with the lessening of the Christian onus upon suicide in modern times, suicide on the stage must be made convincing and intelligible, even though in life it may not often be so. An excellent illustration of the difference between a convincing and an unconvincing suicide may be found among the plays of Sir Arthur Pinero. Paula Tanqueray's suicide is an example of theatrical effectiveness; Zoe Blundell's, of truly dramatic effectiveness. The difference is almost entirely a matter of characterization. There has been nothing indicated in the character or situation of Paula to prepare us for this violent and sudden act of self-destruction. In the case of Zoe, the grounds for her self-destruction have been carefully prepared from the beginning; there has been built up in her a sense of her own defeat, hatred and disgust with herself and her intimates, and an unalloyed bitterness which, we feel, make so desperate an act intelligible.

Dénouement in Comedy

The comic playwright has his own problems of dénouement to solve. If he takes his work seriously, he must not meet more than half way the eagerness of the audience for a happy termination of the hero's difficulties; if he does, he will run the risk of sentimentality, of sacrificing the logic of the situation or character to the too tender feelings of himself or his audience. There must be, as in tragedy, a feeling that the conclusion fits the facts of situation or of character as we have come to know them in the drama or in life. The playwright who takes this problem casually will forfeit something of the respect of his audience, something of the enduring interest his play might have excited. To be sure, the problem is not so acute as that of the tragedian since the audience is more than willing to grant credence to almost any device that will bring the hero safely to his goal.

Especially when the happy ending requires the conversion of one of the major characters, must the playwright pay particular attention to the preparations in character and motivation for the eleventh-hour transformation. The audience, in this as in other respects connected with comedy, is willing to do more than its share, but it is within its rights to insist that the conversion shall not take place merely in response to the exigencies of the plot. For instance, the conversion almost at the end of Plautus' *The Haunted House* is only moderately successful. One can grant only partial credence to the transformation of a stern and angry father into an indulgent and forgiving parent as the result of one brief scene between the father and the erring son's emissary, even though the emissary takes on here, as he does not elsewhere in the play, his most ingratiating appearance and manner. A particular formula of conversion which may be designated by the phrase, the triumph of the worm that turns, is of particular assistance to the writer of comedy. An audience's sympathy can almost certainly be counted on to flow out to the persecuted and abused character who, at long last, proves to be more successful and more efficient than his oppressors. This is certainly one of the elements, among many others, in the perennial appeal of the Cinderella story, an appeal particularly alluring to sentimentalists. An instance of an unabashed use of this formula is Sir James Barrie's *A Kiss for Cinderella,* where the pathetic self-sacrificing heroine escapes death, and finds the fulfilment of her dreams in the form of a handsome and agreeable policeman. But the theme and its appeal take on a hundred disguises. There is a suggestion of it in Orlando, the oppressed brother in Shakespeare's *As You Like It,* and it is noteworthy that in Shakespeare's development of the theme he transforms the wicked brother, in one of the most preposterous conversion scenes in all dramatic literature. The turning of a royal worm is exhibited in so undramatic and intellectual a piece as Shaw's *The Apple Cart.* George Kelly's *Craig's Wife* furnishes a striking example of the use of this formula; here, the transformation of a cowed and circumvented husband into a rebellious and dominant male is brought about with a rather implausible rapidity and completeness, but there is at least theatrical effectiveness in the climax (and incidentally, the turning-point) of the play, when, at the end of the second act, the husband rather childishly smashes a favorite shelf-ornament of his wife's.[7]

Dénouement in Tragicomedy

The writer of tragicomedy faces problems in the treatment of the dénouement that his colleagues, content with simpler solutions,

[7] A considerable collection might rather easily be made of climaxes marked by the smashing of bric-a-brac. Such plays as Noel Coward's *Easy Virtue* and *Private Lives,* Rose Franken's *Another Language,* and D'Annunzio's *Gioconda* will furnish convenient examples.

avoid. One of the major difficulties is that of tone; a play that seems through most of its course, to be heading for tragedy is brought around to a happy conclusion only with difficulty. In periods of the drama less technically self-conscious than our own, this effect could be managed without too great a strain on the credulity of the audience. But it is significant that even Shakespeare at the height of his powers could not make thoroughly acceptable the strained and contrived "happy" endings of *Measure for Measure* and *All's Well that Ends Well.* In the former play, in particular, one's moral sensibilities are painfully violated by the off-hand disposal of the saintly heroine to an utterly unworthy suitor. Even *The Merchant of Venice,* if seen from the Elizabethan point of view, is much more successful. To the Elizabethan, Shylock was a grotesque, that is, a horrifying but somehow diverting villain. If Shylock were played on the modern stage in this manner instead of as a heartbroken gentleman financier, the punishment of Shylock would seem appropriate, and the moonlit romance of the ring-plot in the final act, unblemished loveliness. In drama of the early Stuart period, when the excitement of novel and striking plots frequently took the place of sound motivation, forced happy endings are frequent. One of the most notorious is that of Beaumont and Fletcher's *A King and No King.* Throughout the play, we are given what seems to be a dramatic study of incest, in this case, the incestuous love of a brother and sister. In the dénouement, we learn that the major characters were not actually brother and sister, in fact, shared no blood relationship. This surprise ending for a play directed definitely toward tragedy gives the audience a sense of being tricked and cheated of the tragic emotions for which it has been prepared.

Functions of Dénouement

A major function of the dénouement is what may be designated as dramatic recall. This device is the reverse of the process of foreshadowing which we have considered in connection with the functions of exposition. Dramatic recall points back to the objects, circumstances, or motifs which have been prepared for by the process of foreshadowing. A convenient example of dramatic recall is the fulfilment, one after the other, of the three prophecies as to Macbeth's fate which that hero had wrung from the witches in the third act of that play. A more subtle instance, less evidently a part of the plot-structure of the play is the recurrence at the very end of *Rosmersholm* of the symbolic figure of the white horses, with which that play had prophetically opened. Almost any play, if carefully studied, will furnish some instances of this particular effect. It has a peculiarly gratifying emotional result; it furnishes on the affective level instances of expectations gratified, and goals achieved, which the dénouement as a whole exhibits on the sides of plot and characterization. It frequently gives the audience an opportunity, self-congratulatorily to say, "I told you so," as it recalls its own alert seizings upon unobtrusive foreshadowings as probably significant. Like the device of foreshadowing, it is a not unimportant device of coherence, serving to tie up neatly ends of motifs that otherwise might seem untidy and frayed; it assists in making the play seem an efficient structural entity.

One other aspect of the dénouement needs brief consideration. A desirable feature of any satisfying dénouement is a feeling of completeness, of adequacy, arising from the contemplation of an appropriate conclusiveness. In comedy, this emotion is likely to be much simpler than it is in tragedy. In comedy, it is usually nothing more subtle than the warm pleasant glow induced by a more or less beatifically happy ending, or, in realistic comedy, a moral delight in that accurate distribution of rewards and punishment which art furnishes rather more frequently than life. The emotion of appropriate conclusiveness in tragedy is more complex. It was first indicated by Aristotle by the much discussed term *catharsis.* Whatever meaning Aristotle intended to attach to this rather unfortunate metaphor, it is true that most classical or romantic tragedies succeed in creating in connection with the catastrophe an emotion that is singularly agreeable and serene. The source of this emotion is not so easy to distinguish as the existence of the emotion itself. It is likely to be associated, curiously enough, with the death of the protagonist. If the audience has shared at all deeply in the sequence of emotions provoked by the hero's career, his death means, at the least, a termination of his sufferings, with the accompaniment of more or less alleviation. The alleviation may arise from the consciousness that at the worst the hero is beyond suffering, that, in the magnificent dying words of Hamlet, "The rest is silence." The alleviation may also arise from the perception that something at least of the hero's mission has been attained despite his death. More subtly, it may be projected from the hero's desperate serenity in the face of the worst that life can do to him. There is certainly a point beyond which further suffering is impossible. Once the hero and the audience reach this point, as in the finale of *Œdipus Rex,* a kind of stoical calm develops which promises serenity of a kind, even though it be the serenity of despair.

In certain plays, it is possible to study the mechanism of this ultimate emotion. In Euripides' *Hippolytus,* for example, a very effective example of this alleviating emotion is furnished by the appearance of Artemis, with her words of consolation to the tortured and dying hero, and her capacity to lessen the pain of the immediate circumstance by viewing it *sub specie æternitatis*. The use of the *deus ex machina* here does not involve a cutting of the threads of the problem created by the plot; instead, the goddess's mission is purely emotional and consolatory.

Many modern tragedies follow the models of ancient tragedy in their conclusiveness, but the modern drama has occasionally experimented with the indeterminate conclusion on the theory that life goes on indefinitely instead of coming to a standstill as the definitely conclusive drama implies. A trivial instance may be found in Noel Coward's *Hay Fever,* where the final curtain descends on this family of temperaments wrangling as they did at the beginning of the play, and as we are certain they will go on doing till the end of their days. A more subtle example of the indeterminate conclusion is the conclusion of Granville-Barker's *The Madras House,* where the curtain falls in the midst of the exceedingly well-bred argument between Philip and Jessica over the place of woman in modern society, for the very good reason that this argument is itself without end.

But an ending of the indeterminate type has its dangers, since most audiences feel that a work of dramatic art should be as definitely and distinctly cut off by a curtain from life, as a painting is by its frame.

CHAPTER XIII

CHARACTERIZATION

Aristotle's critical dictum that of the two elements, character and plot, plot is the indispensable element, raised a critical controversy over which gallons of ink have been spilt. Fortunately, it is not necessary for us to come to a definite conclusion as to the validity of this observation. But the raising of the question points, at any rate, to the obvious fact that the problem of characterization is one of the major technical problems forced upon the dramatist, even if it is not the major problem. And a moment's consideration of the elements of the art of telling a story, in or out of the dramatic form, will suggest the reasons for the importance of this problem. The outline of a story, a coherent sequence of events, may be so striking, so novel, that our curiosity and interest may be awakened by the barest summary of it. But such an interest is of only the most superficial sort. The summary of the plot of *Hamlet,* with no touches of characterization, might well attract us by the fullness, diversity, and violence of its incidents. But *Hamlet* becomes eternally absorbing, over and above our interest in what happens, through our tremendous preoccupation with the sort of persons involved in this particular sequence of events. So, in both life and art, while we may be struck at once by the novelty or strangeness of an incident, we are at once moved to inquire the sort of persons involved, and it is only when we have learned something of their nature that the incident begins to arouse a complex series of feelings and emotions and values that give the incident significance.

Before entering upon a consideration of the technique of dramatic characterization, we should make clear some of the practical limitations of characterization in the drama. In respect to characterization in particular, it is never safe to forget that the drama is not life, and that life is not drama. Since drama is a form of art, it always involves a process of selection, simplification, and abstraction from the raw materials that life or literature furnishes the artist. Therefore, we may expect to find in the drama a simplification and clarification of traits and motives which only highly analytical persons ever arrive at in their contemplation of real people.

For it is the duty of the dramatist to make his characters and their traits and motives so clear that they will be almost if not quite intelligible to an attentive audience. In life, although we are forced to arrive at some hypothesis as to the motivation of characters with whom we are closely associated, and although we are sometimes accurate in our diagnosis, yet we can never be perfectly sure of it as the playwright is perfectly sure of the traits and motives of his characters, since he has a means of access to the characters he has created which is denied us in even intimate relations with human beings.

By reason of the artist's process of simplification and clarification, we are likely to feel that we *know* certain characters in the drama better than we know persons with whom we have been closely associated in real life. In all probability, we know Hamlet's mother more intimately than we know our own. Certainly it is possible for us to know a completely rendered character like Falstaff better than we know ourselves. Moreover, since the drama is an art and not life, we should guard against the tendency to bring all the characters we encounter in the drama to the test of our conception of human nature and human conduct. We should never allow ourselves to echo Judge Brack's remark in *Hedda Gabler,* "People don't do such things." Very probably people in Judge Brack's set did not do such things, but Hedda, it turned out, did not behave exactly in accordance with the conventions of her set, because she was not a perfectly conventional woman. We must allow the playwright to represent and to interpret, according to the conventions of his time and in the light of his own psychological insight, any kind of human being, and we must attempt to understand such a human being and to measure his plausibility on the playwright's own terms. Such an open-mindedness is of the very essence of æsthetic development and education.

Type and Individual Characterization

Nor should we allow ourselves to be enslaved by the realistic dictum that all characters must be characterized as individuals. The number of type-characterizations in the drama is infinitely larger than the number of individual characterizations. Logically it is possible to conceive of a character that is completely a type, and not at all an individual, or of an individual that is in no respect a type. Practically, and artistically, such a complete severance of type and individual is incredible. In actual life, of course, every living organism is an individual, no matter how completely his individual nature may be submerged beneath the characteristics of the class or type to which he belongs. He may share most of the views, most of the feelings and attitudes, most of the habits of his type, and yet, there are elements in his physical and psychological entity which give him individual existence and separate identity.[1] Probably the farthest reach in the direction of the typical in characterization is the universalized type of the morality plays.[2] Everyman, Humanum Genus, and Mankind are in varying degrees universalized, but even here the dramatist is forced to give his typical figures some characteristics that are less than universal. Everyman, for instance, unlike every human being, is wealthy, worldly, sophisticated, self-centered, and forgetful of his religious obligations and responsibilities; certainly an audience witnessing a powerful production of *Everyman* is likely to see him in terms of the personality of the actor taking the part.[3] On a less abstract scale are the characters that represent classes. Dramatists have profited heavily from the attempt to distinguish the characteristics appropriate to a particular professional or social type. The merchant, the lawyer, the slave, the soldier, the parasite, the nurse—all these and many others are instances of convenient and credible type-characterizations. Indeed, in Roman comedy, as we have seen, the only characterization the dramatist attempted was type-characterization, and there seems to have been no sense of constraint in his limitation of characters to types already defined in the New Comedy of the Greeks. Interesting illustrations of skill in type-characterization in the early English drama exist in John Heywood's farce, *The Four PP's*. Here, the method of characterization, the dramatic monologue, shows an incomplete break from the technique of characterization in fiction; harks back, indeed, to the method of Chaucer in his *Prologue*. Yet, the fullness of the detail and the richness of the reflected experience succeed in convincing us that we are viewing, not a typical Pardoner, 'Pothecary, Pedlar, and Palmer, but fairly highly individualized examples of their particular trades and professions.

Types are, of course, of various sorts: professional, domestic,

[1] So telling a type-characterization as Sinclair Lewis' Babbitt could after all be distinguished by certain earmarks of individuality from Smith and Robinson and Jones. Indeed, having established Babbitt successfully as a national type, Lewis was driven, by the necessity of action, to show Babbitt emerging from his typical nature and habits, developing a lively dissatisfaction with them, in other words, in becoming far more individualized than he seemed on first acquaintance.

[2] Professor W. Roy Mackenzie, in his *English Morality Play* (Boston: Ginn and Company, 1914) has distinguished between personified abstractions and universalized types. Of the former sort, are Mercy, Charity, Backbiting, Corrupt Collusion, etc. Certainly, in some of these instances, one can be said to have "character" in only a superficial and mechanical sense.

[3] An interesting illustration of the tendency of the type-character to take on individual characteristics may be found in the sixteenth-century morality play, *Mankind,* where the evil characters, New Guise, Nowadays, and Nought (figures which indeed would seem to be beyond anyone's powers to characterize even as types) are not abstract types at all, but contemporary realistic knaves with a vulgarity and earthiness that is repellent but theatrically effective.

national, and social. Most types have had an amazing vitality in the history of the drama. For many types a direct line of descent can be traced from New Greek Comedy to the present day. The "heavy" and the indulgent father, the prostitute with a heart of gold, the witty and resourceful servant, the good-natured hero, sowing his wild oats—all these and others are instances of the vitality of types and of the persistence of a dramatic tradition through Roman comedy, the classical comedy of Jonson, Restoration comedy, the satirical comedy of Sheridan, and the social comedy of the end of the nineteenth century.[4]

On the other hand, certain types are of a more immediate and limited significance. Such social types as the parasite, the boastful soldier, the procurer and the procuress, the slave-girls of Greek and Roman comedy tend to disappear from the drama as they disappeared from the actual life from which the dramatist drew his material. But convention is so strong in the drama that frequently a type survived long after it had disappeared from real life, or after real life had exposed its implausibility. There seems to be almost undying vitality in the stage-types of the Jew, the Irishman, the Swede, the Scotchman, the Negro, and the Yankee. Generations after the public has come to realize the inadequacy of the representation, it will get a certain amount of amusement from the caricature of its own or other nationals to which it has become accustomed in the theater.

As one moves away from the universalized type through the national or professional type, he approaches the realm of individual characterization. But even here, there remains some element of the typical. Logically, the completely individualized character would be unique, and therefore unintelligible, since he would have nothing in common with any sort of recognizable person. So it is, that, in even highly individualized characterization, the character is, at least in some aspects of his character, typical. Even such individualized characters as Hamlet and Falstaff have some of the traits of certain familiar Renaissance types. In one aspect of his nature, Hamlet is the "melancholy malcontent." In one aspect of Falstaff's nature, he is the braggart soldier; in another, the alehouse jester; in still another, the parasite. What we call individual

[4] The persistence of such types is clearly demonstrated by an actor's description of conditions in late nineteenth-century English stock companies. "In a full company of actors there was always to be found a representative for every particular style of character in the plays—'the leading man,' 'the heavy man,' 'the first old man,' 'the juvenile tragedian,' 'the low comedian,' 'the walking gentleman,' 'the leading lady,' 'the juvenile lady,' 'the first old woman,' 'the chamber-maid or *soubrette*' etc. etc." Frank Archer, *How to Write a Good Play* (London. Sampson Low, Marston, 1892), p. 121.

characterization is really a unique combination of recognizable, because typical, qualities. It is this sense of a hitherto unencountered combination of elements that are in their disparate state recognizable, that gives the effect of uniqueness to preëminently successful characterization.

Very few realistic playwrights have succeeded in individualizing all their characters. Even Ibsen, one of the greatest artists in realistic characterization, fell back on easily available types for some of his minor characterizations, though, at his best, he achieves, as in *The Wild Duck,* highly individualized characterizations for all the major personages, and most of the minor, and, in some of his plays, like *Hedda Gabler* and *John Gabriel Borkman,* where he is less prodigal of incidental figures, all the characters may be said to be individual creations.

In most plays of almost any period, some of the characters are not characterized at all. In drama of the classical type, where the personages are few, the dramatist usually attempts to indicate at least the major elements in each of the main persons of the drama, though in the neo-classical drama it is utterly impossible to distinguish between one shadowy confidant and another. In dramas of the romantic type, where the technique encouraged or necessitated the introduction of figures not only of secondary importance, but of fourth or fifth-rate importance, there is an inevitably descending scale of characterization. Four or five of the major characters will be depicted with some care, a half dozen others will be the merest type-sketches, and the rest will be walking ladies and gentlemen to whom at most a name and a few lines of indistinguishable blank verse will be assigned. Whatever they contribute to the drama, it is not characterization.

But, despite the limitations in the responsibility of the playwright in the matter of characterization, it remains an inevitable and persistent problem. Yet, just as there are in life ways of discovering and understanding character, so the dramatist is able to borrow from life one or another of the methods by which we come to know the natures of the persons with whom we are concerned.

Characterization by Appearance

Chronologically, in most instances, the first material that is available for the understanding and interpretation of character is personal appearance. Even the first sight of a person furnishes the observant individual a great deal of material for consideration and analysis. For good and all, we bring to the observation of new acquaintances a formidable apparatus of assumptions as to the significance of physique in terms of character. Size, form, build, posture, grossness of form, or emaciation are our first notations, and a more careful scrutiny will reveal details of feature and gesture that may almost immediately repel or attract us, or at least keep our curiosity alive. The shape of the nose, the clearness of the eye, the condition of the coiffure, the teeth and mouth, the shape and care of the hands—all furnish more or less dependable guides to the nature of the individual. And almost a part of the physique of the individual are his clothes, and their richness or poverty, their extravagance or tastelessness, their neatness or shabbiness, enter immediately into our consciousness and furnish material for interpretation and analysis.

The dramatist, in particular, cannot afford to neglect this significant element in characterization, and a glance at almost any drama will furnish illustrations of the importance of this means of characterization.[5] It is obvious that this method of characterization has distinctly different values for the novelist and the dramatist, respectively. At first sight, it would seem that this method is more suitable to the medium of prose-fiction than to that of the drama. For the novelist can, and sometimes does, take all the time he needs to describe in the greatest detail the physical appearance, the gestures, and the clothes of his characters. The historical novels of Scott are rich in illustrations of this method. But there is a distinct limitation to its effectiveness. As Lessing demonstrated in his epoch-making study of æsthetics, *Laocoön,* certain methods are more appropriate to one medium than to another, and although the art of description, especially in modern literary prose, has been carried to a very high point of skill and charm, elaborate and detailed description is likely to defeat its own end since it imposes on the reader the necessity of visualizing every detail and of combining all the details into an intelligible composition. This task is rendered the more difficult, inasmuch as the novelist is forced to give us one detail after another in point of time and cannot, like the sculptor or the dramatist, give us a total impression and a considerable number of details at a glance. The writer or the reader of the unacted drama is, of course, no better off than the novelist or his reader; indeed, he can almost be said to be worse off, since it is a convention of the drama that elaborate descriptions of the *dramatis personæ* are out of place in stage directions. But the author of an acted drama has an opportunity to profit by this method that is closed to the novelist. For the figures of the dramatist's imagination are embodied in living actors, and even though they may fall far short of being exactly what the creator of the characters

[5] Nice historical and æsthetic problems have been raised by the Queen's remark that Hamlet is fat and scant of breath.

had imagined, they give an immediate and vivid impression that is of the greatest assistance in stamping a figure on the imagination and memory of the audience.[6] And at the beck and call of the dramatist are not only the familiar plasticity of the actor's temperament, but all the resources, various in various ages, of the costume-designer and the make-up box. So, although the importance of the physical element in characterization has varied tremendously from age to age, and, indeed, from dramatist to dramatist, it is a resource that neither the dramatist nor the producer can entirely neglect.

One may hazard the generalization that the physical element in characterization is of little or no importance in classical drama. One gets, to be sure, an impression of physical grandeur from the personages of Greek tragedy, but this effect is due to psychological rather than to physical elements. In the comedies of an Elizabethan classicist like Ben Jonson, there is a wealth of physical notations, but Shakespeare and the other Elizabethan romantics furnish little in the way of descriptive detail. Even so essential an element as Othello's color has been a matter of critical disagreement. But Cleopatra was tawny, Portia's locks hung on her shoulders like a golden fleece, and Rosalind was just as high as Orlando's heart. It is, however, with modern realism that this method of characterization has come into its own in drama. So far indeed did naturalism go in its microscopic notation that there has been a sharp veering away from highly individualistic detail in the work of an expressionist like Georg Kaiser.[7]

Characterization by Speech

A method of characterization closely allied to physical description is speech, since it involves an organ of utterance as well as something uttered.[8] Though, in actual life, the voice or the impression of the voice will be of importance according to the subtlety of the observer, perhaps no part of the physical equipment of personality is so significant for characterization as the voice, quite apart from what the voice says. The depth, range, size, volume, the nasal or throaty, the thin or rich quality of the voice has enormous significance for dramatist and audience alike. Both novelist

[6] The most telling illustration of the divergence between characters as shaped by the author's imagination and characters as distorted by embodiment in conventional actors and actresses is Pirandello's *Six Characters in Search of an Author,* an experimental drama that furnishes dozens of illustrations of dramatic and theatrical technique and of the abyss that lies between the drama and life.

[7] See, in particular, his *Gas* trilogy, in which the central figures are no more detailed than the Billionaire, the Billionaire's Son, and the Billionaire Worker.

[8] We shall consider dialogue as a separate technical element later, but its significance for characterization necessitates mention of it here.

and dramatist can indicate the qualities of the voices they have imagined, but the dramatist, if he is lucky, will find actors and actresses with voices that enhance his imagined utterances.

But, beyond the physical qualities of the voice, is the significance of what the voice utters. Of this method, the novelist and the dramatist are equally free. Both can endow their mannikins, if they have the power, with characteristic telling utterances. Through the language chosen, the freshness or sterility of the phrasing, the degree of cultural elevation, the refinement or vulgarity, the range and brilliance of the figures, many of the intellectual and emotional attributes of the characters can be suggested. Wit, stupidity, crassness or sensitiveness, the prosaic or the imaginative—impressions of all these qualities come to us through the words put into the mouths of characters by novelist or dramatist.

Speech can furnish, then, a variously trustworthy guide to an understanding of the character we would learn to know. The primary critical consideration, perhaps, is whether or not the speech *is* characteristic, whether or not the language, the ideas, the feelings indicated are those which we can associate plausibly with the characters as otherwise indicated. Another question that criticism of speech must raise is that of the reliability of the utterance. Does the character express himself honestly or hypocritically? Can one believe what the character says of himself and of others? The novelist may indicate the reliability of a remark or a habit of speech by a comment approximating a stage direction. The dramatist, like the novelist, may imbed in the speech itself some hint of irony or hypocrisy; he may indicate the nature of the remark by an aside or a stage direction. But the dramatist, while he must rely upon the actor to carry out his intention, can trust experienced actors to achieve an effectiveness that the novelist's stage directions can never give.

Characterization by Opinion

Only less important than what the character says is what the other characters say about him. Here again, art has adapted a familiar technique of actual social intercourse. In our understanding and judgment of a newly encountered individual, we are constantly in the habit of checking the conclusions based upon our impressions of the individual's appearance and speech with the conclusions of other persons more familiar with the object of our interest. The process involves, of course, weighing the evidence offered on the ground of the reliability of the witness. If he is unobservant, malicious, conventional or sentimental, the weight we give his observation will be correspondingly lessened. If, on the other hand, he is shrewd, subtle, worldly, and tolerant, we shall endeavor to make our judgment coincide with his.

No dramatist can afford to neglect this method of characterization, for, if skilfully used, it will go perhaps as far as any technical method can go, in giving us a rounded impression of the character by furnishing a social atmosphere with its approvals and disapprobations, and by creating a world of personality values through which the figure moves successfully or unsuccessfully. The most elaborate use of this technique that comes to mind is to be found in *Hamlet.* Certainly one of the reasons why Hamlet seems perhaps the most complex and complete of Shakespeare's characterizations is the fact that Shakespeare has taken pains, sometimes at the cost of slowing up the development of the plot, to show us Hamlet in isolated and distinct relationship with all the major figures of the play, and some of the minor. The lucid soul of Horatio furnishes perhaps the clearest mirror for the reflection of Hamlet's most attractive side, but Claudius, Gertrude, and Ophelia, in their comments upon him and reactions to him, offer innumerable clues to his many-sided nature. One of the most elaborate instances of Shakespeare's use of this device is Polonius' consciously assumed and conscientiously pursued intention of plumbing the secret of Hamlet's behavior, and, if his well-meant efforts avail little in the elucidation of Hamlet's mystery, they have a tremendous import for the not unenigmatical character of the professional observer, himself. No less significant is Hamlet's sportive impatience with the doting counselor and his jestful stimulation of the latter's imagination. Even such colorless figures as Rosencrantz and Guildenstern, dull and unethical and bawdy University students, give us a view, however mean and distorted, of Prince Hamlet. With the possible exception of Lear, no other character in Shakespeare is illuminated from so many and so diverse points of view. Unquestionably, this is one of the reasons why Hamlet is perhaps the greatest piece of characterization in all dramatic literature.

Characterization by Thoughts

To the novelist is available a means of characterization that, in the main, is denied the dramatist, namely, the revelation of character through the thoughts of the person concerned. The degree, of course, to which the novelist exerts his privilege of taking off the lid and looking into the minds of his characters will depend upon the degree of objectivity or subjectivity that he adopts for the telling of his story. Like most dramatists, he may deny himself the taking of this unfair advantage of the characters that he has created. But, by and large, novelists have not been able to resist the temptation to use the directest road to knowledge of their creations by letting us behold their most secret and intricate mental processes, processes of which in even the modern psychoanalytical novel, the character himself may not be entirely aware.

But the dramatist has not always been able to resist the utilization of this important device of characterization. In the highly conventional neo-classical drama of the seventeenth and eighteenth centuries, dramatist after dramatist had recourse to the somewhat preposterous expedient of supplying each of his major characters with a confidant to whom the hero might unburden himself. The confidant's lot was certainly not a happy one. He was not permitted to have personality or emotions or opinions of a marked or individual sort. At worst and at best, he was an animated confessional, an almost passive recipient of the unburdened ideas and emotions of the figure to whom he was attached. He was condemned not only to listen interminably and unperturbedly but also to take no part in an action that was obviously inclined in a tragic direction.[9]

But the confidant is not the only technical device by which dramatists have found it possible to utilize the rich psychological material of thought and feeling. More economical devices than the confidant are the aside and the soliloquy. Under the influence of the realistic movement, both these technical devices have fallen into disrepute, but the temporary contempt that has been visited upon them is not altogether deserved in the light of their ancient and honorable history.

The Aside

The aside has been a more important element in the history of comedy than of serious drama, probably because it was one of the most obvious means of emphasizing the element of incongruity, which is so significant for most comic effects. The aside is an almost too easy device for revealing directly and immediately to the audience the discrepancy between what the character says and what he feels, between the appearance of courage and the actuality of cowardice, between the innocence of the announced intention and the malice of the actual purpose. The comedies of Plautus are to our taste over-ridden with this device, but its antiquity is but a

[9] It is worth observing, perhaps, that to a certain extent the chorus of Greek tragedy fulfilled the function of a confidant. Here, too, the exigencies of the situation and the convention prevented the chorus' taking part in the action, even when acting on the information imparted to them might have prevented disaster.

circumstance to its vitality, since it has thriven in almost all types of comedy and is still one of the devices surest to arouse laughter in vaudeville sketches or revue skits.

To us, the objections to the aside are more obvious than its advantages. With our insistence that at least in modern drama the action and the dialogue shall be, within limits, an exact representation of the surfaces of life as we know it, there is no place for a momentary interruption of the illusion that we are innocently eavesdropping on a conversation conducted as conversations are conducted in real life. Such an interruption of the conscious give-and-take of talk seems to us crude and unwarrantable. We expect our dramatists to use more subtle means of conveying to us their characters' inner mental and emotional life. But it may very well be argued that the demands of realism are excessive, and that, since the drama is art and not life, and since it is, accordingly, permeated with conventions, the convention of the aside should be accepted, not only theoretically but practically. If the dramatist uses it effectively, the argument against its illogicality or its unreality is entirely beside the point.

The Soliloquy

The soliloquy is a dramatic device for the revelation of character to which more serious attention must be given. Logically and practically, it is a speaking aloud of the character's feelings and ideas, an objectification of intimate and personal psychological material. The source in life of this convenient device is obvious, since what has come to be called in recent times the "interior monologue," the stream of consciousness in which observation, perception, sensation, feeling, emotions, and ideas are all involved, is an omnipresent phenomenon in the experience of any normally self-observant person. The soliloquy, then, is merely a conventional device by which the dramatist utilizes the material of this aspect of experience. The plausibility of it is considerably increased by the phenomenon of "thinking out loud," a habit common enough not to be regarded as psychopathic.

Once the device had been hit upon, its utility was obvious. It is the directest, the most unhampered method of placing the audience in immediate rapport with the character's opinion of himself and others, his interpretation of the preceding action, and his intention with regard to future action. It brings us as close to the heart of a character as it is possible for the dramatist to get. Nor is the device less convenient in other functions. The soliloquy in classical tragedy was frequently used at the beginning of a piece as a prologue, to refresh the memories of the audience as to the circumstances of the story to be revealed, to indicate, sometimes with considerable distinctness, the lines of the ensuing action, and to establish a mood and tone. In classical comedy, the opening soliloquy has something of the nature of a prologue, and something less of the nature of the true soliloquy. Unlike the opening soliloquy in tragedy, the prologue in comedy may be spoken by a personage, hardly at all connected with the ensuing action. His ingratiating addresses to the audience and his gratuitous summaries of the drama to be revealed suggest a degradation in the sensibility of the audience of which the history of the theater supplies other evidence. Even in this crude utilization of the soliloquy-prologue, the *raison d'être* is apparent: to establish a friendly relation between audience and play; to enlighten the audience, if in need of enlightenment; and to serve, in a manner of speaking, as the unprinted program of the piece to be witnessed. The frequent utilization of the soliloquy in the drama of the English Renaissance is one of the many evidences of the classical influence on that romantic period. Here again there is a slight confusion between the opening soliloquy spoken usually by a figure traditionally and somewhat absurdly called the Chorus and the veritable soliloquy which reveals the nature and intent of a major personage. Within the structure of the drama itself, playwrights of the English Renaissance utilized the soliloquy to expose an emotional crisis or a process of weighing plans of action or motives before embarking upon one or another potential enterprise. Such is obviously the case with a number of the most famous of all soliloquies, those of Hamlet. The soliloquy beginning "To be or not to be" debates the pressing problem of suicide; the soliloquy occasioned by Hamlet's catching the King at prayer debates whether or not it will serve his purpose to murder the King under such circumstances. In other situations, the soliloquy is a means of self-analysis, self-estimation, or reproach, which adds immeasurably to our knowledge of Hamlet's complex nature. Indeed, the contribution of the soliloquies to the complication of Hamlet's character can be tested crudely by reading the play without the soliloquies. Neo-classical French tragedy avoided, as we have seen, the unreality of the soliloquy by the device of the confidant. In plays written under some semblance of the romantic tradition, the soliloquy is to be found in even quite recent times. A noteworthy soliloquy in French romantic drama is that of Charles V at the tomb of Charlemagne in Hugo's *Hernani.* It does, to be sure, prepare the way for a decision on Charles' part significant for the dénouement of the drama, but it is somewhat too rich in poetic and historical ornamentation to impress English readers, as it does, traditionally, the French.

The realistic movement in the drama has been markedly hostile to so unrealistic a technical device as the soliloquy, and in the serious drama since Ibsen the soliloquy is an infrequent occurrence. Its place is sometimes taken by a passage of pantomime which goes a little distance in suggesting the psychological subtleties of which the soliloquy is capable. Enough perhaps has been said to explain the appearance of the soliloquy as a device of characterization, and to suggest its potentialities in the way of psychological notations, of emotional stresses and strains, and of intellectual elevation and beauty.

The tremendous psychological riches which modern science has revealed to contemporary playwrights have tempted a number of them to revert to devices similar to, or identical with, the aside and the soliloquy. The most striking example familiar to American readers is Eugene O'Neill's *Strange Interlude* which with some over-elaborateness but with great effectiveness utilizes this ancient device with some traditional and some modern effects. German Expressionists as well, in their attempt to stage the essential reality behind the mask of appearances, have reverted to the soliloquy as a medium for setting forth most private feelings and attitudes. Note for instance the soliloquy which composes the third scene of Kaiser's *From Morn to Midnight,* where the absconding cashier speaks with a poetic and imaginative intensity alien to his customary habits of expression.

Characterization by Action

Since the essence of the drama is the representation of action, in drama, whether of a serious or trivial sort, one of the major modes of characterization is action itself. For, in life as in art, what a person does or does not do, his behavior in and out of crisis, and the exactness or inexactness with which he achieves his objectives, have undeniable significance in terms of character.

The particular problem involved in exhibiting character through action (a problem utterly different from that of what action can be successfully exhibited on the stage or what action should be exhibited on the stage) is that of achieving a convincing relationship between character and action. The character may be strikingly appealing or repellent; the action may be picturesque or terrifying or mirth-provoking; but unless the relationship between character and action is established and maintained, plausibility and persuasiveness will be sacrificed, and the integrity of the play be seriously threatened. This problem of the relationship between character and action may best be approached from the point of view of motivation. Underlying the relationship is the assumption that there are, there must be, adequate reasons, adequate causes for either trivial or consequential actions upon the stage, that nothing must be done that cannot be explained and understood in terms of the natures, the intentions, and the motives of the actors themselves. In other words, the assumption is that of the basic psychological causation of behavior. It is not implied that all actions are the consequences of the reasoning powers of the character; such a representation of human action would be a falsification of all we know of human nature, but it *is* implied that every action must be explicable in terms of the temperament, the feelings and emotions, the instincts and appetencies, the reasoning powers and the ideas of the character in question. The actions must be intelligible in the light of what we have been told and what we can safely assume with regard to the characters involved.

Motivation

The demands in the way of motivation vary directly with the general nature of the particular play. In plays of a tragic or problem type where momentous actions are concerned, the demands in the way of motivation are very much higher than in lighter plays of the comedy or farce-comedy types. We are certainly justified in refusing to take seriously a supposedly serious drama in which life-changing or death-bringing action is inadequately motivated. Such a negligence of psychological plausibility turns tragedy into travesty. But in comedy, farce, and the play of fantasy, we admit a willing suspension of unbelief. Within limits, we are willing to accept amusing action whether or not it is firmly grounded in character. But the seriousness with which comedy is regarded depends directly on the seriousness of the motivation, and in the greatest comedies, such as Molière's *Misanthrope* and *Tartuffe,* or Jonson's *Volpone* or the *Alchemist,* there is a vigorous attempt to make character and action counterbalance. In the romantic comedies of Shakespeare, which take place in an enchanting world of their own, we do not feel compelled to demand the precision of motivation that is necessary in realistic or classical comedy. In farce, the motivation may be of the most mechanical sort. In Goldsmith's *She Stoops to Conquer,* the heroine's little habit of dressing as a lady in the morning and as a bar-maid in the evening is an excellent illustration of an action that has a mechanical rather than a psychological motivation. On the other hand, Young Marlow's aggressiveness with bar-maids and his diffidence with ladies have, we feel, an element of psychological plausibility.

Successful motivation, it will be found, is characterized by some or all of the following qualities: appropriateness, adequacy, consistency, and availability.

It goes almost without saying that the action should strike the beholder as appropriate to the character from whom it proceeds. Cleopatra, whether in classical or romantic guise, must behave in accordance with our conception of her. A king, however unkingly, must attain at moments some manifestations of kingliness. Petulant, magnanimous, caddish, or courageous action must proceed from similar qualities established by the dramatist. There is, of course, an interaction between character and action. Just as characterization by other methods than action will throw light on the motives of action, so action itself may throw perhaps the strongest of all lights on character.

Of even greater importance in successful motivation is the quality of adequacy. It is fairly easy for authors to conceive of characters appropriate to certain actions, or actions appropriate to certain characters; it is not always so easy to convince an audience that the motives given or suggested are adequate to the actions performed. A crucial instance in which adequacy of motivation plays an all important part is that of the suicide of the central figure of a tragedy. Dozens of playwrights have been tempted to dispose of their hero or heroine by some act of picturesque violence, in order to bring a striking or decisive conclusion to a supposedly tragic series of events. Here, admittedly, the seriousness with which we insist upon adequate motivation will depend upon the mode of drama under scrutiny. In romantic tragedy or melodrama, its debased descendant, an audience can be made to accept suicide as a shocking but perfectly plausible conclusion to the career of the hero or heroine. In the austerer classical drama, and much more certainly, in drama that aims at being an exact representation of "real" life, the audience's demands are admittedly greater. Excellent cases in point are the suicides that conclude Ibsen's *Hedda Gabler* and Sir Arthur Pinero's *The Second Mrs. Tanqueray*. Each of these suicides has the effect of concluding the play with a "short sharp shock," but while the first is dramatically effective, the second is effective only theatrically. That is, the first will bear psychological scrutiny; the second will not. Hedda's violent action is made intelligible by one of those perfect coördinations of character and situation for which the tragic writer strives: she is a malignant destructive creature; she discovers that she cannot have life on the preposterous terms which her sick imagination demands; she is trapped by circumstances for which she herself is chiefly responsible; she sees nothing ahead but ugliness and sordidness and degradation;

she achieves, too, we may hope, the sort of "beautiful death" which she had wished to contrive for Eilert Lövborg. Her suicide has an immense appropriateness; the motives that lead up to it are perfectly adequate. At first thought, and certainly under the influence of a performance by a skilled and attractive tragedienne, the suicide of Paula Tanqueray seems equally well motivated. But her pettiness and querulousness, her irritation at not winning the love and respect of Ellean, which she had by no means earned, her "tragic" but unreasonable behavior upon the reappearance of Captain Ardale (who, since their relationship was over and done with, might have been regarded as an appropriate step-son-in-law for a woman supposedly as sophisticated as Paula)—all these motives seem somehow inadequate preparation for violent action on the part of a woman who was loved by a man who knew the world and from whom she had nothing to conceal.

One of the most famous problems of motivation in the English drama is that of the motivation of Iago in *Othello*. It was Coleridge who described Iago's conduct as the expression of "motive-hunting malignity." This is an excellent phrase, but it does not help very much to persuade us of the plausibility of Iago's behavior. Iago is represented to us as rational and not insane; consequently, we are within our rights to demand adequate grounds for his perfidious and supremely cruel behavior. What we have is an instance of behavior that again is theatrically effective but psychologically implausible. In the face of a skilful performance of *Othello,* we are willing to believe that Shakespeare has motivated Iago's behavior adequately. Upon a painstaking scrutiny of the text, however, we must conclude that the motives suggested by Shakespeare, whether taken together or severally, do not constitute adequate grounds for the enormity of Iago's behavior. His thwarted ambition, his sense of mistreatment by Othello, his utterly groundless suspicion of Othello's misconduct with his wife, these are hardly sufficient grounds for the colossal cruelty of Iago.[10]

Another test of success in motivation, the establishing of a plausible relationship between character and action, is consistency. Here, too, our demands in the way of consistency depend directly on the nature of the character. Consistency is a variable in our acceptance or interpretation of the character as an individual or a type, as static or dynamic, as simple or complex.[11]

The author who contents himself with type-characterization finds

[10] For a consideration of the close relationship between Iago's inadequate motivation and the Elizabethan assumptions about the nature of the Moors, see below page 218.

[11] These classifications, to be sure, are not precisely parallel, but type-characters tend to be simple and static, and individual characters complex and dynamic.

a great deal of the work of motivation already done. The audience is in a state of faith in which it is willing to assume that in a character of a certain type certain motives will predominate. The availability of a nexus of motives in well-established type-characters is certainly one of the reasons for the appeal of type-characters to a dramatist of not very high creative powers. He can assume for himself and his audience a group of constant and unmodified motives upon which he can draw at will. He cannot afford, moreover, to disappoint his audience and permit a miser to be other than miserly, a parasite to be other than parasitic. For the audience, the problem of estimating the consistency of motivation differs critically in the case of a play of an early or the contemporary period. In the case of the modern play, the audience will accept uncritically the motivation of such types as the gangster, the hard-boiled chorus girl, the flapper, and the politician. To estimate the consistency of the motivation of such types, it will be necessary for the auditor to escape from the psycho-æsthetic assumptions of the time. In the case of a play of an earlier period, it will be easy enough for him to see the adequacy or the inadequacy of the motivation of unfamiliar types from the modern point of view. It will be more difficult for him to build up a sense of the adequacy of the motivation of a particular type from the point of view of the period in which the play was produced. Such an effort will require a considerable development of the historical imagination coupled with equal knowledge.

A famous instance of the weight of type-motivation is that of Othello and Iago. We have already noticed the inadequacy, from the modern point of view, of the motivation of Iago. The motivation turns out to be somewhat more satisfactory when we realize that, however individual Iago may seem to us to be, he is also a superb example of a common Elizabethan stage-type, the complete, one hundred per cent, Machiavellian villain.[12] The Elizabethan found it possible to assume, as we do not, that a person could be completely and unmitigatedly evil. To this convenient but preposterous figure, Elizabethan dramatists recurred again and again. If Shakespeare's Iago is the most imagination-compelling of the complete Elizabethan villains, it is because of the effect of plausibility which Shakespeare succeeds in creating here. In earlier plays, he had been less scrupulous and less successful. When Richard III in his opening soliloquy announces, "I am determined to be a villain," we are struck at once, in the study if not on the stage, with

[12] It is impossible to trace here the dramatic evolution of this type. Interested students may be referred to Clarence V. Boyer, *The Villain as Hero in Elizabethan Tragedy* (New York: E. P. Dutton and Company, Inc., 1914).

the preposterousness of the underlying psychological assumption. From such an over-simplification of character and motivation only melodrama can arise.

In the case of Othello, the contribution of type-motivation is less obvious. Othello is a rather highly individualized character. But he is not only a brave soldier, an impassioned lover, a brilliant commander, and a noble gentleman; he is also a Moor. Now the Elizabethan audience had very definite associations with Moorish characters. Most Moors on the stage of the English Renaissance had been represented as cruel, bloodthirsty, utterly unscrupulous and malignant villains, violent, hot-tempered, and revengeful. Shakespeare was bold indeed in attempting to make a hero out of a Moor. In this attempt he was notably successful, but he found it necessary to draw on some at least of the traits conventionally associated with Moors. Othello shows little evidence of being blood-thirsty or cruel until his jealousy has been aroused, but Iago's success in alienating him from Desdemona and precipitating the tragedy depends psychologically on Othello's lack of self-control, his hot-bloodedness, and his vengeful nature. Othello reverts to the primitive, or at least to the Renaissance conception of the primitive, and Iago's plot succeeds.

The problem of consistency in motivation also depends on whether the character is static or dynamic, whether it is a fixed or developing personality. It is obvious that it is more difficult to give an effect of adequacy and consistency in characterization if the character develops or deteriorates in the course of the play than if he remains fixed in nature and fundamental traits. The dramatist will do well to avoid the representation of an elaborate process of development or deterioration. The classical drama, of course, made the representation of such a process almost impossible, since the most extended "ideal day" is hardly likely to involve major alterations in a character although it may represent the turning-point in a character's development or deterioration.

There is hardly any marked change in the essential character of Clytemnestra in Æschylus' *Agamemnon.* By processes available to any dramatist Æschylus is able to reveal something of what she has been and the reasons for the changes that have been completed in her at the beginning of the play, but there is little or no actual change in her during the course of the play itself. In the Œdipus of Sophocles' *Œdipus Rex,* there is an appalling and terrifying change in his status and morale; there is a progressive revelation of that haughty, violent, and contentious soul, but there is little actual change in the essence of the character. At least, within the limits of this particular play, Sophocles did not even forecast the changes that tragedy was to bring to Œdipus. It required another play, *Œdipus at Colonnus,* to demonstrate with compelling power, how the horror of tragedy can be transmuted in a great soul intc spiritual elevation and peace.

Even in the looser technique of the romantic drama, the fact that the action is presented to the audience during a period of two or three hours tends to undermine the plausibility of a representation of elaborate deterioration or development. The dramatist who elects to represent a major process of development or deterioration must take particular pains to indicate the basic reasons for such alteration, present visually to the audience the major successive stages in the process, and satisfy it that the final result is psychologically credible. A convenient illustration of such a process is the characterization of Macbeth. We watch Macbeth deteriorate from the status of a trusted and successful officer, through that of an imaginative man stung with the gadfly of ambition. We see his horrified reaction to his first murder, and then the gradual hardening and coarsening of his nature until his saturation in bloody crimes makes him a maddened and desperate megalomaniac. In the case of Lady Macbeth, the process is suggested rather than represented elaborately. The early steps in the process of her deterioration are presented with considerable fullness; then, her successive stages of collapse are hinted to us; we are given a vivid impression of her unhinged and tortured spirit in the sleep-walking scene, but her death is merely, though touchingly, reported.[13]

In the work of a playwright like Ibsen, who is interested primarily in character and whose technique in some respects approximated some features of the classical technique, it is interesting to note his advance in skill in handling the problem of developing or deteriorating characters. In *The Pillars of Society* (1877) the conversion of Bernick in the climax scene is theatrically but not dramatically effective. There is an effort to motivate this sudden volte-face of character, but the process is mechanically represented, and the actual conversion seems a matter of external rather than of internal circumstance. In *A Doll's House* (1879), working in a more constricted technique, Ibsen attempted a much more subtle exhibition of character development. Here, the process of development moves on two distinct planes—there is the actual process of development that has been going on several years before the play begins, and there is the process represented as taking place within the time limits of the acted play. By the rather elaborate exposition, we are made aware of what Nora has been, and we

[13] For a more subtle representation of the psychological deterioration of a great character, the student is recommended to study *Lear.*

are shown her as she appeared superficially at the opening of the play; but, in the remainder of the play, we have, not merely a progressive revelation of various facts in her character as we have in the case of Hjalmar, who is a static not a developing character, but a revelation of her entire psychological history. If one feels finally that the attempt to suggest a long psychological history by action restricted to a very limited period of time is not perfectly successful, one's dissatisfaction with what is after all an extraordinarily effective piece of work arises from the rather tricky and over-plotted means by which Nora's conversion is precipitated.

In the field of comedy, the process of conversion does not demand the most scrupulous motivation. We are, moreover, willing to take the last minute conversions of comedy much more lightly than we do those of sentimental or high comedy. In Plautus' *The Haunted House,* which is almost steadily farcical in tone, the last minute conversion of the harsh father is acceptable only in the realm of farce-comedy. But even here, some theatrical ingenuity is devoted to bringing it about. The erring son, the object of his father's wrath, is not presented in a direct plea for mercy. Instead, he sends an amiable and tactful friend, who has endeared himself to the audience earlier in the play by his verve for revelry, and who now appears as a sober and repentant ambassador. The process of conversion is hurried by the exigencies of the closing drama, but it is not conspicuously clumsy. On a somewhat higher level, the field of romantic comedy, Shakespeare contented himself with a number of offhand conversions. A case in point is the last minute conversion of the usurping duke in *As You Like It.*

Greatness in Characterization

Undoubtedly it is far more profitable to consider the reasons for the greatness of a particular character than it is to raise the general question of the basis of greatness in characterization. But several elements in great characterization may be discussed briefly: consistency, roundedness, expressiveness, vitality, and visibility. In the light of what we have already said, it follows that greatness in characterization depends in part upon consistency. The character may be simple or complex; he may be integrated or disintegrated; he may be normal or wracked by neuroses; but he must furnish us with a consistent and comprehensible formula of character. All the parts must fit into the formula the playwright creates and projects. Greatness of characterization is also likely to be associated with an effect of completeness or roundedness. We feel that we are able to see the character not in two but in three dimensions. All the facts, or at least all the essential facts, are revealed in thought or speech or action, in relation to himself or to one or another figure in the play. Characters done in the flat, in two dimensions, may be vivid and memorable, but they tend to be motionless and unalive. And great characters are likely to be endowed with expressiveness; that is to say, though they may say very little, what they say will proceed from some important center of the character; it will be appropriate, suggestive, illuminating. Certainly, one of the tests of great character is the achievement of an individual style of expression by the character, a style so unmistakable that it could hardly be approached by any other character of even an approximate type. Finally, a desirable quality in characters, great or small, is visibility. Not that, in the case of the classical or the romantic drama, we should be able to tell the height and shape and color of a particular character under consideration. Such detail is alien to the tenets of both classical and romantic art. But we should be able to associate with the character impressions of height and movement, of posture and gestures, which are built up from subjective and psychological notations. But perhaps the supreme test of greatness in characterization is vitality. By some miracle of observation, imagination, creation, or craftsmanship, the great character comes alive. He may be bully or consumptive, genius or ruffian, but he must be vital in every nerve and sinew. This is at once the greatest mystery, the greatest miracle of the dramatist's craft, for in it he becomes godlike; out of words, he moulds beings that are far more real than himself, that live longer, and are more intimately known.

CHAPTER XIV

DIALOGUE

It will assist us in defining the characteristics of dramatic dialogue as distinct from those of conversation if we attempt to differentiate the major functions of the two forms of discourse. In the case of both dramatic dialogue and conversation, there are utilitarian and non-utilitarian functions. For example, conversation of the utilitarian sort transacts business, buys railroad tickets, demonstrates propositions, conveys serious information, makes love; conversation of the non-utilitarian sort has no more serious function than to exchange gossip, to express opinions, or to offer observations on oneself, one's neighbors, and the universe. Similarly, dramatic dialogue has its utilitarian functions: to further the plot, to reveal the characters' thoughts, emotions, and their essential natures, and to describe setting.[1] A non-utilitarian function of dramatic dialogue is that of interesting us in itself by its poetic elevation and imagination or by its wit or humor.

The basic difference between dramatic dialogue and conversation is that dialogue is more steadily and more noticeably utilitarian than conversation, or, conversely, conversation is more frequently non-utilitarian in function than is dramatic dialogue. From this basic distinction rise the major distinctions between dialogue and conversation. If a non-utilitarian conversation is closely listened to, or jotted down and studied, its most striking feature is its lack of direction. It dwells for a few moments with one topic, then leaps to another in response to some unexpressed association of some member of the group. In half an hour it may touch lightly upon a dozen subjects. It may be pleasant, and usually is, but from the point of view of the dramatist, it is painfully inefficient: it does not get anywhere; it does not accomplish anything. It is constantly digressive, wilfully non-purposive. Dialogue, in the main, is controlled by the function of the particular scene of which it is a part; it advances the plot one or more stages in its progress, or sheds a further bit of illumination on the nature and motives of the major figures, or, at its best, accomplishes both these purposes at

[1] The function of dialogue in defining and describing setting will be discussed at length in Chapter XV, but since it is, or may be, a major function of dialogue, it requires mention here.

one and the same time. (At its very best, it also interests us in itself by various stylistic devices.) The dramatist, then, cannot allow his delight in writing winsome or lively or stirring dialogue to run away with him. He must prune and cut and trim until, while there is an appearance of spontaneous movement, underneath the whirls and eddies of the surface a strong current is carrying persons and plot to their coincident goal. Good dialogue, then, is purposive, directed, efficient.

The Functions of Dialogue

Of the functions of dramatic dialogue, the most important is unquestionably that of furthering the plot. As a rule, the dramatist must get on with his story from scene to scene or else the interest and suspense that he has struggled to arouse will subside, and the attention of the audience will be fatally lost. The dialogue may further the plot in a number of ways, but of these, two are of especial importance—the accompaniment of action represented on the stage and the reporting of off-stage action.

The attractions of good dialogue are so many, its effect at its best is so vivid, that one is inclined to forget the very severe limitations on the kinds of action that can be represented on most stages in most types of theaters. These limitations vary, of course, with the type of theater characteristic of a particular age or civilization. The Greek theater, for instance, permitted the stately procession of horses and chariots into the orchestra. The triumphal return of Agamemnon in Æschylus' tragedy is an effect that might be possible in the largest of modern opera houses or *Grossschauspielhäuser,* but horses and chariots are far more manageable properties in an open air auditorium than on even the largest of opera house stages. But even the resources of the Greek theater did not permit the representation of Hippolytus and his chariot being menaced and destroyed by the strange beast sent by Poseidon to destroy him. Similarly, the pageant wagon stage of the English religious drama, the platform stage of the Elizabethans, or the modern picture-frame stage, limit very sharply the sort of action that can be presented. Characters may be seen arguing, quarreling, fighting, making love, drinking, eating (at unrealistic speed), and sleeping, but only the naïveté of the Middle Ages permitted Noah to build the ark and marshal his menagerie in the presence of the audience; and the battles staged in the Elizabethan theaters seemed ridiculous, if not to the groundlings, at least to the more exacting classicists of the time.

Since, then, the overt action that can be represented on the stage is comparatively limited, it is natural that dialogue that accompanies such action is perhaps of less importance and bulk than that which represents action of a more subjective sort. Here the dramatist finds his greatest opportunity for representing action convincingly through dialogue. For if the audience is of any degree of sophistication at all, it is more interested in the meaning of action to the characters concerned than in the objective action itself. Thus the revelations of the feelings and emotions aroused in a group of characters by some essential change in their status and relationship is as exciting as the liveliest of pitched battles that can be staged. In dramas of the more serious sort, indeed, a critical inspection of the dialogue will show that at least one of the most important sources of our interest in it is its power to reveal a sequence of psychological states in response to events either directly represented or merely reported.

Since the kinds of objective or subjective action that can be represented on the stage both have their limitations, dialogue has another very important function in the reporting of action that for one or another reason cannot be represented. Of actions of this sort, two varieties may be distinguished—action that is expository in nature and action that is necessary to the development of the already initiated plot but that it is inconvenient to represent. For the reporting of events that occurred before the actual opening of the play, dialogue is the all important means, and, as we have seen in our consideration of plot, expository dialogue may be painfully obvious or remarkably adroit. But in all dramas, the more or less onerous burden of exposition is one that dialogue must assume. A less inevitable function of dialogue is that of reporting action essential to the development of the plot but inappropriate for stage representation. As in the case of the dialogue of exposition, the dialogue of dramatic narration may be tedious and boring or, at its best, supremely exciting. In the cheaper forms of melodrama, where exciting action is the major source of interest, off-stage events of an unwieldy sort are frequently represented by description and the reactions of the spectators on the stage. This is a kind of compromise between action represented on the stage and action narrated, and, like most compromises, its results are not very satisfactory to any of the persons concerned. It is rather difficult to work up very much excitement over a horse-race or a football match, described incoherently and ecstatically by a segment of the spectators in a grand-stand.[2] The dramatic reporting of off-stage

[2] The ineffectiveness of this sort of compromise may be illustrated by the boat-race scene in O'Neill's *Strange Interlude,* or by the bicycle-race in Georg Kaiser's *From Morn to Midnight.* The best use of this technique that comes to mind is the bull-fight described from adjacent boxes in the final act of Benavente's *The Governor's Wife.*

action was developed to a higher degree of effectiveness by the Greek tragic writers than by the dramatists of any other period. Whatever the reasons were for the banishment from the stage of the Greek theater of anything like violent physical action, the convention of such banishment led irresistibly to the development of the part of the Messenger, and so great was the skill of the tragic writers in exploiting the possibilities of this convention that their success has proved to be unparalleled. Part of their success is due to the fact that the dramatic narrative is usually introduced at a point of great emotional tension for both characters and audience, a point at which both are acutely curious or deeply concerned emotionally with the action about to be reported. For an audience can be counted on to listen with unbroken patience to an account, however lengthy, of an action or series of actions that seems to concern them vitally.[3] Moreover, it is plain that the tragic writers lavished a great deal of imagination and art on the construction of these dramatic narratives, and in consequence the messengers' speeches are frequently the most purple patches in even a distinguished play.

Non-utilitarian Dialogue

As we have said, dramatic dialogue may have a non-utilitarian as well as a utilitarian function. It may not only further the plot, illuminate the characterization, and describe the setting, but it may also be interesting in itself. Dialogue of the non-utilitarian sort has its dangers, for, unless it retains our interest, unless it woos us into forgetting that the action is for the moment being neglected, it becomes a disturbing and annoying intrusion. Yet, in both serious and comic drama, non-functional dialogue is a fairly frequent intrusion. The relatively loose form of the English drama of the Renaissance offered a particular temptation to the dramatist to introduce essentially non-dramatic passages. For example, the discussion of national drinking habits in the fourth scene of *Hamlet* strikes most readers as a dull and unwarranted intrusion. It does not further the plot; it does not advance the characterization; and, although, in the study, it may lead us into unprofitable discussion of Shakespeare's personal views on drinking, it seems in the theater an unjustifiable interruption of the business of this engrossing scene. A less obtrusive instance of a non-utilitarian passage is Mercutio's Queen Mab speech in *Romeo and Juliet.* But supreme as it is as an example of Elizabethan fairy-poetry, one cannot feel that it is an expression of imagination particularly appropriate to

[3] An admirable modern example of a long narrative introduced at a point of great suspense is the heroine's account of her past in Sidney Howard's *Alien Corn.*

Mercutio, nor can it be justified as a plot-forwarding or character-building device.

If there are more non-functional passages of dialogue in comedy than in tragedy, the reasons are obvious. In comedy of most types, and certainly in comedy of the less elevated sorts, plot and character are frequently subordinated to the obligation on the comic writer's part to keep his audiences not only interested but amused. To the furthering of this purpose almost any means can be utilized, and the justification of whatever means is used is the degree to which the particular device amuses us. Almost any farce will furnish a dozen examples of passages of dialogue extraneous to the development of plot or character, and even masterpieces of high comedy contain some of the best known examples of this type of dialogue. In the English drama, perhaps the most famous of such scenes of dialogue are the scandal mongering scenes of *The School for Scandal.* These, of course, find some justification on the ground that they assist in creating the atmosphere in which the main actions of the piece are conducted, but such justification is hardly adequate to explain their extent and their elaborateness. Their *raison d'être* is that, entirely non-dramatic as they are, they are as brilliant passages of conversation as have ever been written in English. They interest and delight us by their wit, their malice, their imagination, and the accuracy of their portraiture, and we are, consequently, in no mood to object that they do not contribute anything relevant to the conduct of the play and the exploitation and exhibition of the major characters.

Indeed, the playwright is well advised to make his dialogue as interesting as possible whether or not it has immediately utilitarian functions. A very brief consideration of the major types of dialogue will suggest the potentialities in the direction of interest.

Dialogue in Verse

It would not be possible to discuss with any adequacy here the important æsthetic problem of why for centuries dramas, both tragic and comic, were almost without exception written in verse. Whether the impulse was to raise drama above the level of life, to embellish it with the attractions of beautiful and imaginative language, or to emphasize the abstract and ideal qualities of drama, the fact is incontrovertible that the verse tradition has been one of the most powerful of the traditions associated with the technique of the drama. It was astonishingly late in the long history of the drama when prose came to be considered an appropriate medium at least for a serious play. Dramatic verse, then, has shared the vicissitudes of taste and style characteristic of non-dramatic verse, although since most dialogue is and must be functional, the particular style of an epoch must be adapted (more or less radically) to the exigencies of the dramatic form. And yet, it is one of the marvels of dramatic verse that the greatest possible complexity and subtlety of thought and imagination and style have not been shunned by dramatists; the greatest periods in the history of the drama have been those in which the dramatists were the greatest poets.

The attractions of dramatic poetry are the attractions of all poetry, with the addition of all that the drama can contribute of excitement, preoccupation, and concern. And it is therefore worthwhile to study with meticulous attentiveness the poetic technique of a particular poet or a particular period. Diction, meter, and imagery —all the elements of poetic technique—must be taken into consideration in any adequate consideration of a poetic-dramatic work.

Of perhaps the most obvious importance in the study of the technique of dramatic verse is the metrical form. Certainly in the drama of Western Europe, no playwrights have ever used exceedingly intricate metrical forms with the power and beauty of the Greek tragic writers. Their only rivals in intricacy (and they are rivals so unworthy as hardly to deserve mention) were certain anonymous English medieval playwrights, who struggled, with perhaps the least poetic gift in the world, to write plays in involved stanzaic forms with rime-schemes of unbelievable and unwieldy complexity. Even when this handicap was thrown off, English playwrights of the sixteenth century experimented with a variety of metrical forms (including the unfortunate fourteener), none of which proved thoroughly and magnificently useful until Christopher Marlowe demonstrated the dramatic possibilities of unrimed iambic pentameter. From the time of his success to the present day, most English plays in poetic form have utilized this metrical medium with a variety and subtlety that it would take volumes to describe and analyze.

Prose Dialogue

A consideration of why prose has, in the main, taken the place of poetry as the form for modern dramatic dialogue, would take us too far astray. Prose appears, to be sure, in some of the greatest of English poetic dramas, and some of the comedies of Shakespeare's influential predecessor, John Lyly, were written almost entirely in prose. The introduction of prose into verse-plays of the English Renaissance seems to have followed rather vaguely defined principles. Comic scenes, especially in low comedy, tend to be written in prose; letters and official proclamations are almost invariably written in prose. It may be suggested that the early appearance of prose in the drama arose from the desire to come a little nearer to an effect of reality than poetry permits. At any rate, as we observe the slow development of realism in the drama, we also observe the long drawn out process of the evolution of a style of prose dialogue approaching closer and closer to the style of real conversation. There is perhaps, no better illustration of the persistent artificiality of the drama—its basic difference from life—than the slowness of the evolution of realistic dialogue. In English, at any rate, it has been only within the present century that dialogue has learned to give the effect, without being the actuality, of real conversation. In this slow evolution, two intentions of the dramatist are in conflict: the desire to write dialogue that sounds real, and the desire to write dialogue that shall be efficient and interesting. The accurate reproduction of conversation in the drama runs the not inconsiderable risk of boring the auditor while it preserves its authenticity, and no dramatist can afford to bore his audience for the sake of being linguistically precise.

It is then both historically and æsthetically unsound to measure prose dialogue by the criterion of realistic accuracy alone. Prose dialogue, like every other element in dramatic technique, is an artifice; the legitimate question is, whether or not the artifice is an attractive one. Here, as elsewhere, there are artifices that please and artifices that alienate. Take for instance the elementary artifice of the pun. At the moment, most persons affect to be alienated by this rather mechanical variety of word-play. And yet it is, historically, one of the most ancient and honorable devices of wit. The Elizabethans, in fact, were so enamored of word-play of all sorts that they did not feel puns to be out of place even in tragedy. So the characters in *Romeo and Juliet* decorate their emotions, both pleasurable and painful, with puns that seem to us distressingly out of place. The antipathy to puns is a modern one, and should not blind us to the skill with which comic writers of almost every period have indulged in this particular manifestation of a sense of humor.

On the credit side of artifice in good prose dialogue may be set down all the qualities associated with good prose style of any sort: terseness, conciseness, polish, wit, agility, appropriate and suggestive imagery and figures. On the debit side stand extravagance of diction, banality, pomposity (except as a comic device), over-elaborateness, and inflated rhetoric. For good prose dialogue one need go no further than the lighter passages in Shakespeare, Beaumont, and Fletcher, or to the Irish comedies of Lady Gregory and John Millington Synge. For bad prose dialogue, more than ample illustration may be discovered without difficulty in the sentimental comedies and dramas of the eighteenth century and from practically all nineteenth-century prose drama. Tom Robertson, of course, in the eighties, made a vigorous effort to bring stage prose closer to the conversation of real life, but even his dialogue is divertingly stagey. A convenient illustration of the evolution of prose dialogue within our own time is furnished by the plays of Sir Arthur Pinero. In all his serious work up to *Mid-Channel,* the dialogue, while it aims at an appearance of reality, is inflated and rhetorical in the worst sense. One of his favorite figures, the *raisonneur,* is particularly prone to burst into tirades of dismaying rhetorical exuberance. It was not until he achieved the æsthetic maturity of *Mid-Channel* that he wrought an effective dramatic dialogue that one can imagine cultivated persons actually speaking.

One of the greatest writers of dialogue in the modern period is undoubtedly Ibsen. But, even as his plot structure is deceptively simple, so his dialogue in the maturer plays is only apparently realistic. In actuality, it is beautifully efficient, shaped, pointed, directed to the furthering of plot and the illumination of character. It is never flat and prosaic, since it is always lighted up by feeling, rises directly out of the innermost consciousness of the characters, and thus is a perfect expression of their natures.

Probably the playwright of our time who has come nearest to giving the effect of actual conversation is Anton Chekhov. In his plays, one gets the incoherence, the desultoriness, the self-absorption of actual conversation, an effect that is made possible by his constant minimization of the element of plot and his emphasis on the meticulous depiction of domestic interiors and psychology.

But in whatever period of drama, the student of dialogue will be well advised to estimate its effectiveness in terms of its functions: the furtherance of plot, the illumination of character, the description of setting; and in terms of its interest in itself through the available resources and the individual gifts of fine prose and verse.

CHAPTER XV

SETTING

Since all events occur, not only in time, but in space, one of the playwright's tasks is that of indicating in more or less detail the setting of the particular events composing his plot. But, since almost all playwrights, except the most inventive, have had in mind the form of theater characteristic of their time, the element of setting may perhaps be best considered in terms of the major types of theaters which playwrights have found available for the production of their plays.

For the playwrights of western Europe, four major types of stages have been available at one or another period: the permanent-set stage of the classical or neo-classical drama; the moving or stable platform-stage of the English medieval and Renaissance drama; the picture-frame stage characteristic of the theater from the Restoration to the end of the nineteenth century, and the mechanized stage of the twentieth century. Since these stages and the theaters of which they were a part differed widely, the opportunity and the obligation of the playwright in the treatment of setting differed as well.

Setting in the Classical Drama

From the point of view of setting, the permanent-set stage of the classical and neo-classical theater gave the playwright the least opportunity and the lightest obligation. For tragedy, the permanent set represented, with almost no alteration, the façade of a temple or a palace. It needed no description, and it allowed the dramatist to evoke, by reference only to its austerity and magnificence, the particular atmosphere with which he hoped to invest his play. For comedy, at least of the New Greek or Roman period, the typical setting was a street, on which most of the major characters lived. Greater demands were sometimes made of course on stage producer and manager. In the period of the Old Greek Comedy, plays like Aristophanes' *Birds* and *The Clouds* demanded an elaborateness of setting and costuming that must have challenged the imagination of the producers of the day, but, if we remember the willingness of audiences to make-believe when anything but make-believe is out of the question, we shall not assume too romantic or too realistic an embellishment of even the great plays of Aristophanes. Occasionally, even Roman comedy demanded a setting other than the conventionalized street of houses. Plautus' *Rudens* (*The Rope*), for instance, required the representation of the façade of the Temple of Venus, a dwelling place, and a rocky ascent from the beach so extensive that two characters could hear each others' voices for a considerable time before they saw each other.[1]

All in all, the problem of setting was solved for the classical playwright before he began his play. The problem for him was not to choose or describe a setting, but to contrive to represent the major events of his story before the setting that the theater of his time made available. The street scene that served as the background for most classical comedies after the Old Greek period unquestionably presented difficulties in the representation of some scenes. Scenes and dialogue that would naturally occur within doors must be brought out into the street with more or less plausibility. In Plautus' *The Haunted House,* for example, it is preposterous that roisterers should have their drinking bout with their mistresses on couches in the street in front of Theopropides' house, and in many another play the excuse which brings the characters into the street to talk over private affairs is incredibly thin. Similarly, in *Ralph Roister Doister* Dame Custance enters on one occasion, saying, "I come to see if any more stirrying be here;" and, again,

> I come forth to see and hearken for newes good,
> For about this houre is the tyme, of likelyhood,
> That Gawyn Goodlucke, by the sayings of Suresby,
> Would be at home; and lo, yond I see him, I.

Another limitation imposed by the street scene of New Greek Comedy precipitated a conflict between this theatrical convention and the Greek social convention that women of good reputation, married or single, were unaccustomed to make frequent public appearances on the street. Perhaps this conflict helps explain the fact that most of the female characters in New Greek and Roman comedy are women of rather bad reputation. Frequently, of course (and this is a further illustration of the irksomeness of the theatrical convention) the heroine's reputation remained under suspicion long enough to permit her to get in one or more appearances on the stage but was carefully whitewashed before the happy conclusion of the piece.

[1] But the modern reader of this play should take care not to imagine this set in too great detail, for it is one of the stage conventions of all time that no character shall see another character until the playwright is ready for him to do so. See the recognition scene in the fifth act of Shakespeare's *Twelfth Night* or the interminable recognition scenes (a sturdy and recognized convention) in Greek tragic treatments of the Electra story.

Setting in the Medieval Drama

With the platform-stage, whether stationary or ambulatory, of the English medieval drama, new problems in setting were imposed on the dramatist. Certainly, in the case of the ambulatory platform-stage, the pageant wagon of the medieval religious drama, the problem of setting was minimized by the fact that all four sides of the platform were open to the audience. What setting was necessary had to be indicated by the lines themselves or by three dimensional properties of a relatively simple sort. In the case of the latter, we may feel sure that there was little or no attempt to indicate the setting with any fullness of detail; the use of properties might almost be said to be symbolical, that is to say, they were intended to suggest the setting rather than to represent it with what we should call realism. The medieval playwright, it would seem, planned to get his effect of period and place through costume rather than through actual setting. The rather elaborate lists of costumes that have come down to us indicate the importance that this element of production had in the medieval biblical drama. But, apart from the use of three-dimensional properties like tables and cradles, thrones and Hellmouths, the setting had to be suggested by the lines of the play itself, and, although there is for the modern reader a rather delightful naïveté [2] in the confusion of English and Oriental local color and atmosphere, occasionally the atmosphere is conveyed with a rather compelling vividness. The descriptive-expository passage that opens the Wakefield *Second Shepherd's Play* conveys a painfully vivid impression of the physical and economic miseries of medieval shepherd life.

Setting in the Elizabethan Drama

The platform-stage of the English theater of the Renaissance had vastly greater resources than the elementary platform-stage of the medieval period. In the public theaters, at least, the platform extended out into the auditorium in such a way as to permit the groundlings to stand around three sides of it. In one instance, at least, that of the Fortune Theater, the platform-stage was 43 feet wide and 27½ feet deep. This basic structural element in the English Renaissance theater was inevitably in the mind of every playwright who wrote for a theater of this type. On this apron of the platform-stage, nothing in the way of scenery could be used except properties of the three dimensional type. The other resources of the

[2] Perhaps the most delightful example of naïveté in the treatment of setting in the medieval drama occurs in the Chester play of *Noah's Flood*. Here the manuscript gives sufficiently explicit stage-directions for the important process of building the ark.

Renaissance stage undoubtedly varied from theater to theater, and perhaps from decade to decade, but it can be stated with some assurance that, in addition to the projecting platform-stage, there was, in a number of important theaters of the period, the following constant elements: an inner stage,[3] that is to say, a space that could be cut off from the outer stage by a curtain, behind which properties could be shifted at will; a balcony [4] above the inner stage, of like dimensions, and similarly capable of being cut off at intervals by the drawing of a curtain; and two entrances at either side of the inner stage, with perhaps a window above each entrance. Preposterous as this arrangement may seem to us architecturally (since the stage represented neither an outdoor nor an indoor scene, but in a sense both at once), this curious structure encouraged and made possible the wonderfully free and flexible structure of the Elizabethan drama.

Whatever may have been the use to which the Elizabethan stage was put, it is obvious that a theater of this sort placed a far heavier burden upon the playwright than a theater of the classical sort, for, while it permitted him to shift the ground of his action as frequently as the plot required, it also imposed upon him the necessity of indicating, in each case, the setting of each important scene and of creating the proper atmosphere for a long series of scenes instead of the single unchanging scene of the classical drama. Sir Edmund Chambers is undoubtedly correct in his contention that a great many scenes in Elizabethan and Stuart plays are unlocalized; that is to say, a great many scenes happen in an undetermined spot vaguely connected spatially with the particular spots designated for the major scenes. But, after we have deducted from the total number of scenes in a play the unlocalized scenes, we still have left a very considerable number of scenes for which the dramatist must indicate a setting. Here, as in the case of the medieval drama, the setting provided by the lines of the dramatist was frequently of the simplest sort. Here, too, the setting was likely to be symbolic rather than realistic. Moreover, the playwright was usually disinclined, for reasons of dramatic tactics, to introduce an elaborate description of the scene in question. He preferred to make informa-

[3] The inner stage at the Fortune Theater probably measured about twenty by ten feet.

[4] The balcony of the Elizabethan stage lent itself to a variety of uses. Perhaps its most frequent use was as the wall of a city. In the chronicle plays of the period, there are innumerable scenes of parley between a beleaguering army and a city, whose rulers, whether kings or citizens, carry on negotiations, from this vantage point. When not needed for the staging of some scene in the play, it was occasionally used by the musicians who furnished incidental music or accompaniments for singing, or even, it would seem, for privileged spectators, whose view of the actors' backs would be unimpeded.

tion concerning place and atmosphere incidental to dialogue that furthered action or developed character. There are, of course, set descriptions of setting in the Elizabethan drama: one recalls Macduff's illusive if unconsciously ironical description of Macbeth's castle, and the moonlit loveliness of the Jessica-Lorenzo dialogue at the opening of the final scene of *The Merchant of Venice.* But the more frequent and the more effective means was the introduction of details incidentally and the notation of the effect of the supposed surroundings on the minds and emotions of the characters involved. There is little or no precise description of the garden in the balcony scene in *Romeo and Juliet,* but the frequent references to the moon and Juliet's lines,

> The orchard walls are high and hard to climb
> And the place death considering who thou art,
> If any of my kinsmen find thee here

are far more effective dramatically than the most elaborate nondramatic description of the setting would be. Another instance of the effectiveness of a setting implied through the emotions aroused occurs in Juliet's lines after Romeo has descended from the balcony:

> Methinks I see thee now thou art below,
> As one dead in the bottom of a tomb;
> Either my eyesight fails, or thou look'st pale.

These lines give an astonishingly vivid impression of the height of the balcony, altogether out of proportion to the balcony that the Elizabethan or the modern stage has been able to furnish the star-crossed lovers.

An interesting illustration from the same play of the use of both the set description and the incidental description concerns the tomb of the Capulets which plays so important a part in the dénouement of the tragedy. It is first presented to us in the monologue before Juliet takes the sleeping potion, with an extravagance of horror that strikes the modern reader as a little excessive even in view of Juliet's distraction and terror. An entirely different atmosphere, and perhaps a more convincing one, is invoked by the tomb scene itself, by such indirect description as Friar Lawrence's,

> Saint Francis be my speed! how oft to-night
> Have my old feet stumbled at graves!

and Paris's,

> Under yon yew-trees lay thee all along,
> Holding thine ear close to the hollow ground
> So shall no foot upon the churchyard tread

> Being loose, infirm, with digging up of graves,
> But thou shalt hear it.

The vividness of the setting and atmosphere of certain scenes in the Elizabethan drama seems to be due to the imaginative power with which playwrights, great and small, visualized the settings of scenes required, and transmitted the effect of these settings through the characters concerned to the audience. Never, perhaps, has any type of theater placed so heavy a burden in scene depiction upon the playwright, and never have dramatists of any period risen to the responsibility with so powerful and ravishing an imagination.

Setting Since the Restoration

The picture-frame stage, characteristic of the English and the Continental theater from the Restoration to the end of the nineteenth century, and still typical of theaters built before the Great War, furnished a form midway in flexibility between the unchanging scene of the classical theater and the rapidly changing scenes of the Elizabethan theater. It permitted a more frequent change of scene than the first, and a less frequent change of scene than the second, for the framing in of the stage by the proscenium arch encouraged the attempt to secure, and created in the audience the expectation of getting, a fullness of detail in setting that neither of the earlier types of stage had demanded. This demand for relatively realistic sets was met for generations by the mechanisms of back-drops and wings slid onto the stage in grooves; thus it was possible to make a considerable number of changes of scene within a given play. In the earlier theaters of this type scenes were sometimes changed without lowering the curtain. At any rate, this type of setting initiated the evolution of the scene-painter's art, and prepared the way for the infinitely more plausible box sets for interiors characteristic of the later nineteenth-century and twentieth-century theaters.

The burden on the playwright, from the Restoration to the late nineteenth century, was considerably lightened. It was necessary for him to indicate the type of setting required and the absolutely essential stage properties, but he could depend upon the scene-painter and the costumer to supply most of the atmosphere that his drama needed. Scenes suitable to the mechanism of the picture-frame stage rapidly became conventionalized, and at least until the onslaught of modern romanticism, the number of scenes required for most plays was remarkably restricted: a noble and a humble interior, a wood, a dungeon, a church, a city street, a village street. These, with some slight alterations in the matter of properties, would serve to stage most plays of the Restoration and the eighteenth century. With the appearance of modern romanticism in the drama, the demands upon the scene-designer and painter became more extravagant. Mountain glades, seascapes, barren heaths, towers and castles, Peruvian, Spanish, and Oriental interiors and exteriors were demanded and obtained. And still, the number of sets in common use was so restricted that even the opera houses of modest American towns could be counted on to supply almost any touring company with adequate if somewhat familiar and time-worn sets.[5]

From the point of view of the playwright, the picture-frame stage has been a great boon in limiting his responsibility for the description of setting, either in stage directions or in the lines of his dialogue. The student, consequently, is likely to find that plays written since 1660 give him less to stimulate his imagination as tc setting than the plays of any other period.

With the coming of realism the burden of playwright and scene-designer was again increased, for one of the major manifestations of realism in both the novel and the drama was an intense localization of setting and atmosphere. The student of the realistic drama is likely to find in the printed modern play a minute and specific description of the sort of setting the playwright expects the stage-designer to create, though even so great a realist as Ibsen contented himself usually with exceedingly brief notations of setting. With playwrights active since the onset of that intensified realism known on the Continent as naturalism, the description of setting through the medium of stage directions often goes to very great lengths. Certain playwrights, indeed, more or less consciously rebellious against the limitations of the dramatic form, have developed the stage direction to a point where it has the function, not merely of indicating and describing the scene but of furnishing expository, historical, analytical, or critical information that is manifestly non-dramatic in nature. One is willing to forgive Barrie's non-dramatic stage directions for their humor, or Bernard Shaw's for their wit, but the elaborate psychological and historical analyses of characters that Granville-Barker frequently furnishes, though they are illuminating for both actors and readers, are veritable intrusions of an essentially non-dramatic technique into the dramatic form.[6]

Although the picture-frame stage is still the characteristic form

[5] One of the largest collections of nineteenth-century scenery extant is in the possession of the *Théâtre Français,* where the casual visitor can see at almost any performance the tastes and modes of that remote period, unaffected by the revolution in stagecraft in the world outside France.

[6] For examples, see Granville-Barker's *The Madras House* and the opening stage direction of Shaw's *Candida.*

of the stage in most American and British and many European theaters, the student of the drama should not be unaware of the fact that a very basic revolution in theatrical mechanism and structure is one of the most conspicuous features of the theatrical history of our time, a revolution that must be taken into consideration in any study of the Continental drama, outside France. In so far as the stage is concerned, the impulse behind the current revolution in stage forms is the desire to increase the resources of the stage itself, and to escape from the very definite restrictions of the picture-frame stage. In consequence, the chief characteristic of what may be called the mechanized stage is its adaptation from earlier types of theaters of their most useful features, and the utilization, in connection with the stage, of all the mechanical and illuminating devices produced by modern ingenuity. In many theaters, there are structural arrangements designed to bring the performers and the audience into as close contact as was the case in the classical theater and the theaters of the English Renaissance. The stage has been made more flexible by the use of elaborate mechanisms to raise or lower various portions of the stage itself. Furthermore, developments in stage mechanics of the nature of the wagon stage or the revolving stage, are making it possible to stage a series of scenes with a speed characteristic of the Renaissance theater but with an elaborateness unknown to it. Finally, while scene painting has developed a very high degree of taste and beauty, the resources of the modern electrician have made it possible to achieve by such relatively simple means as screens and draperies illusive and suggestive effects impossible in the candle-lighted or gas-lighted auditorium.

The effect of the mechanized theater on the drama is obvious only to one more or less familiar with the mechanized theater itself. In general, it has tended to liberate the contemporary dramatist from the rather petty realism encouraged by the nineteenth-century picture-frame stage, to free him to use a larger number of scenes than the older theaters allowed, and to encourage his imagination to enter the fields of fantasy, symbolism, and the byways of the unconscious. At the moment, it would be difficult to defend the position that contemporary dramatists have in any considerable numbers risen to the opportunities the mechanized theaters affords them. Here, as in other phases of modern life, the machine seems to have been developed beyond man's powers to adjust himself to it, and to make the finest possible use of it. But at any rate no student of the drama can afford to overlook the contribution of the contemporary theatrical architect, the electrician, and the mechanician to the enhancement of dramatic opportunities.

It is important that the student of the drama should take into consideration in his study of any play the type of theater for which it was written or in which it was produced. He should then be in a position to judge of the extent to which the playwright has utilized the resources of his theater and the effectiveness of his use of such resources. For only if he keeps in mind the resources and the limitations of the theater of the epoch in which the play was written, will he be in a position to decide whether or not the playwright has shirked or met the responsibilities inevitably imposed upon him by the necessity of indicating and describing the settings requisite for the action of his play.

CONCLUSION

Drama in the theater produces the most complex of the experiences induced by literature. By reason of this complexity, the drama offers to students the greatest variety of approaches. As we indicated in the Introduction to this book, the drama, like any other form of literature, may be studied as a literary type, as a strand in the closely woven history of national or comparative literature, as a reflection, always more or less distorted, of the life and ideas of the age in which it is produced, or as a manifestation of the emotional and intellectual experience of the individual dramatist.

But the drama, as this book has attempted to show, can also be studied in the theater, and it is this study, we believe, that will yield most students the richest returns. We have attempted to define the relationship, in various periods in the history of the drama, between the theater and the form and spirit of the drama. We have attempted to suggest the important contributions that scenery, lighting, acting, and direction have made to the art of the theater, and the effects of different types of theatrical architecture on the nature and form of the drama itself.

The returns yielded by any serious study of the drama in the theater are immense.[1] They are different in certain respects from the returns made by any other form of literature, any other form of art. In the first place, the drama in the theater is capable of communicating a vividness of impression of which no other literary form is capable. The novel, at its most vivid, cannot hope to communicate the poignant sense of being an intimate observer of the places and persons, the emotions and actions of the playwright's imagining. The vividness and the immediacy inseparable from the effect of the drama in the theater are akin, not to the subjective vividness of the lyric or the epic, but to the vividness of the plastic arts. The drama comes closer than any other form of literature to rivaling the color and form, the brilliance and the firmness of

[1] Not *all* the returns are available to *every* spectator. Certainly the ideal spectator is inadequately described in the following valiantly democratic assertions: "No well-written play is above the understanding of the boy in the gallery." W. T. Price, *The Technique of the Drama* (New York: Brentano's, 1892), p. 166. "If the spectator be confused, baffled, irritated or bored, or any or all of these, he has a legitimate complaint against the dramatist." Richard Burton, *How to See a Play* (New York: The Macmillan Company, 1914), p. 153.

painting, the roundedness and mass of sculpture. But the vividness peculiar to the drama is a more intense vividness than that of even the most richly colored painting, the most alluringly rounded sculpture. The drama is the art that most closely approximates life because it represents not merely a high moment in experience and imagination like painting and sculpture, but a sequence of striking events and emotions in time, and because it uses as one of its indispensable mediums actual human personalities. Indeed, the approximation of the drama to life, especially in its realistic modes, is so close that much false criticism has its origin in the assumed identification of the two. But as we have iterated, the drama is art, and not life. Yet it comes closer than any of the other arts to the immediacy and the reality of life.

Therefore, the theater offers its devotees incomparable and memorable experiences. Here is at once an escape from life and a confrontation of it. Here is life being lived, photographed or idealized, sentimentalized or satirized. Here are intenser emotions, vivider personalities, more startling action, more graces and humors of dialogue than life can ever offer. Here life is seen under a steady glow of unreality that is somehow poignantly real. Here is life, even at its most tragic, as one dreams that it might be.

INDEX

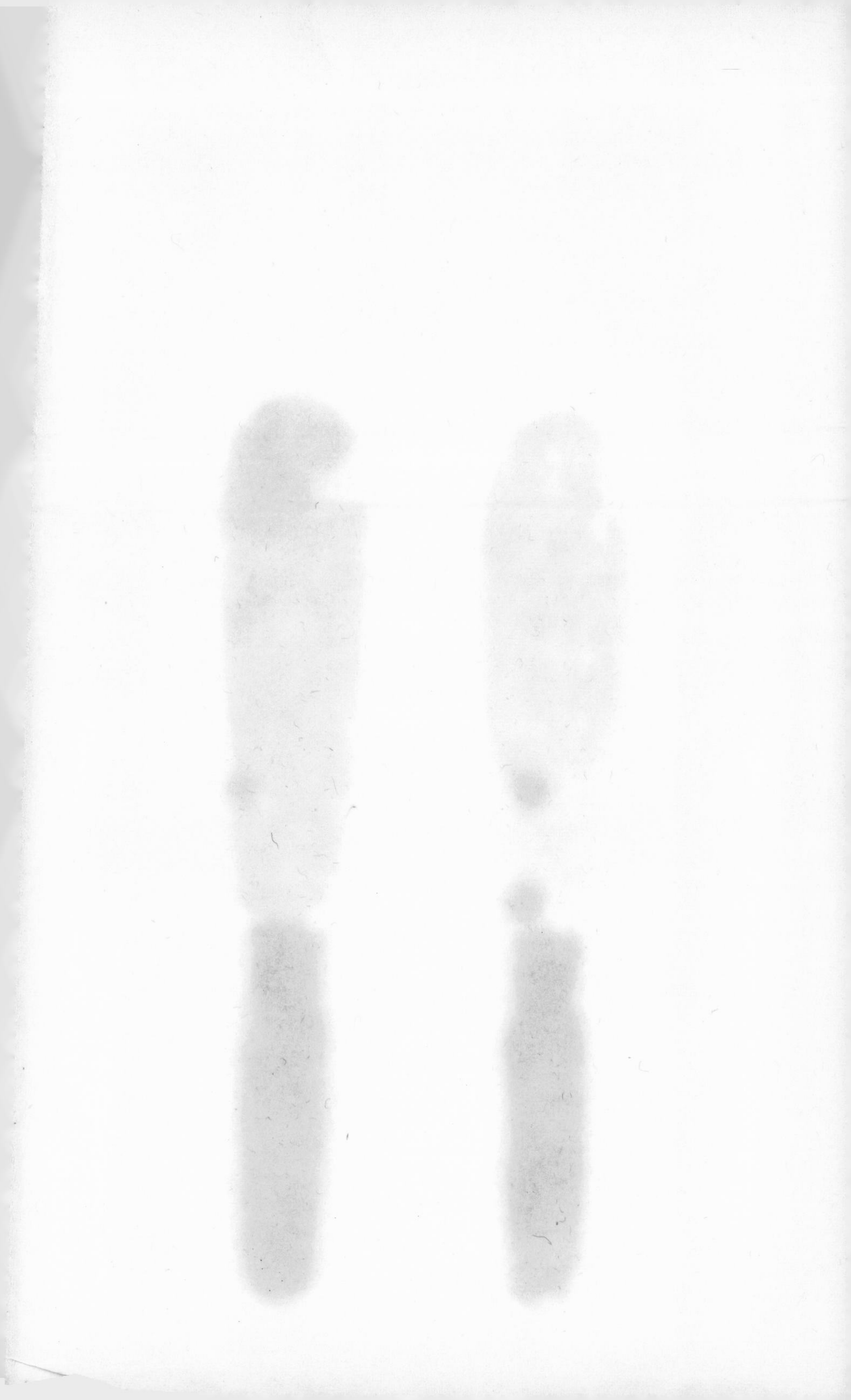